THE GROWTH OF
THE AMERICAN ECONOMY
TO 1860

THE GROWTH OF
THE AMERICAN ECONOMY
TO 1860

edited by

DOUGLASS C. NORTH

&

ROBERT PAUL THOMAS

UNIVERSITY OF SOUTH CAROLINA PRESS

Columbia, S.C.

THE GROWTH OF THE AMERICAN
ECONOMY TO 1860

Contents

Contents

General Introduction

Douglass C. North & Robert Paul Thomas

The history of the American economy from its founding to the outbreak of the Civil War records a tremendous achievement, embracing the transformation of a wilderness continent into the most prosperous economy in the world. This effort to assess that achievement is based on a selection of original sources—the stuff of history—chosen and presented within an interpretative framework. It is hoped that this combination will allow the reader a better understanding of the elements and forces shaping the growth of the American economy.

The Analytical Framework

To provide an analytical framework within which to evaluate the documents presented below, it is necessary first to discuss briefly the determinants of economic growth. While it is true that no general theory of economic growth currently exists, much of recent economic research has been devoted to this subject. Resultant insights into the sources of economic growth have provided, at the least, rough guides to our understanding of this complex phenomenon.

The term economic growth is generally defined as an increase in the quantity of goods and services produced by an economy. Such increase can come about in two ways. First, the quantity of inputs, or factors of production, in the economy may be amplified—that is, the amounts of land, labor, capital, and managerial or entrepreneurial services available in the society may be increased. Clearly, a proportioned increase in all of these inputs will result in a larger total output for the economy. The augmentation of output occurring in this manner is generally called extensive growth, and this sort of process accounted for much of the economic expansion of the United States before the Civil War. However, extensive growth guarantees only a larger economy; in itself it does not imply a higher standard of living for society. Yet it is precisely such a rise in the standard of living—or a higher per capita income—that we custom-

1

arily associate with the desirability of economic growth. An increase in per capita income, termed *intensive* growth, is, then, the second way in which economic growth occurs. Such growth can be generated, for example, by increases in the quantity of land and physical capital relative to the population. Each laborer, having more capital and land to work with, should as a result produce a larger output. Most of the increase in per capita incomes during the colonial or preindustrial period of the American economy probably stemmed from this source. This source of growth, however, accounts for only a small part of recent increases in the per capita income of the United States.

The major credit for intensive growth in our economy must be accorded most probably to quite a different cause—namely the progressively improving efficiency with which goods and services have been produced. In other words, from a given amount of inputs, the American economy has been able to obtain a larger output because it has utilized the inputs in an increasingly more productive manner. Essentially this bettering of efficiency has stemmed from three main sources: technological change, the improving quality of the factors of production, and improvements in economic organization.

Typically, economic historians have given preeminence to technological progress when explaining improved efficiency in an economy. Certainly, technology's dramatic changes in the past three or four centuries would make a *Mayflower* passenger feel more at home in the world as it existed at the time of Christ than in the modern era, only 350 years after the settlement at Plymouth. Technology has transformed our world in three major ways. First, it has substituted machines for the hand of man in creating products. Second, new sources of energy have been developed (here we think immediately of the steam engine of the industrial revolution, and the more recent examples of electric power, the internal combustion engine, and nuclear power). Third, matter itself has been molded and reshaped to make it more useful to mankind—a striking example is the transformation of by-products of petroleum into complex synthetic fabrics and other materials for industrial use.

These technological improvements result from man's increased knowledge of his world. Their economic importance depends upon his ability to put this knowledge to practical uses. Although changes in technology during the past two and a half centuries are of titanic proportions, a moment's reflection suggests that in themselves they are not a sufficient explanation for the economic advances made by the American economy. The reason for this is clear. Once introduced, technological innovation is more or less available to all the world; the latest scientific and engineering journals provide all the technical information necessary to adapt and adopt the improvements. Therefore, if technology were the whole answer, all the literate nations of the world should be as prosperous as the United States. But in fact most nations in the world have not been able to make efficient use of the striking improvements in technology. The widely varying economic experience among countries in the past two centuries essentially reflects the degree to which each has been able to profit from the advances in technology during this time.

Two factors that directly influence a nation's ability to realize its potential for technological growth are: the motivation, education, and knowledge of the populace; and the structure and efficiency of the economic organization. The production process has become increasingly complex in step with technological advance. Increasingly, better education and longer training are required to make efficient use of these innovations. This is especially true for underdeveloped economies. First of all, not only are skilled engineers and scientists essential to adapt the technology to the particular and usually rather unique conditions under which each economy operates, but highly trained operators are also a requisite to handle, service, and use the equipment effectively. Furthermore, significant improvements in technology often demand large-scale economic organization and an increasingly sophisticated society that evolves with economic growth to accommodate the growing army of professional people—engineers, chemists, physicists, lawyers, economists—essential to the operation of the economy. Thus there exists a necessary complementary relationship between improvements in physical capital embodying the new technology, and increasing demands for human capital embodying more knowledge and better training.

The type of economic organization constructed by a country is another important factor in determining the pace at which it may realize the growth potential offered by technological change. In general, an economy can be organized in one of three ways: by tradition, by planning, and by the free market system.

A traditional economy is one in which economic activities are undertaken in the present exactly as they were undertaken in the past; the economy of much of medieval Europe and several present-day African economies provide examples. A planned economy is centrally directed, and may thus be extremely progressive, with the economic system responding to a set of orders developed by planners; current examples may be seen in a number of more or less developed communist countries. The market system relies upon the self-interest of all individuals to provide the proper goods in the proper amounts and in the most efficient manner. As hypothesized by Adam Smith's famous "invisible hand," the self-interested activity of the individual, limited by the competition of other similarly self-motivated individuals, will result in society's receiving the maximum economic benefit from its resources. This follows because the largest profit or individual gain is to be earned by producing the goods consumers most desire. Also, as an individual discovers a new and profitable product or process, his success will cause others to imitate his efforts that they may share in the profits. The result is that society receives the new product as soon as it is economically feasible; because of the competition of rival producers, it is soon produced as efficiently as possible. Thus the free market system is conducive to rapid economic growth because it is in the self-interest of individuals to behave in a manner that results in economic growth.

The free market system presupposes two crucial conditions. First, people must be economically motivated; that is, they must be sufficiently eager to improve their economic position to respond to changes in prices and profits which are the orders of the market system. This assures that as conditions change resources will be reallocated so that society will continue to obtain the maximum benefit from its resources. Second, the individual must be free to enjoy the fruit of his labors; this is why the existence of private property is necessary to a market economy. Individuals will be most highly motivated economically if they alone are entitled to the rewards of their efforts.

THE SELECTION OF DOCUMENTS

The original sources presented in this history were selected because of their particular relevance to the growth of the American economy. They generally either illustrate the source of such growth or describe the organization of the economy. Only occasionally have we included documents from the rich storehouse of contemporary controversies concerning the adoption of economic policies. Generally such debates concerned, not the furtherance of economic growth, but simply the redistribution of income among members of society. Occasionally, debates focused on both those topics; in some such cases we have included excerpts from a relevant document, as on the tariff question, and on the Second National Bank. Many other debates, however, while forming a vital part of our economic history, usually were not central to the specific area of American economic growth.

The Interpretative Framework

The colonialization of America was a direct outgrowth of the significant changes in Europe that historians call the decline of feudalism and the rise of capitalism. The European economy during the fifteenth and sixteenth centuries was moving away from the small, local, self-contained economies we know as manorialism and toward regional and national economies in which trade and commerce played an important role. The ideological climate also underwent a radical change. There was violent ferment in religious and political views, and science as a body of knowledge made significant progress. This knowledge also began to be applied to economic problems as the improving economic organization of European society allowed and as the new spirit of individual gain directed. One of the manifestations of the new spirit of capitalism was the expansion of world trade and almost as an accident the rediscovery of America.

The rediscovery of America by Europe late in the fifteenth century greatly increased the stock of available resources in the Western world. Improved efficiency in the shipping industry during the sixteenth century allowed the beginning of European exploitations of these resources. Spain was the first country to do so on a large scale, and her great success and consequent increased world power both aroused the envy of other European nations and stimulated them to embark upon explorations of their own. These nations, among them the English, naturally first turned their attentions to that part of the New World to which the Spanish could not successfully contest their entry—the North American continent and the Caribbean.

Before they could exploit the unfamiliar resources of this unknown part of the New World, the English were forced to spend much of the first half of the seventeenth century in investigation and exploration. These initial efforts required a significant capital outlay by Britain, and it was suggested that this was the proper realm of the Crown. As it turned out, however, it was merchant companies that organized the first English settlements in the New World.

The Virginia Company, a private business, was formed to establish a colony on the North American continent for the purpose of earning profits for its shareholders, but the economic pursuits which would earn these profits remained unclear. The Spanish success had proved that wealth would be found in the New World. The company's problem was simply to find how to make profitable use of Virginia's resources. The original colonists were instructed to establish trade with the Indians, to search for the Northwest Passage, to prospect for precious metals, and to attempt to produce goods that could not be profitably produced in England. As it turned out, the establishment of a colony required significant investments of labor and capital which the company persistently underestimated, with the result that the colony faced starvation while it searched for profitable economic pursuits. The Northwest Passage was not found, nor were precious metals discovered; trade with the Indians proved insufficient to support the colony, and attempts to produce iron and glass and to grow wine grapes were economic failures. These experimental efforts cost dearly, for in the process a majority of the original colonists died, the company went bankrupt, and title to the colony reverted to the Crown. Despite these losses, and although British North America proved not to be the instant financial success that Spain had found South and Central America to be, the first permanent English settlement in the New World was established. In the process the colony did succeed in discovering tobacco and developing it as a profitable export crop.

After Virginia's initial experience, except for the small settlement at Plymouth it was two decades before another major English colony was established in North America. New England was settled in the 1630's by religious dissenters whose prospects in Europe were limited because of their unconventional sectarian views. The fear of a bleak economic future coupled with a desire to make their own society away from Europe's persecutions gave this group courage to endure a temporarily lower standard of living and to undertake the substantial risks of migration. To live, these colonists too were forced to seek goods that could be profitably traded to Europe in exchange for manufactures. Despite the export of fish and furs which initially served this purpose, the first New Englanders, like their predecessors in Virginia, suffered a time of near starvation while they were adjusting to their new environment.

At approximately the same time that New England was settled, the colony of Maryland was founded, also in the behalf of a religious minority. But the new colony's close proximity to Virginia allowed Maryland's settlers to make use of the experience gained earlier by their sister colony. They immediately took up the growing of tobacco; also, since they could obtain foodstuffs in Virginia when needed, their hardships were less rigorous.

Once established, each of the colonies depended for future economic growth upon the profitability of producing one or more export staples. To attract labor and capital from Europe in the amounts needed to ensure a viable economy, the colonies had to be able to offer for each factor of production a higher reward than it could earn in Europe. While there were other motives for immigration at this time, it is probable that laborers were attracted to the colonies in large numbers only if the standard of living in the colonies was higher than the immigrants would have enjoyed in the mother country. And, clearly, European owners of capital would lend to colonists, or invest directly in the New World, only if they expected to gain a greater return than could be earned at home.

On the other side of the ledger, since labor and capital could be paid these higher rewards only if they were more productive in the colonies than they would have been in Europe, it was requisite that both be put to their optimum use, which meant combining them with factors that were relatively abundant in the colonies—namely, land and natural resources. Thus the colonies naturally turned to mining the resources of the New World, and the production of agricultural products—tobacco, wheat, sugar, rice, and indigo—as well as fishing and developing forest products, became their major economic activities. Had the colonies been forced instead to be self-sufficient and to produce for themselves the range of goods which by these exports they obtained from Europe, there is no question that their productivity would have been less and their incomes lower. Thus the economic growth of the American colonies was set in motion by the search for suitable staple products to export, and gained momentum through international trade.

Since the pace of colonial economic growth was so closely geared to the profitability of producing these staple exports, any increase in their price, with resultant increase in profits, would lead to extensive growth. Eager to increase production in such circumstances, colonists offered higher returns to labor and capital. These higher rewards attracted labor and capital from Europe or from other economic activities within the colonies. Subsequent increases in output as a result reduced the price of the product to the point where further expansion was unprofitable. Expansion thus ceased until European demand once more caused the price of the product to rise, or improvements in the process of production lowered costs, thereby setting off another wave of economic expansion in the colonies.

The enactment by Britain in the 1660's of a set of regulations known as the Navigation Acts, designed to ensure a self-sufficient empire, substantially affected the pattern of colonial trade. While each American colony developed some direct trade with the mother country and with Europe, only certain colonies were well adapted to large scale international trade within this legal framework. The West Indies, for example, were able to specialize in the production of sugar; Virginia and Maryland, in the production of tobacco; and South Carolina, in the production of rice and indigo. New England and the Middle Colonies were unable to develop a large direct trade with the mother country, either because their major products could not be profitably shipped to Europe or, as in the case of foodstuffs produced in the Middle Colonies, because they were denied entry to the home market. These colonies, however, were able to find markets for their products in other colonies, sending foodstuffs to New England, the West Indies, and, to a lesser extent, the other staple-producing colonies. In turn, New England supplied the other colonies with fish, forest products, and especially merchant and shipping services.

This mutual interdependence grew during the colonial period and was a broad influence for extensive economic growth. An increase in demand for the export products of the staple-producing colonies caused their prices to rise and led to their accelerated production at the expense of the local production of foodstuffs. The Middle Colonies and New England then responded to an increased demand for foodstuffs on the part of the staple-producing colonies, which in turn induced further economic expansion in the former area, thus translating the initial demand for colonial staples into an extensive growth stimulus for the Atlantic colonies in general.

The substantial extensive growth of the American colonies is attested by the growth in population and is shown in the statistics for colonial trade. But it is doubtful that this growth was matched by similar improvements in the standard of living. Clearly the increase in the size of the colonial economy, leading to specialization, and probably some augmentation of capital and land per laborer produced small improvements in per capita incomes during the period. Technological advances did occur, but when compared to those in the nineteenth century, they appear extremely modest. In short, the conditions for rapid increase in per capita income were generally lacking during the colonial period. However, this was also true throughout the world, and doubtless the standard of living in the American colonies, even if not rapidly rising, was as high as anywhere, especially during the latter part of the colonial period.

The period between the American Revolution and the end of the War of 1812 was a period of disruption and readjustment for the American economy. The traditional trade patterns were forever destroyed, first by the Revolution, and then by the new nation's consequent position outside the British Empire, which caused American ships and to some extent exports to be treated by Britain as coming from a foreign nation. The British West Indies for example were closed to American ships, restricting this profitable trade outlet. The economy was forced to cope also with a swarm of vexatious domestic problems which were not resolved even by the ratification of the Constitution.

The economy's health during this period has been the topic of vigorous debate by economic historians. Unquestionably, the Revolutionary War severely disrupted the American economy; but descriptions of the period between 1783 and 1793 range from an assessment of acute depression to that of rapid economic growth. The lack of statistical data has made this question difficult to resolve. However, recent research suggests that the decade following the close of the Revolutionary War fits neither extreme. Rather, it was a period in which the economy reorganized itself and attempted to develop new export markets outside the British Empire.

The outbreak of war in Europe solved the problem of finding new markets: the Americans became the suppliers and carriers of goods to both sides. The years between 1793 and 1807 were extraordinarily prosperous as a result, until the embargo of 1808 suddenly cut off the source of this prosperity, bringing about unemployment and ultimately driving resources once employed in trading into manufacturing. In fact, this first wide-scale attempt to develop American manufacturing was premature and was made possible only by artificial conditions created by the embargo and the ensuing war. The end of the war and the resumption of normal trade relations with Great Britain allowed the importation of lower-priced English manufactures, destroying the market for American manufactures and causing a wave of bankruptcies among the new domestic industrial firms.

The period between the outbreak of the Revolution and the end of the second war with Great Britain saw the American economy emerge from colonial status, struggle through a period of turmoil under the Confederation, and establish stability under the Constitution. Her advantage as a neutral nation in a world at war brought about an era of prosperity for America until she too was drawn into the maelstrom. Except for the brief interval between 1793 and 1807, it is doubtful whether Americans enjoyed any substantial increase in their overall standard of living, even though the economy grew extensively as the population continued to increase at the substantial rate established in the colonial period. Shortly before the outbreak of the Revolution, population totaled 2,150,000; by 1790, it had increased to 3,930,000; and by 1815, to 8,420,000. During this period large numbers migrated beyond the Appalachians, so that by 1790 over 200,000 persons were settled there. The substantial rate of population increase continued through the pre-Civil War period, as did the westward movement. The population of the United States increased from 17,120,000 in 1840 to 31,500,000 in 1860. Between 1815 and 1860 the area east of the Mississippi River became fairly densely settled, as did Louisiana, eastern Texas, Arkansas, Missouri, and eastern Iowa.

Sometime between 1815 and the outbreak of the Civil War the rate of growth in per capita income accelerated. Exactly when this occurred remains uncertain, but it can easily be shown that it must have happened. If we but extrapolate backward from 1839 the rate of intensive growth of the economy which statistics show occurred after that date, we soon reach incomes for the earlier period that contemporary evidence suggests are absurdly low. The interpretation must follow that for most of the period before 1839 per capita incomes (if increasing at all) were increasing at a slower rate than after that date. Also, the acceleration in the rate of growth in per capita income must have occurred not very long before 1840.

This crucial period was characterized, as were previous expansions, by a substantial increase in international trade. The rapid extensive growth that occurred after 1815 differed from previous expansions in that it probably set in motion forces which made the United States actually less dependent upon international trade as the "engine of growth" and increasingly dependent upon the domestic market.

The main expansive force during this period was the export of cotton to Europe, particularly to England, which was in the midst of the Industrial Revolution and experiencing a rapid expansion of her cotton textile industry. This led to ever-increasing demands for raw cotton which the American South was particularly suited to supply. Before 1840 the expansion of the Northeast and West was influenced by the income they received indirectly from the cotton trade.

As might be expected, during those periods in which the demand for cotton was increasing more rapidly than the supply, the price of cotton rose substantially; this increased the profitability of the crop and induced planters to switch to cotton some of the land previously devoted to foodstuffs. The consequent increased demand for foodstuffs to feed themselves and their slaves caused the price of corn and pork to increase throughout the South and West.

The increased profitability of cotton also caused planters to seek to augment their total acreage, and a movement to the Southwest (the "new" South) ensued. In the West (or northern West) the increase in the price of foodstuffs led to the same phenomenon— attempts to increase acreage and production, and a general migration westward. The rapid increase in the supply of cotton, once new southern lands were put into production, then caused the price of cotton to fall, reducing the profitability of the crop. Part of the former cotton lands were again planted in foodstuffs because of the now relatively high price of corn and hogs; the decline in southern demands for foodstuffs in turn resulted in a decline in prices of these commodities, a reduction in profits of agriculture in the West, and a temporary halt in the westward movement.

During the expansion part of the cycle, increased southern and western incomes would lead predictably to increased demands by these regions for manufactured goods. Although these goods initially came from Europe during the period under consideration, they were carried, insured, and distributed by firms located in the Northeast. Thus agrarian expansion in the South and West induced complementary expansion in the eastern part of the country.

The major growth originated by cotton exports occurred during the 1830's. Increasingly during the 1820's and especially during the 1830's the Northeast discovered that it could profitably produce certain crude manufactures in competition with Europe to supply to the South and West. Thereafter, aided by a protective tariff and by substantial internal improvements in the form of canals and railroads which lowered the costs of interregional transportation, manufacturing in the Northeast rapidly expanded. These improvements in the transportation sector were not the result of private enterprise alone, but were joint ventures between governments at various levels and American entrepreneurs. The results of such mixed enterprise in generating social overhead capital were important to the growth of the economy.

A flexible pattern of domestic trade resulted from these developments. The Northeast, increasingly engaging in manufacturing, came to need foodstuffs to nourish its industrial population, so that a substantial direct East-West trade developed over the Great Lakes and the Erie Canal independent of the price of cotton or of any other export. Likewise it is clear in retrospect that all three major regions contributed to the substantial increase in per capita income experienced between 1815 and 1860. The rise of industry in the Northeast as a result of the expansion of the domestic market was obviously extremely important but cannot claim full credit. Productivity was increasing in the agricultural regions as well. Incomes in these areas rose with the migration onto new and richer lands which was made economically feasible by improvements in transportation. And, of course, the export trade of the South remained important even though its fortunes no longer dominated those of the United States as a whole.

The characteristics discussed earlier that are responsible for intensive growth—technical change, improvements in the quality of the factors of production, and improvements in economic organization—were all three very much in evidence during this period. The first, technological change, was obviously present, as Yankee ingenuity adapted European industrial techniques to the American scene. Second, this improved technical knowledge was not the result of formal research, as it is today, but stemmed mainly from the specialization allowed by an enlarged domestic market, coupled with the native abilities of a fairly literate, economically motivated populace. The investment made by society was large (for the time) in equipping its individual members with those motives and skills that made for economic advance when employed in specialized activities. And finally, the growth of international trade, especially of the export of cotton, stimulated market-oriented regional specialization and thereby ensured an efficient economic organization within a market economy.

I

Background to Colonization

The economic growth of the United States begins with the discovery of North America by Europeans. In an attempt to discover a less expensive way of obtaining the luxury goods of the East, European nations had been stimulated to search for a sea route to Asia, and the discovery of the New World was an accidental by-product of this search. The early discoverers, much to their chagrin, found the New World blocking a direct westward passage to the Orient. Portugal and Spain led in these voyages of exploration; Spain in the process discovered and claimed most of the continent of South America with its substantial stocks of gold and silver. While Spanish explorers were able to appropriate large amounts of precious metals from the Indians, these gains were small when compared to the wealth remaining to be exploited, and permanent Spanish settlements were established during the sixteenth century to operate mines. Spain was aided in this endeavor by the fortunate existence of an indigenous population suitable for use as labor. The precious metals obtained from the mines served as valuable exports which could be profitably exchanged for European goods and services needed by the new Spanish colonies. The output of the mines soon made Spain the most prosperous nation in Europe and aroused the envy of her neighbors. By the latter half of the sixteenth century, Spain's success had created an interest in colonization on the part of other European nations.

1. Reasons For Planting Colonies

England's interest in overseas trade and the establishment of colonies increased steadily from the 1570's onward. This awakening interest is attested by the publication of several pamphlets listing the advantages of establishing English colonies in the New World. Richard Hakluyt, the great sixteenth-century proponent of colonization, collected and published such documents, and the following selection is from one of his works.

SOURCE: A true Report of the late discoveries, and possession taken in the right of the Crowne of England of the Newfound Lands, By that valiant and worthy Gentleman, Sir Humfrey Gilbert Knight.

15

The second Chapter sheweth, that it is lawfull and necessarie to trade and traffique with the Savages: And to plant in their Countries: And divideth planting into two sorts.

And first for traffique, I say that the Christians may lawfully travell into those Countries and abide there: whom the Savages may not justly impugne and forbidde in respect of the mutuall societie and fellowshippe betweene man and man prescribed by the Law of Nations.

· · ·

The first, when Christians by the good liking and willing assent of the Savages, are admitted by them to quiet possession.

The second, when Christians being unjustly repulsed, doe seeke to attaine and mainteine the right for which they doe come.

· · ·

Moreover, it shall be requisite eyther by speeche, if it be possible, either by some other certaine meanes, to signifie unto them, that once league of friendship with all loving conversation being admitted betweene the Christians and them: that then the Christians from thenceforth will alwayes be ready with force of Armes to assist and defend them in their just quarrels, from all invasions, spoyles and oppressions offered them by any Tyrants, Adversaries, or their next borderers: and a benefite is so much the more to be esteemed, by how much the person upon whom it is bestowed standeth in neede thereof.

For it appeareth by the relation of a Countryman of ours, namely David Ingram, (who travelled in those countries xi. Moneths and more) That the Savages generally for the most part, are at continuall warres with their next adjoyning neighbours, and especially the Cannibals, being a cruell kinde of people, whose foode is mans flesh, and have teeth like dogges, and doe pursue them with ravenous mindes to eate their flesh, and devoure them.

Wherein is also briefly set downe, her highnesse lawfull Title thereunto, and the great and manifold commodities, that are likely to grow therby, to the whole Realme in generall, and to the Adventurers in particular: Together with the easinesse and shortnesse of the Voyage.

Written by Sir George Peckham Knight, the chiefe adventurer, and furtherer of Sir Humfrey Gilberts voyage to Newfound Land.

From Richard Hakluyt, *The Principal Navigations, Voyages, Traffiques, and Discoveries of the English Nation* (Glasgow: James MacLehose and Sons, 1904), VIII, 97–101, 108, 110–13, 119–21, 130.

And it is not to be doubted, but that the Christians may in this case justly and lawfully ayde the Savages against the Cannibals. So that it is very likely, that by this meanes we shall not only mightily stirre and inflame their rude mindes gladly to embrace the loving company of the Christians, proffering unto them both commodities, succour, and kindnesse: But also by their franke consents shall easily enjoy such competent quantity of Land, as every way shall be correspondent to the Christians expectation and contentation, considering the great abundance that they have of Land, and how small account they make thereof, taking no other fruites thereby then such as the ground of it selfe doeth naturally yeelde. And thus much concerning the first sort of planting, which as I assuredly hope, so I most heartily pray may take effect and place.

But if after these good and fayre meanes used, the Savages neverthelesse will not bee herewithall satisfied, but barbarously will goe about to practise violence eyther in repelling the Christians from their Ports and safe-landings, or in withstanding them afterwards to enjoy the rights for which both painfully and lawfully they have adventured themselves thither:

Then in such a case I holde it no breach of equitie for the Christians to defend themselves, to pursue revenge with force, and to doe whatsoever is necessarie for the atteining of their safetie: For it is allowable by all Lawes in such distresses, to resist violence with violence: And for their more securitie to increase their strength by building of Forts for avoyding the extremitie of injurious dealing.

. . .

The third Chapter doeth shew the lawfull title which the Queenes most excellent Majestie hath unto those Countries, which through the ayde of Almighty God are meant to be inhabited.

And it is very evident that the planting there shal in time right amply enlarge her Majesties Territories and Dominions, or (I might rather say) restore to her Highnesse ancient right and interest in those Countries, into the which a noble and worthy personage, lineally descended from the blood royall, borne in Wales, named Maddock ap Owen Gwyneth, departing from the coast of England, about the yeere of our Lord God 1170 arrived and there planted himselfe and his Colonies, and afterward returned himselfe into England, leaving certaine of his people there, as appeareth in an ancient Welsh Chronicle, where he then gave to certaine Ilands, beastes, and foules sundry Welsh names, as the Iland of Pengwin, which yet to this day beareth the same.

. . .

The fourth chapter sheweth how that the trade, traffike, and planting in those countreys, is likely to prove very profitable to the whole realme in generall.

Now to shew how the same is likely to proove very profitable and beneficiall generally to the whole realme: it is very certaine, that the greatest jewell of this realme, and the chiefest strength and force of the same, for defence or offence in marshall matter and maner, is the multitude of ships, masters and mariners, ready to assist the most stately and royall navy of her Majesty, which by reason of this voyage shall have both increase and maintenance. And it is well knowen that in sundry places of this realme ships have beene built and set forth of late dayes, for the trade of fishing onely: yet notwithstanding the fish which is taken and brought into England by the English navy of fishermen, will not suffice for the expense of this realme foure moneths, if there were none els brought of strangers. And the chiefest cause why our English men doe not goe so farre Westerly as the especiall fishing places doe lie, both for plenty and greatnesse of fish, is for that they have no succour and knowen safe harbour in those parts. But if our nation were once planted there, or neere thereabouts; whereas they now fish but for two moneths in the yeere, they might then fish so long as pleased themselves, or rather at their comming finde such plenty of fish ready taken, salted, and dried, as might be sufficient to fraught them home without long delay (God granting that salt may be found there) whereof David Ingram (who travelled in those countreys as aforesayd) sayth that there is great plenty: and withall the climate doth give great hope, that though there were none naturally growing, yet it might as well be made there by art, as it is both at Rochel and Bayon, or elsewhere. Which being brought to passe, shall increase the number of our shippes and mariners, were it but in respect of fishing onely: but much more in regard of the sundry merchandizes and commodities which are there found, and had in great abundance.

Moreover, it is well knowen that all Savages, aswell those that dwell in the South, as those that dwell in the North, so soone as they shall begin but a little to taste of civility, will take marvelous delight in any garment, be it never so simple; as a shirt, a blew, yel-low, red, or greene cotten cassocke, a cap, or such like, and will take incredible paines for such a trifle.

. . .

To what end need I endevour my selfe by arguments to prove that by this voyage our navie and navigation shalbe inlarged, when as there needeth none other reason then the manifest and late ex-ample of the neere neighbours to this realme, the kings of Spaine and Portugall, who since the first discovery of the Indies, have not onely mightily inlarged their dominions, greatly inriched them-selves and their subjects: but have also by just account trebled the number of their shippes, masters and mariners, a matter of no small moment and importance?

Besides this, it will proove a generall benefit unto our countrey, that through this occasion, not onely a great number of men which do now live idlely at home, and are burthenous, chargeable, and unprofitable to this realme, shall hereby be set on worke, but also children of twelve or fourteene yeeres of age, or under, may bee kept from idlenesse, in making of a thousand kindes of trifling things, which wil be good merchandize for that countrey. And more-over, our idle women (which the Realme may well spare) shall also be imployed on plucking, drying, and sorting of feathers, in pulling, beating, and working of hempe, and in gathering of cotton, and divers things right necessary for dying. All which things are to be found in those countreys most plentifully. And the men may imploy themselves in dragging for pearle, woorking for mines, and in mat-ters of husbandry, and likewise in hunting the Whale for Trane, and making caskes to put the same in: besides in fishing for cod, salmon, and herring, drying salting and barrelling the same, and felling of trees, hewing and sawing of them, and such like worke, meete for those persons that are no men of Art or science.

Many other things may bee found to the great reliefe and good employments of no small number of the naturall Subjects of this Realme, which doe now live here idlely to the common annoy of the whole state. Neither may I here omit the great hope and like-lyhood of a passage beyond the Grand Bay into the South Seas, confirmed by sundry authours to be found leading to Cataia, the Moluccas and Spiceries, whereby may ensue as generall a benefite to the Realme, or greater then yet hath been spoken of, without either such charges, or other inconveniences, as by the tedious tract of time and perill, which the ordinary passage to those parts at this day doeth minister.

· · ·

The fift chapter sheweth, that the trading and planting in those countreis is likely to prove to the particular profit of all adventurers.

I must now according to my promise shew foorth some probable reasons that the adventurers in this journey are to take particular profit by the same. It is therefore convenient that I doe divide the adventurers into two sorts: the noblemen and gentlemen by themselves, and the Merchants by themselves. For, as I doe heare, it is meant that there shall be one societie of the Noblemen and Gentlemen, and another societie of the merchants. And yet not so divided, but that eche society may freely and frankely trade and traffique one with the other.

· · ·

The sixt Chapter sheweth that the traffique and planting in those countries, shall be unto the Savages themselves very beneficiall and gainefull.

Now to the end it may appeare that this voyage is not undertaken altogether for the peculiar commodity of our selves and our countrey (as generally other trades and journeis be) it shall fall out in proofe, that the Savages shall hereby have just cause to blesse the houre when this enterprise was undertaken.

First and chiefly, in respect of the most happy and gladsome tidings of the most glorious Gospel of our Saviour Jesus Christ, whereby they may be brought from falshood to trueth, from darknesse to light, from the hie way of death to the path of life, from superstitious idolatrie to sincere Christianity, from the devill to Christ, from hell to heaven. And if in respect of all the commodities they can yeelde us (were they many moe) that they should but receive this onely benefit of Christianity, they were more then fully recompenced.

· · ·

The seventh Chapter sheweth that the planting there, is not a matter of such charge or difficultie, as many would make it seeme to be.

Now therefore for proofe, that the planting in these parts is a thing that may be done without the ayde of the Princes power and purse, contrary to the allegation of many malicious persons, who wil neither be actors in any good action themselves, nor so much as afoord a good word to the setting forward thereof: and that worse is, they will take upon them to make molehilles seeme mountaines, and flies elephants, to the end they may discourage others, that be very well or indifferently affected to the matter, being like unto Esops dogge, which neither would eate Hay himselfe, nor suffer the poore hungry asse to feede thereon:

I say and affirme that God hath provided such meanes for the furtherance of this enterprise, as doe stand us in stead of great treasure: for first by reason that it hath pleased God of his great goodnesse, of long time to hold his merciful hand over this realme, in preserving the people of the same, both from slaughter by the sword, and great death by plague, pestilence, or otherwise, there are at this day great numbers (God he knoweth) which live in such penurie and want, as they could be contented to hazard their lives, and to serve one yeere for meat, drinke and apparell only, without wages, in hope thereby to amend their estates: which is a matter in such like journeyes, of no small charge to the prince. Moreover, things in the like journyes of greatest price and cost as victuall (whereof there is great plentie to be had in that countrey without money) and powder, great artillery, or corselets are not needefull in so plentifull and chargeable maner, as the shew of such a journey may present: for a small quantitie of all these, to furnish the Fort only, will suffice untill such time as divers commodities may be found out in those parts, which may be thought well worthy a greater charge. Also the peculiar benefit of archers which God hath blessed this land withall before all other nations, will stand us in great stead amongst those naked people.

. . .

To conclude, since by Christian dutie we stand bound chiefly to further all such acts as do tend to the encreasing the true flock of Christ by reducing into the right way those lost sheepe which are yet astray: And that we shall therein follow the example of our right vertuous predecessors of renowned memorie, and leave unto our posteritie a divine memoriall of so godly an enterprise: Let us I say for the considerations alledged, enter into judgement with our selves, whether this action may belong to us or no, the rather for that this voyage through the mighty assistance of the omnipotent God, shall take our desired effect (whereof there is no just cause of doubt). Then shal her Majesties dominions be enlarged, her high-nesse ancient titles justly confirmed, all odious idlenesse from this our Realme utterly banished, divers decayed townes repaired, and many poore and needy persons relieved, and estates of such as now live in want shall be embettered, the ignorant and barbarous idol-aters taught to know Christ, the innocent defended from their bloodie tyrannicall neighbours, the diabolicall custome of sacrificing humane creatures abolished.

II

The Founding of the First English Colonies

The first wave of English colonization of the New World came between 1607 and the outbreak of civil war in England. Thirteen colonies were successfully established during this period, seven on the North American continent and six in the West Indies. The English civil war and its aftermath left England with little time to supervise her colonies, so that American colonial development before 1660 occurred with very little interference from abroad. Each colony produced staples for export to Europe: fish and furs from New England; tobacco and furs from Virginia and Maryland; and from the West Indies, tobacco, cotton, and (after 1640) sugar. Before 1660 a large portion of the trade of the American colonies, especially the tobacco trade, was carried on with the Dutch. During this period a vigorous trade between the colonies also developed, with residents of New England serving as both merchants and shippers for the Atlantic colonies.

2. The Establishment of Virginia

Peace with Spain in 1604 had cleared the way for the successful planting of the first non-Spanish colonies in the New World. During the first three decades of the seventeenth century, thirteen permanent English colonies were established in the Caribbean and on the North American continent. On the continent, Virginia and Maryland were planted in the South and Massachusetts Bay, Plymouth, Rhode Island, Connecticut, and New Haven were established in the North. In the West Indies, the islands of St. Christopher, Antigua, Nevis, Monteserrat, Barbados, and Bermuda were settled. While Spain still claimed all of the New World, her effective control did not extend north of Florida, nor did Spain control the lesser islands of the West Indies or the Guinea coast of South America. In these three areas the English as well as the French, Dutch, and other European nations established their colonies during the seventeenth century. The English came to the New World seeking to share the wealth which Spanish success had proven to exist there. The exact method by which wealth could be obtained was uncertain. Whether it would come as a result of the discovery of gold and silver, the discovery of the Northwest Passage, or from the exploitation of the New World's natural resources was a matter to be determined by the first colonists. Exploration and experimentation were therefore to be the main activities of the colonists during their first several years in the New World.

Colonizing ventures required a legal title to the land, the accumulation of capital, and the migration of labor—and the bringing together of these three factors of production by promoters or entrepreneurs. The promoters of the first permanent English colony at Jamestown in Virginia were, in the main, merchants, who formed a joint-stock company patterned after the Muskovy, Levant, and East India companies. Their expectations, and the way in which the Virginia Company set out to colonize the New World, are described in the following document.

The country it selfe is large and great assuredly, though as yet, no exact discovery can bee made of all. It is also commendable and hopefull every way, the ayre and clymate most sweete and wholsome, much warmer then England, and very agreeable to our Natures: It is inhabited with wild and savage people, that live and lie up and downe in troupes like heards of Deare in a Forrest: they have no law but nature, their apparell skinnes of beasts, but most goe naked: the better sort have houses, but poore ones, they have no Arts nor Science, yet they live under superior command such as it is, they are generally very loving and gentle, and doe entertaine and relieve our people with great kindnesse: they are easy to be brought to good, and would fayne embrace a better condition: the land yeeldeth naturallie for the sustentation of man, aboundance of fish, both scale and shell: of land and water fowles, infinite store: of Deere, Kaine and Fallow, Stags, Coneys, and Hares, with many fruits and rootes good for meate.

There are valleyes and plaines streaming with sweete Springs, like veynes in a naturall bodie: there are hills and mountaines making a sensible proffer of hidden treasure, never yet searched: the land is full of mineralles, plentie of woods (the wants of England) there

SOURCE: "Nova Brittania: offering most excellent fruites by planting in Virginia.—Exciting all such as be well affected to further the same.—
London, Printed for Samuel Macham, and are to be sold at his shop in Pauls Church-yard, at the signe of the Bul-head . . . 1609."
From Peter Force (ed.), Tracts and Other Papers Relating Principally to the Origin, Settlement and Progress of the Colonies in North America (4 vols.; New York: Peter Smith, 1947), I, vi, 11–12, 16–19, 21–6.

are growing goodly Okes and Elmes, Beech and Birch, Spruce, Walnut, Cedar and Firre trees, in great aboundance, the soile is strong
and lustie of its owne nature, and sendeth our naturally fruitfull
Vines running upon trees, and shrubbes: it yeeldeth also Rosin,
Turpentine, Pitch and Tarre, Sassafras, Mulbery-trees and Silke-
wormes, many Skinnes and rich furres, many sweete woodes, and
Dyers woodes, and other costly dyes: plenty of Sturgion, Timber
for Shipping, Mast, Plancke and Deale, Sope ashes, Caviare, and
what else we know not yet, because our daies are young. But of this
that I have said, if bare nature be so amiable in its naked kind, what
may we hope, when Arte and Nature both shall joyne, and strive
together, to give best content to man and beast? . . .

· · ·

And now it followes, how it can be good for this Commonwealth:
which is likewise most apparent many waies. First, if we consider
what strength of shipping may be raysed and maintained thence,
in furnishing our owne wants of sundrie kindes, and the wants of
other Nations too, in such needfull things arising thence which can
hardly now be obtained from any other part of the world, as planck
and tymber for shipping, with Deale and Wainscot, pipestaves and
clabbord, with store of Sope ashes, whereof there grow the best
woods to make them in great aboundance, all which we may there
have, the wood for the cutting, and the Ashes for the burning,
which though they be grosse commodities, yet no Marchandize is
better requested, nor will sooner yeelde golde or silver in any our
bordering Nations. England and Holland alone, spend in these
about three hundreth thousand poundes sterling every yeare. We
may transport hether or unto Hamborough, Holland, or other
places, fiftie *per centum* better cheape, then from Prusia or Polonia,
from whence they are onely now to be had, where also the woods
are so spent and wasted, that from the place where the wood is cut
and the ashes burnt, they are brought by land at least two hundred
miles to ship. And from thence we may have Iron and Copper also
in great quantitie, about which the expence and waste of woode, as
also for building of Shippes, will be no hurt, but great service to
that countrey; the great superfluity whereof, the continuall cutting
downe, in manie hundred yeares, will not be able to overcome,
whereby will likewise grow a greater benefite to this land, in preserving our woodes and tymber at home, so infinitely and without

measure, upon these occasions cutte downe, and falne to such a sicknesse and wasting consumption, as all the physick in England cannot cure.

We doubt not but to make there in few yeares store of good wines, as any from the Canaries, by replanting and making tame the Vines that naturally grow there in great abundance, onely send men of skill to doe it, and Coopers to make caskes, and hoopes for that and all other uses, for which there is woode enough at hand.

There are Silke-wormes, and plenty of Mulberie-trees, whereby Ladies, Gentlewomen and little children, (beeing set in the way to doe it) may bee all imploied with pleasure, in making Silke, comparable to that of *Persia, Turkey,* or any other. We may bring from thence Sturgion, Caviare, and new land-fish of the best. There grows hempe for Cordage, an excellent commoditie, and flaxe for linnen cloth; which beeing sowen and well manured, in such a clymate and fertile soyle, will make great benefite, and will put downe that of other countries.

And for the making of Pitch, Tarre, Turpentine, Sope-ashes, Deale, Wainscott, and such like, wee have alreadie provided and sent thither skillfull workemen from forraine parts, which may teach and set ours in the way, whereby we may set many thousands a worke, in these such like services.

For as I tolde you before, there must be Art and industry with our helps and means extended, with a little pacience to bring these things to passe, wee must not looke to reape with joy, except we sow in teares: The aboundance of King *Solomons* golde and silver, did not raine from heaven upon the heads of his subjects: but heavenly providence blessed his Navigations and publike affayres, the chiefe meanes of their wealth.

Experience hath lately taught us by some of our neighbour Provinces, how exceedingly it mounts the State of a Commonwealth, to put forth Navigation (if it were possible) into all parts and corners of the world, to furnish our owne wants, and also to supply from one kingdome to another, such severall needfull things, as for want of shipping and other meanes they cannot furnish of themselves, for this will raise experience, and men of skill, as also strength at Sea and land, with honour, wealth, and riches, returning still to the heads and fountaines, from whence their first occasions grew.

Wee may but looke a little backe, and wee shall see what a novice our nation was within these sixscore yeeres, in case of forraine trade, not knowing whence to fetch, nor which way to transport, but onely to some marte or staple towne, within two daies sailing, and that was counted so great a matter then, that therefore they were called Marchant adventurers, and the great Hulkes of *Italy*, which in those daies brought spices Corants and such like, and landes at *South-ampton*, (the Storehouse then for Marchandize) are Chronicled for wonders in our *English* Stories for indeede we knew no better then, but were content (as babes) with *Easterlings* on the one hand and *Lumbards* on the other, which were continuall Liegers in *London*, and fed us as they listed.

And take this ever as a rule, that Domesticke Marchandizing brings forth but poore effects in a Commonwealth, whereof I needed not have shewed example further then our owne doores.

· · ·

And now to our present businesse in hand, which so many stumble at, in regard of the continuall charge, I would have them know, that it cannot be great nor long, as the businesse may be handled. Two things are especially required herein, people to make the plantation, and money to furnish our present provisions and shippings now in hand: For the first wee neede not doubt, our land abounding with swarmes of idle persons, which having no meanes of labour to relieve their misery, doe likewise swarme in lewd and naughtie practises, so that if we seeke not some waies for their forreine employment, wee must provide shortly more prisons and corrections for their bad conditions, for it fares with populous common weales, as with plants and trees that bee too frolicke, which not able to sustaine and feede their multitude of branches, doe admit an engrafting of their buds and sciences into some other soile, accounting it a benefite for preservation of their kind, and a disburdening their stocke of those superfluous twigs that suck away their nourishment. . . .

Yet I doe not meane, that none but such unsound members, and such poore as want their bread, are fittest for this imployment: for we intend to have of every trade and profession, both honest, wise and painefull men, whereof our land and Citie is able to spare, and furnish many (as we had experience in our last sending thither) which will be glad to goe, and plant themselves so happily, and their children after them, to holde and keepe conformitie, with the lawes, language and religion of England for ever.

· · ·

And as for the generall sort that shall goe to bee planters, bee they never so poore, so they be honest, and painefull, the place will make them rich: all kinde of Artificers wee must first imploy, are Carpenters, Ship-wrights, Masons, Sawyers, Brickemakers, Bricklayers, Plowmen, Sowers, Planters, Fishermen, Coopers, Smiths, Mettel-men, Taylers, Turners, and such like, to make and fitte all necessaries, for comfort and use of the Colony, and for such as are of no trades (if they bee industrious) they shall have there imployment enough, for there is a world of means to set many thousands a worke, partly in such things as I mentioned before, and many other profitable workes, for no man must live idle there.

•　　•　　•

Wee intend to plant there (God willing) great plentie of Sugar Canes, for which the soyle and clymate is very apt and fit; also Linseed, and Rapeseeds to make Oiles, which because the soyle is strong and cheape, may there be sowed and the oyle made to great benefite: wee must plant also Orenges, Limons, Almonds, Anniseeds, Rice, Cummin, Cotton wool, Carowey seeds, Ginger, Madder, Olives, Oris, Sumacke, and many such like, which I cannot now name, all very good Marchandize, and will there grow and increase, as well as in *Italy* or any other part of the streights, whence we fetch them now. And in searching the land there is undoubted hope of finding Cochinell, the plant of rich Indico, Graine-berries, Beaver Hydes, Pearles, rich Treasure, and the South sea, leading to *China*, with many other benefites which our day-light will discover.

But of all other things, that God hath denied that countrie, there is want of Sheepe to make woollen cloth, and this want of cloth, must alwaies bee supplied from England, whereby when the Colony is thorowly increased, and the *Indians* brought to our Civilitie (as they will in short time) it will cause a mighty vent of *English* clothes, a great benefit to our Nation, and raising againe of that auncient trade of clothing, so much decayed in England: whose lifting up againe (me thinkes I see apparantly approching,) by the good dispositions of our best sort of Citizens, who willingly engage themselves to undertake all new discoveries, as into this of the West, and by the North West to finde out *China*. And unto the East beyond the *Cape*, into the *Red Sea*, the gulfe of *Persia*, the streights of *Sunda*, and among all the Kings of *India*, for the good and honour of our Nation: Which calles to minde, a blind Prophesie in one of the *Sibells*, that before the ende of the world there shall be a discoverie of all Nations: which shall come to bee knowne and acquainted together, as one neighbour with another, which since the confusion of tongues have lyen obscure and hid.

But however that bee, yet these good mindes and resolutions, doe serve for imitation to others, and doe deserve assuredly the best encouragement, whereby wee shall not still betake our selves to small and little Shipping (as we dayly do beginne,) but shall reare againe such Marchants Shippes both tall and stout, as no forreine Sayle that swimmes shall make them vaile or stoope: whereby to make this little Northerne corner of the world, to be in short time the richest Store-house and Staple for marchandize in all Europe.

The second thing to make this Plantation is money, to be raised among the adventurers, wherein the sooner and more deeply men engage themselves, their charge will be the shorter, and their gaine the greater, as in this last point which I have to speake for the good of each particular Adventurer, I will make it plaine.

First you shall understand, that his Majestie hath granted us an enlargement of our Charter, with many ample priviledges, wherein we have Knights and Gentlemen of good place: Named for the Kings counsell of *Virginia* to governe us: As also every Planter and Adventurer shall be inserted in the Patent by name. This ground being laide, wee purpose presently to make supply of Men, Women and Children (so many as we can) to make the Plantation. Wee call those Planters that goe in their persons to dwell there: And those Adventurers that adventure their money and go not in person, and both doe make the members of one Colonie. We do account twelve pound ten shillings to be a single share adventured. Every ordinary man or woman, if they will goe and dwell there, and every childe above tenne yeares, that shall be carried thither to remaine, shall be allowed for each of their persons a single share, as if they had adventured twelve pound ten shillings in money. Everie extraordinarie man, as Divines, Governors, Ministers of State and Justice, Knights, Gentlemen, Physitions, and such as be men of worth for special services, are all to goe as planters, and to execute their several functions in the Colonie, and are to be maintained at the common charge, and are to receive their Divident (as others doe) at seven yeares end, and they are to be agreed with all before they goe, and to be rated by the Councell, according to the value of their persons: which shall be set downe and Registred in a booke, that it may alwaies appeare what people have gone to the

Plantation, at what time they went and how their persons were valued: And likewise, if any that goe to bee planters will lay downe money to the Treasurer, it shall be also registred and their shares inlarged accordingly be it for more or lesse. All charges of setling and maintaining the Plantation, and of making supplies, shall be borne in a joint stock of the adventurers for seven yeares after the date of our new enlargement: during which time there shall be no adventure, nor goods returned in private from thence, neytheir by Master, Marriner, Planter, nor Passenger, they shall be restrained by bond and search, that as we supplie from hence to the Planters at our owne charge all necessaries for food and apparel, for fortifying and building of houses in a joynt stock, so they are also to returne from thence the encrease and fruits of their labours, for the use and advancement of the same joynt stocke, till the end of seven yeares: at which time wee purpose (God willing) to make a division by Commissioners appointed, of all the lands granted unto us by his Majestie, to every of the Colonie, according to each mans severall adventure, agreeing with our Register booke, which wee doubt not will bee for every share of twelve pound tenne shillings, five hundred acres at least. Now if any thinke that wee shall bee tyed to a continuall charge, of making new supplies for seven yeares, let them conceive thus much, that if we doe it thorowly at the first, by engaging our selves at once, in furnishing many men and other meanes: assuredly after the second yeare, the returnes from thence will be able with an over-plus, to make supplies at large, so that our purses shall be freed, and the over-plus of stock will also grow to greatness, which stock is also (as the land) to be divided equally at seven yeares end or sooner, or so often as the company shall thinke fit for the greatness of it, to make a Divident.

And as by this wee shall be soone freed from charge and expence, so there grows a greater benefit to the planters (by bestowing their labours cheerfully) to make returne of stocke, for hereby the sooner they freeing us from disbursements, the more our shares and portions will be lessened in the Divident of Stocke and land at seven yeeres end, whereby the lesse comming to us, the more will be to them, so that heere is no discouragement any way, if men will be capable to doe themselves good. But if we will be so wise to linger, and lie in the winde, to heare what newes, to bring in our stocke next yeare, and when we are behinde for foure or five Adventures, we come dropping in with one or two and still runne in arrerages for twice so much: (For I know many that would bring in stocke amongst us, but they lie out to see what successe first: and upon such like termes.) Is this Gentleman-like, or Marchant-like, in truth it is paultry, and such as would bring all to naught, if we should bee so minded too, and I tell you true, our single shares will make but a hungry plantation, if we doe not at the least double them now: and therefore I urge it the more, for that the very life of all is now in the beginning by making our supplies thoroughly, and thence will our gaines arise both sooner and certain. Yet I grant that others may come in hereafter at any time, eyther to adventure his person or money, or both, but if there be spent one yeere of the seven before he comes in, or hee that comes in with the first shall notwithstanding bee a yeare behinde in supplies, they shall be both alike shortened in a seventh part of the Divident both of stocke and lands, and if two yeeres behinde, then shortened two sevenths, and if but sixe moneths, yet a fourteenth part, for every man is Registred according to the time, his money or person beganne to adventure, or made supply, so that they which come late, get not the start of those that bore the first brunt of the business, and this will neither advantage him that withholds, nor hinder him that is forward, for whatsoever falles from him that is slack, will be found of him that supplies in due time. But every man that comes in now in the first of these seven yeeres and shall afterwards upon all occasions perform in due time, every twelve pound tenne shillings so brought in shall bee accounted an entire single share, and shall receive accordingly without abridgement, as it had beene brought in, when the enterprise first beganne and not otherwise.

And as for the divisions of landes at seven yeeres ende which (some may object) will be little worth, and unequally divided: let them understand, that no man shall have his lot entirely in one place, to be all of the best, or all of the worst, but each man shall have proportionably to his adventures, in three or foure distinct differences, that may bee made in the goodnesse or badnesse of the groundes by Commissioners equally chosen by the Adventurers heere, and the Planters there; and as for the value and little worth now, of those grounds in Virginia, we know that in England within these thirty or fortie yeeres, the yeerely rent of those grounds (in many places) were not worth five shillings, that now do goe for fourtie and more.

And howsoever those grounds in Virginia are now but little

worth indeede, yet time and meanes will make them better, considering how they passe our grounds in *England*, both in regard of the soile and clymate, fitte for many precious uses: And also in how many severall places we purpose to plant our Colony, and not to bestow our costs upon *James-towne* onely, and upon the grounds lying thereabout, and to let all the rest lie barren: for seeing his Majestie hath graunted to our Colony as much circuite of ground as all *England* almost, we purpose (God willing) if wee may be supplied with sufficient meanes, to settle out of hand, sixe or seven plantations more, all upon, or neare our main-river, as capitall townes, twenty myles each from other, and every plantation shall manure and husband the lands and grounds lying neere unto it, and allotted for the circuite thereof, and shall all endevour for a joynt stocke, and shall be still supplied from hence with more money and provisions, and against any publike injury shall be ready to unite, and joyne themselves together. And by this meanes wee shall come to have our Divident in landes of worth and well manured, which will be eyther bought or rented of us at a good value by the planters, or by such as intend hereafter to inhabite there, as also by these several plantations (which happily one place better fitting then another) wee shall bring forth more severall sorts of Marchandize, and be also better fortified: and besides the Planters will be in such hope to have their owne shares and habitations in those lands, which they have so husbanded, that it will cause contending and emulation among them, which shall bring foorth the most profitable and beneficiall fruites for the joynt stocke.

Whereby undoubtedly, wee shall be soone freed from further expence, our gaines will grow, and our stocke encrease, we shall fell our tymber, saw our planck, and quickly make good shipping there, and shall returne from thence with good imployment, an hundred saile of good shippes yearely, all which good and much more, wee shall withstand and bring our selves into a laborinth, if wee pinch and spare our purses now: therefore not to holde you longer with many wordes, (being neere Exchange time as I take it) remember what I have said in proving my proposition, and take my conclusion in a word or two.

Seeing our provocations are so many, our cause and title good, avaunt all idle oracles that seeke to bar us: The wisedome of the wisest saith in these cases, *Whatsoever thy hand shall find to doe, do it with all thy might.*

3. The Starving Time

The Virginia Company at the outset of its colonizing venture was uncertain which kind of economic activity should engage the colony's efforts. It was equally ignorant about how to establish a viable colony. This led to mistakes that meant hard times for the first settlers, since they found themselves undercapitalized and with insufficient knowledge of their new land to be initially self-sufficient even in the production of food. Surrounded by often hostile Indians and unable to obtain supplies easily or quickly from Europe, the colony was soon reduced to starvation. So drastic did the situation become that several of the colonists resorted to cannibalism. The situation was relieved only by the timely arrival of supplies by ship.

The day before Captaine Smith returned for England with the ships, Captaine Davis arrived in a small Pinace, with some sixteene proper men more: To these were added a company from James towne, under the command of Captaine John Sickelmore alias Ratliffe, to inhabit Point Comfort. Captaine Martin and Captaine West, having lost their boats and neere halfe their men among the Salvages, were returned to James towne; for the Salvages no sooner understood Smith was gone, but they all revolted, and did spoile and murther all they incountered.

Now wee were all constrained to live onely on that Smith had onely for his owne Companie, for the rest had consumed their proportions. And now they had twentie Presidents with all their appurtenances: Master Piercie, our new President, was so sicke hee could neither goe nor stand. But ere all was consumed, Captaine West and Captaine Sickelmore, each with a small ship and thirtie or fortie men well appointed, sought abroad to trade. Sickelmore upon the confidence of Powhatan, with about thirtie others as carelesse as himselfe, were all slaine; onely Jeffrey Shortridge escaped; and Pokahontas the Kings daughter saved a boy called Henry Spilman, that lived many yeeres after, by her meanes, amongst the Patawomekes. Powhatan still, as he found meanes, cut off their Boats, denied them trade: so that Captaine West set saile for Eng-

SOURCE: Captain John Smith, "What happened in the first gouernment after the alteration, in the time of Captaine George Piercie, their Gouernour," (1609), *The Generall Historie of Virginia by Captain John Smith*, 1624; *The Fourth Booke*, in Lyon Gardiner Tyler (ed.), *Narratives of Early Virginia* (New York: Charles Scribner and Sons, 1907), 294–6.

land. Now we all found the losse of Captaine Smith, yea his great-est maligners could now curse his losse: as for corne provision and contribution from the Salvages, we had nothing but mortall wounds, with clubs and arrowes; as for our Hogs, Hens, Goats, Sheepe, Horse, or what lived, our commanders, officers and Salvages daily consumed them, some small proportions sometimes we tasted, till all was devoured; then swords, armes, pieces, or any thing, wee traded with the Salvages, whose cruell fingers were so oft imbrewed in our blouds, that what by their crueltie, our Governours indis-cretion, and the losse of our ships, of five hundred within six moneths after Captaine Smiths departure, there remained not past sixtie men, women and children, most miserable and poore crea-tures; and those were preserved for the most part, by roots, herbes, acornes, walnuts, berries, now and then a little fish: they that had startch in these extremities, made no small use of it; yea, even the very skinnes of our horses. Nay, so great was our famine, that a Salvage we slew and buried, the poorer sort tooke him up againe and eat him; and so did divers one another boyled and stewed with roots and herbs: And one amongst the rest did kill his wife, pow-dered her, and had eaten part of her before it was knowne; for which hee was executed, as hee well deserved: now whether shee was better roasted, boyled or carbonado'd, I know not; but of such a dish as powdered wife I never heard of. This was that time, which still to this day we called the starving time; it were too vile to say, and scarce to be beleeved, what we endured: but the occasion was our owne, for want of providence industrie and government, and not the barrennesse and defect of the Countrie, as is generally sup-posed; for till then in three yeeres, for the numbers were landed us, we had never from England provision sufficient for six moneths, though it seemed by the bils of loading sufficient was sent us, such a glutton is the Sea, and such good fellowes the Mariners; we as little tasted of the great proportion sent us, as they of our want and miseries, yet notwithstanding they ever overswayed and ruled the businesse, though we endured all that is said, and chiefly lived on what this good Countrie naturally afforded. Yet had wee beene even in Paradice it selfe with these Governours, it would not have beene much better withe us; yet there was amongst us, who had they had the government as Captaine Smith appointed, but that they could not maintaine it, would surely have kept us from those extremities of miseries. This in ten daies more, would have supplanted us all with death.

But God that would not this Countrie should be unplanted, sent Sir Thomas Gates, and Sir George Sommers with one hundred and fiftie people most happily preserved by the Bermudas to preserve us: strange it is to say how miraculously they were preserved in a leaking ship, as at large you may reade in the insuing Historie of those Ilands.

4. The Development of an Export Staple

Despite the repeated disasters of the first years in Virginia, persistent struggles within the company, and conflicts between the company and the king, the colony managed to survive to become the first permanent English settlement in the New World. In the process much valuable information was gained about how—and especially how not—to proceed to colonize North America. Because of the company's insistence, attempts were made to produce wine, iron, silk, glass, and other commodities which England at the time was forced to purchase from foreign nations. Each of these attempts turned out less profitably than the growing of tobacco, which had been introduced by John Rolfe in 1612. Thereafter most of the colony's efforts were devoted to the production of that product. Throughout the colonial period, the economic expansion of Virginia was closely linked to the fortunes of the tobacco industry.

If much was learned in the process of establishing the first English colony, the lesson was not without its price. It has been estimated that between 1606 and 1623 some 5,500 persons had migrated to the colonies, but in 1623 only 1,200 persons were still living there. Since only 300 had returned to England from the colony, approximately 4,000 must have lost their lives in establishing Virginia.

A Declaration of the present State of Virginia humbly presented to
  the King's most Excellent Majesty by the Virginia Company.

May it please Your Majesty:

In the end of December, in the year 1618, being the 12th year after the beginning of this plantation, and after the expense of four-

SOURCE: The Virginia Company, "Defence of the Virginia Charter" (1623), Abstract of the Proceedings of the Virginia Company of London (Virginia Historical Society, Collections [8 vols.; Richmond, Va., 1889]), II, 148–51.

score thousand pounds of the publick stock and upwards, besides other sums of voluntary planters, there were remaining there in the colony about six hundred persons—men, women, and children—and cattle about three hundred at the most, and the Company was then left in debt about five thousand pounds.

At this time (through God's blessing), notwithstanding the great mortalities which, in some of these four latter years, have generally seized upon all those parts of America, and besides the late massacre of three hundred and fifty persons, and a great mortality thereby occasioned by being driven from their habitation and provisions, there are remaining, as we compute, above five and twenty hundred persons, sent with the expense only of thirty thousand pounds of the public stock besides the charges of particular societies and planters. And the cattle, what by new supplies and what by increase of the former provision, are multiplied to above one thousand of beasts, and of swine an infinite number; and the old debt of the Company hath been discharged.

At the beginning of these four last years the only commodities of price, and upon which only a valuation was set to maintain the trade, were tobacco and sassafras, for in the two last years before there was no course taken up for the setting up of any others through the poverty of the Company.

During these 4 last years there hath been expended in setting up of iron works (the oar whereof is there in great plenty and excellent) about five thousand pounds, which work being brought in a manner to perfection was greatly interrupted by the late massacre, but ordered to be restored again with all possible diligence.

For the making of wine, it is to be known that the soil there doth of itself produce vines in great abundance and some of a very good sort, besides divers plantations been sent thither of the better hands of Christendom.

There hath also been sent thither eight vigneroons procured from Languedock, and careful order hath been taken for setting up of that commodity, which we doubt not in a short time will show itself in great plenty, and had not the business been interrupted by the massacre e'er this effect had been seen, there being divers vineyards planted in the country whereof some contained ten thousand plants.

For silk the country is full of mulberry trees of the best kind, and general order taken for the planting of them abundantly in all places inhabited. True it is that the silkworm seed hath, till this last year, miscarried, to the great grief of the Company, having had large supplies thereof from your Majesty's store; but in September last we sent near 80 ounces with extraordinary care and provision that we doubt not but that it will prosper and yield a plentiful return, there being sent also men skilful to instruct the planters for all things belonging to bring the silk to perfection, and we have notice that the seed hath been received safe and order given for the disposing and nourishing them through the whole plantation.

There have been sent also, at the great charge of the Company, skilful men from Germany for setting up of sawing mills, and divers shipwrights from hence for making boats and ships, and others for salt works and others for other commodities, the good effect whereof we doubt not will shortly appear.

We will not here enlarge in declaring the great and assidual care which the Council and Company, with their principal officers, have from time to time taken, as well from reclaiming the colony from overmuch following tobacco (every man being now stinted to a certain proportion), as also in setting forward the other staple and rich commodities, as well by the charges and provisions aforesaid as likewise by setting upon them a competent valuation, not doubting but that whosoever will be pleased to take the pains to peruse their frequent letters, instructions and charters to that effect, together with sundry printed books made purposely and published for their help and direction (the full view whereof is prohibited to no man), will be far from censuring them for any omission. Neither may we forbear to do that justice to the Governor and Commission and other principal officers now residing in Virginia as not to testify their solicitous care and industry in putting in execution our desires and instructions, as appeareth by their proclamation and other orders to be seen.

Touching the government, it hath in these four latter years been so reformed, according to your Majesty's original directions, that the people who in former times were discontent and mutinous by reason of their inassurance of all things, through want of order and justice, live now amongst themselves in great peace and tranquility, each knowing his own and what he is mutually to receive and perform.

And to the end that worthy persons may be allured to these places of council and government, and all occasion of rapine and extortion be removed, the Council and Company have now, at their very great charge, caused to be set up a competent annual provision and revenue for maintenance of the Governor, with other magistrates and officers, and particularly the ministry, according to the degree and quality of each place.

Neither have these our cares and courses been ineffectual, but as they have settled the colony there in a great quiet and content, so have they raised here at home so great a fame of Virginia, that not only men of meaner estates, as at the first by necessity, but many persons of good sort, out of choice and good liking, have removed themselves thither, and are dayly in providing to remove.

There have been in these four last years granted forty-four patents for land to persons, who have undertaken to transport each of them at least one hundred men, whereas in the former twelve years there was not above six.

There have come in ten times more adventurers in these four last years than in almost twice that time before, so that whereas in former times there were sometimes hardly got twenty to keep the quarter-court, there are now seldom less than two hundred, and sometimes many more.

There have been employed in these four last years forty-two sail of ships of great burthen, whereas in four years before there were not above twelve.

We may not here omit one extraordinary blessing, which it hath pleased God Almighty in the four last years so as to excite the heart of well-minded people to extend their aid towards the forwarding of this glorious work, that there hath been contributed towards in presents, to the value of fifteen hundred pounds by zealous and devout persons, most of them refusing to be named, of which fruit the preceding years were altogether barren.

．　　．　　．

And if your Majesty, being the first founder and great supporter of this action (which will remain a constant monument of your glorious name forever), will be pleased that the four hundred young and able men desired by the Company and not denied but respited, may now at length be levied, as was petitioned, and sent to Virginia for the rooting out of those treacherous and barbarous murderers, as also for the supply of the plantation in parts yet defective, we doubt not but in a short time to yield unto your Majesty so good and real account of the fruits of our cares, endeavours, and labours as may be answerable to our duty and your princely expectation.

5. Motives for the Settlement of New England

The experience of Virginia illustrated the high risks of being a colonist in the early seventeenth century. Although potential reward remained high, the sizable risk involved might have served to discourage for a long time further ventures of this sort if wealth alone had been the colonists' goal. However, Plymouth was founded in 1620, and three decades after Jamestown two more major North American colonies were established. This time the colonists sought the additional goal of freeing their religion from the controls of the Church and State of England. The great Puritan migration from England to New England and the Catholic migration to Maryland, both in the 1630's, brought to the New World thousands of people whose aspiration for basic political, religious, and social freedoms made them willing to bear the risks of migration. The following document reveals this desire for freedom, combined with a desire to improve their economic position.

1. IT will be a service to the Church of great consequence to carry the Gospell into those parts of the world, to helpe on the comminge of the fullnesse of the Gentiles, and to raise a Bulworke against the kingdome of AnteChrist which the Jesuites labour to reare up in those parts.

2. All other churches of Europe are brought to desolation, and our sinnes, for which the Lord beginnes allreadly to frowne upon us and to cutte us short, doe threatne evill times to be comminge upon us, and whoe knowes, but that God hath provided this place to be a refuge for many whome he meanes to save out of the generall callamity, and seeinge the Church hath noe place lefte to flie into but the wildernesse, what better worke can there be, then to goe and provide tabernacles and foode for her against she comes thether:

SOURCE: John Winthrop, "Reasons to be considered for iustifieing the undertakeres of the intended Plantation in New England, & for incouraginge such whose hartes God shall move to ioyne with them in it," in Robert C. Winthrop, *Life and Letters of John Winthrop* (Boston: Treknor and Fields, 1864), I, 309–10.

3. This Land growes weary of her Inhabitants, soe as man, whoe is the most pretious of all creatures, is here more vile and base then the earth we treade upon, and of lesse prise among us then an horse or a sheepe: masters are forced by authority to entertaine servants, parents to mainetaine there owne children, all townes complaine of the burthen of theire poore, though we have taken up many unnessisarie yea unlawfull trades to mainetaine them, and we use the authoritie of the Law to hinder the increase of our people, as by urginge the Statute against Cottages, and inmates, and thus it is come to passe, that children, servants and neighboures, especially if they be poore, are compted the greatest burthens, which if thinges weare right would be the cheifest earthly blessinges.

4. The whole earth is the Lords garden and he hath given it to the Sonnes of men with a general Comission: Gen. 1:28: increace and multiplie, and replenish the earth and subdue it, which was againe renewed to Noah: the end is double and naturall, that man might enjoy the fruits of the earth, and God might have his due glory from the creature: why then should we stand striving here for places of habitation, etc, (many men spending as much labour and coste to recover or keepe sometimes an acre or twoe of Land, as would procure them many and as good or better in another Countrie) and in the meane time suffer a whole Continent as fruitfull and convenient for the use of man to lie waste without any improvement?

5. We are growne to that height of Intemperance in all excesse of Riott, as noe mans estate allmost will suffice to keepe saile with his æqualls: and he whoe failes herein, must live in scorne and contempt. Hence it comes that all artes and Trades are carried in that deceiptfull and unrighteous course, as it is allmost impossible for a good and upright man to mainetayne his charge and live comfortablie in any of them.

. . .

7. What can be a better worke, and more honorable and worthy a Christian then to helpe raise and supporte a particular Church while it is in the Infancy, and to ioyne his forces with such a company of faithfull people, as by a timely assistance may growe stronge and prosper, and for wante of it may be put to great hazard, if not wholly ruined . . . ?

6. An Early Account of Conditions in New England

In general the New England colonists experienced the same problems that Virginia had faced earlier. While they were adjusting to the severe climate and searching for a staple export, they also suffered near starvation. Some, finding conditions too harsh, chose to return to Europe. Those who stayed soon developed an export staple by trading to the Indians corn and European goods in return for furs. New England differed from Virginia in that the joint-stock company which formed it was dominated not by merchants in England but by the colonists themselves, and their main interest was to make not profits, but a new society in America. The following document, written as a letter by one of the original settlers of Massachusetts nine months after his arrival in the New World, describes events during that period.

Touching the plantacon which wee here have begun, it fell out thus about the yeare 1627 some freinds beeing togeather in Lincolnesheire, fell into some discourse about New England and the plantinge of the gospell there; and after some deliberation, we imparted our reasons by lettres and messages to some in London and the west country where it was likewise deliberately thought uppon, and at length with often negociation soe ripened that in the year 1628 wee procured a patent from his Majestie for our planting between the Matachusetts Bay, and Charles river on the South; and the River of Merimack on the North and 3 miles on ether side of those Rivers and Bay, as allso for the government of those who did or should inhabit within that compass and the same year we sent Mr. John Endecott and some with him to beginne a plantacon and to strengthen such as he should find there which wee sent thether from Dorchester and some places adjoyning; ffrom whom the same year receivinge hopefull news. The next year 1629 wee sent diverse shipps over with about 300 people, and some Cowes, Goates and horses many of which arrived safely. Theis by their too large comendacons of the country, and the comodities thereof, invited us soe strongly to goe on that Mr. Wenthropp of Soffolke (who was well

SOURCE: "Governour Thomas Dudley's Letter to the Countess of Lincoln, March, 1631," in Peter Force (ed.), *Tracts and Other Papers* . . . (4 vols.; New York: Peter Smith, 1947), II, iv, 7–15, 18–19.

knowne in his owne country and well approved heere for his pyety, liberality, wisedome and gravity) comeinge in to us, wee came to such resolution that in April 1630, wee sett saile from Old England with 4 good shipps. And in May following 8 more followed, 2 haveing gone before in Ffebruary and March, and 2 more following in June and August, besides another set out by a private merchant. Theis 17 Shipps arrived all safe in New England, for the increase of the plantacon here theis yeare 1630 but made a long, a troublesome, and a costly voyage beeing all wind bound long in England, and hindred with contrary winds after they set saile and so scattered with mists and tempests that few of them arrived togeather. Our 4 shipps which sett out in Aprill arrived here in June and July, where wee found the colony in a sadd and unexpected condicon above 80 of them beeing dead the winter before and many of those alive weake and sicke: all the corne and bread amongst them all hardly sufficient to feed them a fortnight, insoemuch that the remainder of 180 servents wee had the 2 years before sent over, comeinge to us for victualls to sustaine them wee found ourselves wholly unable to feed them by reason that the provisions shipped for them were taken out of the shipp they were put in, and they who were trusted to shipp them in another failed us, and left them behind; whereupon necessity enforced us to our extreme loss to give them all libertie; who had cost us about: 16 or 20 £s a person furnishing and sending over. But bearing theis things as wee might, wee beganne to consult of the place of our sitting downe: ffor Salem where wee landed, pleased us not. And to that purpose some were sent to the Bay to search upp the rivers for a convenient place; who uppon their returne reported to have found a good place uppon Mistick; but some other of us seconding theis to approove or dislike of their judgement; we found a place liked us better 3 leagues up Charles river—And there uppon unshipped our goods into other vessels and with much cost and labour brought them in July to Charles Towne; but there receiveing advertisements by some of the late arived shipps from London and Amsterdam of some Ffrench preparations against us (many of our people brought with us beeing sick of ffeavers and the scurvy and wee thereby unable to cary up our ordinance and baggage soe farr) wee were forced to change counsaile and for our present shelter to plant dispersedly, some at Charles Towne which standeth on the North Side of the mouth of Charles River; some on the South Side thereof, which place we named Boston (as wee intended to have done the place wee first resolved on) some of us uppon Mistick, which wee named Mead-ford; some of us westwards on Charles river, 4 miles from Charles Towne, which place wee named Watertoune; others of us 2 miles from Boston in a place wee named Rocksbury, others uppon the river of Sawgus betweene Salem and Charles Toune. And the west-erne men 4 miles South from Boston at a place wee named Dor-chester. This dispersion troubled some of us, but helpe it wee could not, wanting abillity to remove to any place fit to build a Toune uppon, and the time too short to deliberate any longer least the winter should surprize us before wee had builded our houses. The best counsel wee could find out was to build a fort to retire to, in some convenient place if any enemy pressed thereunto, after wee should have fortifyed ourselves against the injuries of wett and cold. So ceasing to consult further for that time they who had health to labour fell to building, wherein many were interrupted with sicknes and many dyed weekely, yea almost dayley. . . .

Insomuch that the shipps beeing now uppon their returne, some for England some for Ireland, there was as I take it not much less than an hundred (some think many more) partly out of dis-like of our goverment which restrained and punished their ex-cesses, and partly through feare of famine not seeing other means than by their labour to feed themselves) which returned back againe. And glad were wee so to bee ridd of them. Others also afterwards hearing of men of their owne disposition, which were planted at Piscataway went from us to them, whereby though our numbers were lessened yet wee accounted ourselves nothing weak-ened by their removeall. Before the departure of the shipps wee contracted with Mr. Peirce Master of the Lyon of Bristow to re-turne to us with all speed with fresh supplies of victualls and gave him directions accordingly. . . .

The shipps beinge gone, victualls wastinge, and mortallity in-creasinge wee held diverse fasts in our severall congregations, but the Lord would not yet bee depricated; . . . The people who came over with us from the time of their setting saile from England in Aprill 1630. untill December followinge there dyed by estimacon about 200 at the least— Soe lowe hath the Lord brought us! Well, yet they who survived were not discouraged but bearing God's cor-rections with humilitye and trusting in his mercies, and consider-ing how after a greater ebb hee had raised upp our neighbours at

Plymouth we beganne againe in December to consult about a fitt place to build a Toune uppon, leaveinge all thoughts of a fort, because uppon any invasion wee were necessarily to loose our howses when we should retire thereinto; soe after diverse meetings at Boston, Rocksbury and Waterton on the 28th of December wee grew to this resolucon to bind all the Assistants (Mr. Endicott and Mr. Sharpe excepted, which last purposeth to returne by the next shipps into England) to build howses at a place, a mile east from Waterton neere Charles river, the next Springe, and to winter there the next yeare, that soe by our examples and by removeinge the ordinance and munition thether, all who were able, might be drawne thether, and such as shall come to us hereafter to their advantage bee compelled soe to doe; and soe if God would, a fortifyed Toune might there grow upp, the place fitting reasonably well thereto. I should before have menconed how both the English and the Indian corne beeinge at tenne shillinges a strike, and beaver beeinge vallued at 6 shilling a pound, wee made lawes to restraine the sellinge of corne to the Indians, and to leave the price of Beaver at libertie which was presently sold for tenne and 20 shillinges a pound. I should allsoe have remembred how the halfe of our Cowes and allmost all our Mares and Goates sent us out of England, dyed at sea in their passage hether, and that those intended to bee sent us out of Ireland were not sent at all; all which togeather with the loss of our six months buildinge, occasioned by our intended removeall to a toune to bee fortifyed, weakened our estates, especially the estates of the undertakers who were 3 or £4000 engaged in the joynt stock which was now not above soe many hundreds; yet many of us laboured to beare it as comfortably as wee could, remembringe the end of our comeinge hether and knowinge the power of God who canne support and raise us againe, and useth to bring his servants lowe, that the meeke may bee made glorious by deliverance, Psal. 112.

• • •

I have no leisure to review and insert thinges forgotten but out of due time and order must sett them downe as they come to memory. About the end of October, this year 1630 I joyned with the Governour and Mr. Maverecke in sendinge out our pinace to the Narragansetts to trade for corne to supply our wants, but after the pynace had doubled Cape Codd, shee putt into the next harbour shee found, and there meetinge with Indians who shewed their willingness to Truck, shee made her voyage their and brought us 100 bushells of corne at about 4s a bushell which helped us somewhat. . . .

But now having some leasure to discourse of the motives for other mens comeinge to this place or their abstaining from it, after my breif manner I say this— That if any come hether to plant for worldly ends that canne live well at home hee comits an errour of which hee will soon repent him. But if for spirittuall and that noe particular obstacle hinder his removeall, he may finde here what may well content him: vizt: materialls to build, fewell to burn, ground to plant, seas and rivers to ffish in, a pure ayer to breath in, good water to drinke till wine or beare canne be made, which togeather with the cowes, hoggs and goates brought hether allready may suffice for food, for as for foule and venison, they are dainties here as well as in England. Ffor cloaths and beddinge they must bringe them with them till time and industry produce them here. In a word, wee yett enioy little to bee envyed but endure much to be pittyed in the sicknes and mortalitye of our people. And I do the more willingly use this open and plaine dealeinge least other men should fall short of their expectacons when they come hether as wee to our great prejudice did, by means of letters sent us from hence into England, wherein honest men out of a desire to draw over others to them wrote somewhat hyperbolically of many things here. If any godly men out of religious ends will come over to helpe us in the good worke wee are about I think they cannot dispose of themselves nor of their estates more to God's glory and the furtherance of their owne reckoninge, but they must not bee of the poorer sort yett for diverse yeares. Ffor we have found by experience that they have hindred, not furthered the worke— And for profaine and deboshed persons their oversight in comeinge hether is wondred at, where they shall find nothing to content them. If there bee any endued with grace and furnished with meanes to feed themselves and theires for 18 months, and to build and plant lett them come into our Macedonia and helpe us, and not spend themselves and their estates in a less profittable employment: for others I conceive they are not yet fitted for this busines.

Touching the discouragement which the sicknes and mortality which every first year hath seized upon us, and those of Plymouth, as appeareth before, may give to such who have cast any thoughts this way (of which mortallity it may bee said of us allmost as of the

Egiptians, that there is not an howse where there is not one dead, and in some howses many) the naturall causes seem to bee in the want of warm lodginge, and good dyet to which Englishmen are habittuated at home; and in the suddain increase of heate which they endure that are landed here in somer, the salt meates at sea haveing prepared their bodyes thereto, for those onely theis 2 last yeares dyed of feavers who landed in June and July; as those of Plymouth who landed in winter dyed of the Scirvy, as did our poorer sort whose howses and bedding kept them not sufficiently warm, nor their dyet sufficiently in heart. . . .

Upon the 5 of February arrived here Mr. Peirce with the shipp Lyon of Bristou with supplyes of victualls from England who had sett fourth from Bristou the first of December before.

.   .   .

The shipp now waites but for wind, which when it blowes there are ready to goe aboard therein for England Sr. Richard Saltonstall, Mr. Sharpe, Mr. Coddington and many others, the most whereof purpose to returne to us againe, if God will. In the meane time wee are left a people poore and contemptible yet such as trust in God, and are contented with our condition, beeinge well assured that hee will not faile us nor forsake us.

I had allmost forgotten to add this, that the wheate wee received by this last shipp standes us in 13 or 14 shillinges a strike, and the pease about 11s. a strike besides the adventure, which is worth 3 or 4 shillinges a strike which is an higher price than I ever tasted bread of before.

.   .   .

The like accident of fire also befell Mr. Sharpe and Mr. Colborne uppon the 17 of this March both whose howses, which were as good, and as well furnished as the most in the plantacon were in 2 houres space burned to the ground together with much of their house hould stuff, apparell and other thinges as allsoe some goods of others who sojourned with them in their howses; God so please-inge to exercise us with corrections of this kind, as he hath done with others, for the prevention whereof in our new toune intended this somer to bee builded, wee have ordered that noe man there shall build his chimney with wood, nor cover his house with thatch, which was readily assented unto, for that diverse other howses have beene burned since our arrivall (the fire allwaies beginninge in the woodden chimneyes) and some English wigwams which have taken fire in the roofes covered with thatch or boughs.

7. An Inducement to Settle in Maryland

Maryland was the last major English colony to be established on the continent of North America before the English civil war temporarily brought colonization to a halt. The promotional efforts leading to the establishment of Maryland differed significantly from those employed to establish Virginia or New England. Where the promoters of Virginia had been merchants and the promoters of New England the colonists themselves, the promoter of Maryland was a single nobleman, Lord Baltimore. The land on which Maryland took root had been granted by the king to Lord Baltimore to use as he saw fit. In becoming the proprietor and organizing the colony as his own feudal domain, Lord Baltimore designated it as a refuge for Catholics, who, being a minority in England like the Puritans, also felt restricted by the Church of England. The proprietor granted land to persons who would finance colonists to come to the New World, reserving for himself an annual quitrent from the land. Like New England, Maryland held out to prospective colonists the prospect of wider freedoms than they enjoyed in England and a potentially higher standard of living. The following document was written to entice people to join Lord Baltimore in the venture.

Wherefore the Most Noble Baron intends, by the aid of God, to sail for those parts, about the middle of next September; and to those whom he shall find to accompany and assist him in so glorious an undertaking, he offers many inducements, in the most generous and liberal spirit.

Of which this is the first and most important (to say nothing of those rewards of station and preferment, which will be liberally given in honor of worth, valor, fortitude and noble deeds), that whoever shall pay a hundred pounds, to carry over five men (which will be enough for arms, implements, clothing and other necessaries); whether they shall think best to join us themselves, or intrust the men and money to those, who shall have charge of this

SOURCE: Father Andrew White, S.J., "An Account of the Colony of the Lord Baron of Baltamore, in Maryland, near Virginia: in which the character, quality and state of the Country, and its numerous advantages and sources of wealth are set forth," (1633), in Clayton Colman Hall (ed.), Narratives of Early Maryland, 1633–1684 (New York: Charles Scribner's Sons, 1910), 6–7.

matter, or to any one else, to take care of them and receive their share of the lands: to all the men so sent, and to their heirs forever, shall be allotted the right to two thousand acres of good land. Besides this, if in the first expedition they prove themselves faithful followers, and do good service, they shall receive no small share in the profits of trade—of which hereafter—and in other privileges: concerning which they will be more fully informed, when they come to the aforesaid Baron. Moreover, as to what was said before concerning a hundred pounds, this shall also be understood, in proportion, of a smaller or larger sum of money, whether given by one man, or contributed and furnished by several together.

The first and most important design of the Most Illustrious Baron, which also ought to be the aim of the rest, who go in the same ship, is, not to think so much of planting fruits and trees in a land so fruitful, as of sowing the seeds of religion and piety. Surely a design worthy of Christians, worthy of *angels*, worthy of *Englishmen*. The English nation, renowned for so many ancient victories, never undertook anything more noble or glorious than this. Behold the lands are white for the harvest, prepared for receiving the seed of the Gospel into a fruitful bosom. The Indians themselves are everywhere sending messengers, to seek after fit men to instruct the inhabitants in saving doctrine, and to regenerate them with the sacred water. There are also men here in the city, at this very time, who declare that they have seen ambassadors, who were sent by their kings for this same purpose to Jamestown in Virginia; and infants brought to New England to be washed in the saving waters. Who then can doubt, that by one such glorious work as this, many thousands of souls will be brought to Christ? I call the work of aiding and saving souls glorious: for it was the work of Christ, the King of Glory. For the rest, since all men have not such enthusiastic souls and noble minds, as to think of nothing but divine things, and to consider nothing but heavenly things; because most men are more drawn, secretly or openly, by pleasures, honor and riches, it was ordained by the wonderful wisdom of God, that this one enterprise should offer to men every kind of inducement and reward.

8. The Settlement of Maryland

The geographical proximity of Maryland to Virginia proved a decided advantage to the new colony, allowing Maryland to obtain provisions by trade when needed, and obviating the time of famine that both Virginia and New England had been forced to endure. In addition, the substantial knowledge of the New World acquired by the Virginians during the previous two decades was directly applicable to neighboring Maryland. Following Virginia's example, Maryland immediately turned to the growing of tobacco for export, thus avoiding costly experimentation. Unlike both Virginia and New England this new colony was fortunately able to immediately establish friendly relations with the surrounding tribes, sparing themselves the ravages of Indian wars. The following account of the settlement of Maryland, if accurate, is a sharp contrast to the experiences of Virginia and New England.

His most Excellent Majestie having by his Letters Patent, under the Great Seale of England, granted a certaine Countrey in America (now called Maryland, in honour of our gratious Queene) unto the Lord Baltemore, with divers Priviledges, and encouragements to all those that should adventure with his Lordship in the Planting of that Countrey: the benefit and honour of such an action was readily apprehended by divers Gentlemen, of good birth and qualitie, who thereupon resolved to adventure their Persons, and a good part of their fortunes with his Lordship, in the pursuite of so noble and (in all likelihood) so advantagious an enterprize. His Lordship was at first resolved to goe in person; but the more important reasons perswading his stay at home, hee appointed his brother, Mr. Leonard Calvert to goe Governour in his stead, with whom he joyned in Commission, Mr. Jerome Hawley, and Mr. Thomas Cornwallis (two worthy and able Gentlemen.) These with the other Gentlemen adventurers, and their servants to the number of neere 200. people, imbarked themselves for the voyage, in the good ship called the *Arke*, of 300. tunne and upward, which was attended by his Lordships Pinnace, called the *Dove*, of about 50. tunne. And so

SOURCE: "A Relation of Maryland; together, with a Map of the Countrey, The Conditions of Plantation, with His Majesties Charter to the Lord Baltemore, translated into English" (London, 1635), ch. i, in Clayton Colman Hall (ed.), *Narratives of Early Maryland, 1633–1684* (New York: Charles Scribner & Sons, 1910), 70–1, 73–7.

on Friday, the 22. of November, 1633. a small gale of winde comming gently from the Northwest, they weighed from the Cowes in the Isle of Wight, about ten in the morning; And having stayed by the way Twenty dayes at the Barbada's, and Fourteene dayes at Saint Christophers (upon some necessary occasions) they arrived at Point Comfort in Virginia, on the foure and twentyeth of February following. They had Letters from his Majesty, in favor of them, to the Governour of Virginia, in obedience whereunto, he used them with much courtesie and humanitie. . . .

On the 3. of March, they left Point-Comfort, and 2. dayes after, they came to Patowmeck river, which is about 24. leagues distant, there they began to give names to places, and called the Southerne point of that River, Saint Gregories; and the Northerne point, Saint Michaels.

They sayled up the River, till they came to Heron Island, which is about 14. leagues, and there came to an Anchor under an Island neere unto it, which they called S. Clements. Where they set up a Crosse, and tooke possession of this Countrey for our Saviour, and for our Soveraigne Lord the King of England.

. . .

At their comming to this place, the Governour went on shoare, and treated friendly with the Werowance there, and acquainted him with the intent of his comming thither, to which hee made little answere (as it is their manner, to any new or suddane question) but entertained him, and his company that night in his house, and gave him his owne bed to lie on (which is a matt layd on boords) and the next day, went to shew him the country, and that day being spent in viewing the places about that towne, and the fresh waters, which there are very plentifull, and excellent good (but the maine rivers are salt) the Governor determined to make the first Colony there, and so gave order for the Ship and Pinnaces to come thither.

This place he found to be a very commodious situation for a Towne, in regard the land is good, the ayre wholsome and pleasant, the River affords a safe harbour for ships of any burthen, and a very bould shoare; fresh water, and wood there is in great plenty, and the place so naturally fortified, as with little difficultie, it will be defended from any enemie.

To make his entry peaceable and safe, hee thought fit to present the Werowance and the Wisoes of the Towne with some English

Cloth, (such as is used in trade with the Indians) Axes, Howes, and Knives, which they accepted very kindly, and freely gave consent that hee and his company should dwell in one part of their Towne, and reserved the other for themselves; and those Indians that dwelt in that part of the Towne, which was allotted for the English, freely left them their houses, and some corne that they had begun to plant: It was also agreed between them, that at the end of harvest they should leave the whole towne; which they did accordingly: And they made mutuall promises to each other, to live friendly and peaceably together, and if any injury should happen to be done on any part, that satisfaction should be made for the same, and thus upon the 27. day of March, Anno Domini, 1634. the Governour tooke possession of the place, and named the Towne Saint Maries.

•   •   •

The next day they began to prepare for their houses, and first of all a Court of Guard, and a Store-house; in the meane time they lay abord the ship: They had not beene there many dayes before Sir John Harvie the governor of Virginea came thither to visit them; . . .

After they had finished the store-house, and unladed the ship, the Governour thought fit to bring the Colours on shore, which were attended by all the Gentlemen, and the rest of the servants in armes; who received the Colours with a volley of shot, which was answered by the Ordnance from the ships; At this Ceremony were present, the Werowances of Patuxent, and Yoacomaco, with many other Indians; and the Werowance of Patuxent hereupon tooke occasion to advise the Indians of Yoacomaco to be carefull to keepe the league that they had made with the English. . . .

They brought thither with them some store of Indian Corne, from the Barbado's, which at their first arivall they began to use (thinking fit to reserve their English provision of Meale and Oatemeale) and the Indian women seeing their servants to bee unacquainted with the manner of dressing it, would make bread thereof for them, and teach them how to doe the like: They found also the countrey well stored with Corne (which they bought with truck, such as there is desired, the Natives having no knowledge of the use of money) whereof they sold them such plenty, as that they sent 1000. bushells of it to New-England, to provide them some salt-fish, and other commodities which they wanted.

During the time that the Indians stai'd by the English at Yoacomaco, they went dayly to hunt with them for Deere and Turkies,
whereof some they gave them for Presents, and the meaner sort
would sell them to them, for knives, beades and the like: Also of
Fish, the natives brought them great store, and in all things dealt
very friendly with them; . . .

Their comming thus to seate upon an Indian Towne, where they
found ground cleered to their hands, gave them opportunity (although they came late in the yeere) to plant some Corne, and to
make them gardens, which they sowed with English seeds of all
sorts, and they prospered exceeding well. They also made what
haste they could to finish their houses; . . .

They procured from Virginia, Hogges, Poultrey, and some Cowes,
and some male cattell, which hath given them a foundation for
breed and increase; and whoso desires it, may furnish himselfe with
store of Cattell from thence, but the hogges and Poultrey are already increased in Maryland, to a great stocke, sufficient to serve
the Colonie very plentifully. They have also set up a Water-mill
for the grinding of Corne, adjoyning to the Towne.

Thus within the space of six moneths, was laid the foundation
of the Colonie in Maryland; and whosoever intends now to goe
thither, shall finde the way so troden, that hee may proceed with
much more ease and confidence then these first adventurers could,
who were ignorant both of Place, People, and all things else, and
could expect to find nothing but what nature produced: besides,
they could not in reason but thinke, the Natives would oppose
them; whereas now the Countrey is discovered, and friendship with
the natives is assured, houses built, and many other accommoda-
tions, as Cattell, Hogges, Poultry, Fruits and the like brought
thither from England, Virginea, and other places, which are use-
full, both for profit and Pleasure: and without boasting it may be
said, that this Colony hath arived to more in six moneths, then
Virginia did in as many yeeres. If any man say, they are beholding
to Virginea for so speedy a supply of many of those things which
they of Virginia were forced to fetch from England and other remote places, they will confess it, and acknowledge themselves glad
that Virginea is so neere a neighbour, and that it is so well stored
of all necessaries for to make those parts happy, and the people to
live as plentifully as in any other part of the world, only they wish

that they would be content their neighbours might live in peace by them, and then no doubt they should find a great comfort each in other.

9. A Description of the Economy of Maryland in the 1660's

The following document, in a brief description of the economy of the tobacco region of the American colonies as it had developed by the 1660's, describes the character of a staple economy, its specialization in the production of a few agricultural products, and its dependence upon trading these commodities for the myriad goods not produced locally. Note that by 1660 trade had developed between this staple-producing region and both Europe and New England, thus establishing the inter-dependence between members of the empire that characterized the colonial period.

The three main Commodities this Country affords for Trafique, are Tobacco, Furrs, and Flesh. Furrs and Skins, as Beavers, Otters, Musk-Rats, Rackoons, Wild-Cats, and Elke or Buffeloe, with divers others, which were first made vendible by the Indians of the Country, and sold to the Inhabitant, and by them to the Merchant, and so transported into England and other places where it becomes most commodious.

Tobacco is the only solid Staple Commodity of this Province: The use of it was first found out by the Indians many Ages agoe, and transferr'd into Christendom by that great Discoverer of America Columbus. It's generally made by all the Inhabitants of this Province, and between the months of March and April they sow the seed (which is much smaller than Mustard-seed) in small beds and patches digg'd up and made so by art, and about May the Plants commonly appear green in those beds: In June they are transplanted from their beds, and set in little hillocks in distant rowes, dug up for the same purpose; some twice or thrice they are

SOURCE: George Alsop, "Upon Trafique, and what Merchandizing Commodities this Province affords, also how Tobacco is planted and made fit for Commerce"; from George Alsop, *A Character of the Province of Maryland*, 1666, ch. iv; in Clayton Colman Hall (ed.), *Narratives of Early Maryland*, 1633–1684 (New York: Charles Scribner & Sons, 1910), 363–4.

weeded, and succoured from their illegitimate Leaves that would be peeping out from the body of the Stalk. They top the several Plants as they find occasion in their predominating rankness: About the middle of September they cut the Tobacco down, and carry it into houses, (made for that purpose) to bring it to its purity: And after it has attained, by a convenient attendance upon time, to its perfection, it is then tyed up in bundles, and packt into Hogs-heads, and then laid by for the Trade.

Between November and January there arrives in this Province Shipping to the number of twenty sail and upwards, all Merchant-men loaden with Commodities to Trafique and dispose of, truck-ing with the Planter for Silks, Hollands, Serges, and Broad-clothes, with other necessary Goods, priz'd at such and such rates as shall be judg'd on is fair and legal, for Tobacco at so much the pound, and advantage on both sides considered; the Planter for his work, and the Merchant for adventuring himself and his Commodity into so far a Country: Thus is the Trade on both sides drove on with a fair and honest Decorum.

The Inhabitants of this Province are seldom or never put to the affrightment of being robb'd of their money, nor to dirty their Fingers by telling of vast sums: They have more bags to carry Corn, then Coyn; and though they want, but why should I call that a want which is only a necessary miss? the very effects of the dirt of this Province affords as great a profit to the general Inhabitant, as the Gold of Peru doth to the straight-breecht Commonalty of the Spaniard.

Our Shops and Exchanges of Mary-Land, are the Merchants Store-houses, where with few words and protestations Goods are bought and delivered; not like those Shop-keepers Boys in London, that continually cry, What do ye lack Sir? What d'ye buy? yelping with so wide a mouth, as if some Apothecary had hired their mouths to stand open to catch Gnats and Vagabond Flyes in.

Tobacco is the currant Coyn of Mary-Land, and will sooner pur-chase Commodities from the Merchant, then money. I must con-fess the New-England men that trade into this Province, had rather have fat Pork for their Goods, then Tobacco or Furrs, . . .

Medera-Wines, Sugars, Salt, Wickar-Chairs, and Tin Candle-sticks, is the most of the Commodities they bring in: They arrive in Mary-Land about September, being most of them Ketches and Barkes, and such small Vessels, and those dispersing themselves into several small Creeks of this Province, to sell and dispose of their Commodities, where they know the Market is most fit for their small Adventures.

Barbadoes, together with the several adjacent Islands, has much Provision yearly from this Province. . . .

III

Imperial Regulation of the Colonial Economy

In the 1660's the English government resumed its interest in the American colonies and in that decade passed a series of acts designed to regulate their economic growth and commerce. Generally known as the Navigation Acts, these were designed to ensure that the English colonies provided the maximum benefit to the mother country. In accordance with the economic theories of that period, this was to be accomplished by imposing restraints on the natural course of colonial economic development, among them the following: (1) goods and produce going to or coming from the colonies were to be carried only in ships of the empire; (2) certain specific colonial goods, among which were tobacco, rice, and sugar, were to be shipped only to Great Britain; (3) the mother country was to have a monopoly on the provision of manufactured goods to the colonies; (4) the colonies were forbidden to engage in manufactures competing directly with those of the mother country, and were encouraged to develop manufactures not produced in the mother country; and (5) preferential treatment was to be granted to encourage the production of certain colonial products for the benefit of the mother country. The goal of these acts was to make the empire self-sufficient, a desirable state according to the dictates of the mercantilistic theory prevalent during this era. While these acts certainly imposed costs upon the colonies, they were quite mild compared to restrictions placed by other European nations upon their colonies. The rapid and extensive economic growth of the American colonies during the next hundred years suggests that the burden of the acts was far from prohibitive.

10. An Explanation of the Relatively Rapid Growth of the American Colonies

The great eighteenth-century economist, Adam Smith, writing in 1776, believed the relatively favorable institutional arrangements existing in *the colonies to be responsible for their rapid growth, as he set forth in the following excellent description of the legal framework governing the English colonies.*

. . . . There are no colonies of which the progress has been more rapid than that of the English in North America.

Plenty of good land, and liberty to manage their own affairs their own way, seem to be the two great causes of the prosperity of all new colonies.

In the plenty of good land the English colonies of North America, though, no doubt, very abundantly provided, are, however, inferior to those of the Spaniards and Portugueze, and not superior to some of those possessed by the French before the late war. But the political institutions of the English colonies have been more favourable to the improvement and cultivation of this land, than those of any of the other three nations.

First, the engrossing of uncultivated land, though it has by no means been prevented altogether, has been more restrained in the English colonies than in any other. The colony law which imposes upon every proprietor the obligation of improving and cultivating, within a limited time, a certain proportion of his lands, and which, in case of failure, declares those neglected lands grantable to any other person; though it has not, perhaps, been very strictly executed, has, however, had some effect.

Secondly, in Pennsylvania there is no right of primogeniture, and lands, like moveables, are divided equally among all the children of the family. In three of the provinces of New England the oldest has only a double share, as in the Mosaical law. Though in those provinces, therefore, too great a quantity of land should sometimes be engrossed by a particular individual, it is likely, in the course of a generation or two, to be sufficiently divided again. In the other English colonies, indeed, the right of primogeniture takes place, as in the law of England. But in all the English colonies the tenure of the lands, which are all held by free socage, facilitates alienation, and the grantee of any extensive tract of land, generally finds it for his interest to alienate, as fast as he can, the greater part of it, reserving only a small quit-rent. . . .

SOURCE: Adam Smith, *An Inquiry Into The Nature and Causes Of The Wealth Of Nations* (New York: Random House Modern Library, 1937), vii, 538–51.

The plenty and cheapness of good land, it has already been observed, are the principal causes of the rapid prosperity of new colonies. The engrossing of land, in effect, destroys this plenty and cheapness. The engrossing of uncultivated land, besides, is the greatest obstruction to its improvement. But the labour that is employed in the improvement and cultivation of land affords the greatest and most valuable produce to the society. The produce of labour, in this case, pays not only its own wages, and the profit of the stock which employs it, but the rent of the land too upon which it is employed. The labour of the English colonists, therefore, being more employed in the improvement and cultivation of land, is likely to afford a greater and more valuable produce, than that of any of the other three nations, which, by the engrossing of land, is more or less diverted towards other employments.

Thirdly, the labour of the English colonists is not only likely to afford a greater and more valuable produce, but, in consequence of the moderation of their taxes, a greater proportion of this produce belongs to themselves, which they may store up and employ in putting into motion a still greater quantity of labour. The English colonists have never yet contributed any thing towards the defence of the mother country, or towards the support of its civil government. They themselves, on the contrary, have hitherto been defended almost entirely at the expence of the mother country. But the expence of fleets and armies is out of all proportion greater than the necessary expence of civil government. The expence of their own civil government has always been very moderate. It has generally been confined to what was necessary for paying competent salaries to the governor, to the judges, and to some other offices of police, and for maintaining a few of the most useful public works. . . .

Fourthly, in the disposal of their surplus produce, or of what is over and above their own consumption, the English colonies have been more favoured, and have been allowed a more extensive market, than those of any other European nation. Every European nation has endeavoured more or less to monopolize to itself the commerce of its colonies, and, upon that account, has prohibited the ships of foreign nations from trading to them, and has prohibited them from importing European goods from any foreign nation. But the manner in which this monopoly has been exercised in different nations has been very different.

Some nations have given up the whole commerce of their colonies to an exclusive company, of whom the colonies were obliged to buy all such European goods as they wanted, and to whom they were obliged to sell the whole of their own surplus produce. It was the interest of the company, therefore, not only to sell the former as dear, and to buy the latter as cheap as possible, but to buy no more of the latter, even at this low price, than what they could dispose of for a very high price in Europe. It was their interest, not only to degrade in all cases the value of the surplus produce of the colony, but in many cases to discourage and keep down the natural increase of its quantity. Of all the expedients that can well be contrived to stunt the natural growth of a new colony, that of an exclusive company is undoubtedly the most effectual. This, however, has been the policy of Holland, though their company, in the course of the present century, has given up in many respects the exertion of their exclusive privilege. This too was the policy of Denmark till the reign of the late king. It has occasionally been the policy of France, and of late, since 1755, after it had been abandoned by all other nations, on account of its absurdity, it has become the policy of Portugal with regard at least to two of the principal provinces of Brazil, Fernambuco and Marannon.

Other nations, without establishing an exclusive company, have confined the whole commerce of their colonies to a particular port of the mother country, from whence no ship was allowed to sail, but either in a fleet and at a particular season, or, if single, in consequence of a particular licence, which in most cases was very well paid for. This policy opened, indeed, the trade of the colonies to all the natives of the mother country, provided they traded from the proper port, at the proper season, and in the proper vessels. But as all the different merchants, who joined their stocks in order to fit out those licensed vessels, would find it for their interest to act in concert, the trade which was carried on in this manner would necessarily be conducted very nearly upon the same principles as that of an exclusive company. The profit of those merchants would be almost equally exorbitant and oppressive. The colonies would be ill supplied, and would be obliged both to buy very dear, and to sell very cheap. This, however, till within these few years, had always been the policy of Spain, and the price of all European goods, accordingly, is said to have been enormous in the Spanish West Indies. At Quito, we are told by Ulloa, a pound of iron sold for about four and six-pence, and a pound of steel for about six and nine-pence sterling. But it is chiefly in order to purchase European goods, that the colonies part with their own produce. The more, therefore, they pay for the one, the less they really get for the other, and the dearness of the one is the same thing with the cheapness of the other. The policy of Portugal is in this respect the same as the ancient policy of Spain, with regard to all its colonies, except Fernambuco and Marannon, and with regard to these it has lately adopted a still worse.

Other nations leave the trade of their colonies free to all their subjects, who may carry it on from all the different ports of the mother country, and who have occasion for no other licence than the common dispatches of the customhouse. In this case the number and dispersed situation of the different traders renders it impossible for them to enter into any general combination, and their competition is sufficient to hinder them from making very exorbitant profits. Under so liberal a policy the colonies are enabled both to sell their own produce and to buy the goods of Europe at a reasonable price. But since the dissolution of the Plymouth company, when our colonies were but in their infancy, this has always been the policy of England. It has generally too been that of France, and has been uniformly so since the dissolution of what, in England, is commonly called their Mississippi company. The profits of the trade, therefore, which France and England carry on with their colonies, though no doubt somewhat higher than if the competition was free to all other nations, are, however, by no means exorbitant; and the price of European goods accordingly is not extravagantly high in the greater part of the colonies of either of those nations.

In the exportation of their own surplus produce too, it is only with regard to certain commodities that the colonies of Great Britain are confined to the market of the mother country. These commodities having been enumerated in the act of navigation and in some other subsequent acts, have upon that account been called *enumerated commodities*. The rest are called *non-enumerated*; and may be exported directly to other countries, provided it is in British or Plantation ships, of which the owners and three-fourths of the mariners are British subjects.

Among the non-enumerated commodities are some of the most important productions of America and the West Indies; grain of all sorts, lumber, salt provisions, fish, sugar, and rum.

Grain is naturally the first and principal object of the culture of all new colonies. By allowing them a very extensive market for it, the law encourages them to extend this culture much beyond the consumption of a thinly inhabited country, and thus to provide beforehand an ample subsistence for a continually increasing population.

In a country quite covered with wood, where timber consequently is of little or no value, the expence of clearing the ground is the principal obstacle to improvement. By allowing the colonies a very extensive market for their lumber, the law endeavours to facilitate improvement by raising the price of a commodity which would otherwise be of little value, and thereby enabling them to make some profit of what would otherwise be mere expence.

In a country neither half-peopled nor half cultivated, cattle naturally multiply beyond the consumption of the inhabitants, and are often upon that account of little or no value. But it is necessary, it has already been shewn, that the price of cattle should bear a certain proportion to that of corn before the greater part of the lands of any country can be improved. By allowing to American cattle, in all shapes, dead and alive, a very extensive market, the law endeavours to raise the value of a commodity of which the high price is so very essential to improvement. The good effects of this liberty, however, must be somewhat diminished by the 4th of George III. c. 15. which puts hides and skins among the enumerated commodities, and thereby tends to reduce the value of American cattle.

To increase the shipping and naval power of Great Britain, by the extension of the fisheries of our colonies, is an object which the legislature seems to have had almost constantly in view. Those fisheries, upon this account, have had all the encouragement which freedom can give them, and they have flourished accordingly. The New England fishery in particular was, before the late disturbances, one of the most important, perhaps, in the world. The whale-fishery which, notwithstanding an extravagant bounty, is in Great Britain carried on to so little purpose, that in the opinion of many people (which I do not, however, pretend to warrant) the whole produce does not much exceed the value of the bounties which are annually paid for it, is in New England carried on without any bounty to a very great extent. Fish is one of the principal articles with which the North Americans trade to Spain, Portugal, and the Mediterranean.

Sugar was originally an enumerated commodity which could be exported only to Great Britain. But in 1731, upon a representation of the sugar-planters, its exportation was permitted to all parts of the world. The restrictions, however, with which this liberty was granted, joined to the high price of sugar in Great Britain, have rendered it, in a great measure, ineffectual. Great Britain and her colonies still continue to be almost the sole market for all the sugar produced in the British plantations. Their consumption increases so fast, that, though in consequence of the increasing improvement of Jamaica, as well as of the Ceded Islands, the importation of sugar has increased very greatly within these twenty years, the exportation to foreign countries is said to be not much greater than before.

Rum is a very important article in the trade which the Americans carry on to the coast of Africa, from which they bring back negroe slaves in return.

If the whole surplus produce of America in grain of all sorts, in salt provisions, and in fish, had been put into the enumeration, and thereby forced into the market of Great Britain, it would have interfered too much with the produce of the industry of our own people. It was probably not so much from any regard to the interest of America, as from a jealousy of this interference, that those important commodities have not only been kept out of the enumeration, but that the importation into Great Britain of all grain, except rice, and of salt provisions, has, in the ordinary state of the law, been prohibited.

The non-enumerated commodities could originally be exported to all parts of the world. Lumber and rice, having been once put into the enumeration, when they were afterwards taken out of it, were confined, as to the European market, to the countries that lie south of Cape Finisterre. By the 6th of George III. c. 5. all non-enumerated commodities were subjected to the like restriction. The parts of Europe which lie south of Cape Finisterre, are not manufacturing countries, and we were less jealous of the colony ships carrying home from them any manufactures which could interfere with our own.

The enumerated commodities are of two sorts: first, such as are either the peculiar produce of America, or as cannot be produced, or at least are not produced, in the mother country. Of this kind are, molasses, coffee, cacao-nuts, tobacco, pimento, ginger, whalefins, raw silk, cotton-wool, beaver, and other peltry of America, indigo, fustic, and other dying woods: secondly, such as are not the peculiar produce of America, but which are and may be produced in the mother country, though not in such quantities as to supply the greater part of her demand, which is principally supplied from foreign countries. Of this kind are all naval stores, masts, yards, and bowsprits, tar, pitch, and turpentine, pig and bar iron, copper ore, hides and skins, pot and pearl ashes. The largest importation of commodities of the first kind could not discourage the growth or interfere with the sale of any part of the produce of the mother country. By confining them to the home market, our merchants, it was expected, would not only be enabled to buy them cheaper in the Plantations, and consequently to sell them with a better profit at home, but to establish between the Plantations and foreign countries an advantageous carrying trade, of which Great Britain was necessarily to be the center or emporium, as the European country into which those commodities were first to be imported. The importation of commodities of the second kind might be so managed too, it was supposed, as to interfere, not with the sale of those of the same kind which were produced at home, but with that of those which were imported from foreign countries; because, by means of proper duties, they might be rendered always somewhat dearer than the former, and yet a good deal cheaper than the latter. By confining such commodities to the home market, therefore, it was proposed to discourage the produce, not of Great Britain, but of some foreign countries with which the balance of trade was believed to be unfavourable to Great Britain.

The prohibition of exporting from the colonies, to any other country but Great Britain, masts, yards, and bowsprits, tar, pitch, and turpentine, naturally tended to lower the price of timber in the colonies, and consequently to increase the expence of clearing their lands, the principal obstacle to their improvement. But about the beginning of the present century, in 1703, the pitch and tar company of Sweden endeavoured to raise the price of their commodities to Great Britain, by prohibiting their exportation, except in their own ships, at their own price and in such quantities as they thought proper. In order to counteract this notable piece of mercantile policy, and to render herself as much as possible independent, not only of Sweden, but of all the other northern powers, Great Britain gave a bounty upon the importation of naval stores from America and the effect of this bounty was to raise the price of timber in America, much more than the confinement to the home market could lower it; and as both regulations were enacted at the same time, their joint effect was rather to encourage than to discourage the clearing of land in America.

Though pig and bar iron too have been put among the enumerated commodities, yet as, when imported from America, they are exempted from considerable duties to which they are subject when imported from any other country, the one part of the regulation contributes more to encourage the erection of furnaces in America, than the other to discourage it. There is no manufacture which occasions so great a consumption of wood as a furnace, or which can contribute so much to the clearing of a country over-grown with it.

The tendency of some of these regulations to raise the value of timber in America, and thereby to facilitate the clearing of the land, was neither, perhaps, intended nor understood by the legislature. Though their beneficial effects, however, have been in this respect accidental, they have not upon that account been less real.

The most perfect freedom of trade is permitted between the British colonies of America and the West Indies, both in the enumerated and in the non-enumerated commodities. Those colonies are now become so populous and thriving, that each of them finds in some of the others a great and extensive market for every part of its produce. All of them taken together, they make a great internal market for the produce of one another.

The liberality of England, however, towards the trade of her colonies has been confined chiefly to what concerns the market for their produce, either in its rude state, or in what may be called the very first stage of manufacture. The more advanced or more refined manufactures even of the colony produce, the merchants and manufactures of Great Britain chuse to reserve to themselves, and have prevailed upon the legislature to prevent their establishment in the colonies, sometimes by high duties, and sometimes by absolute prohibitions.

·   ·   ·

While Great Britain encourages in America the manufactures of pig and bar iron, by exempting them from duties to which the like commodities are subject when imported from any other country, she imposes an absolute prohibition upon the erection of steel furnaces and slit-mills in any of her American plantations. She will not suffer her colonists to work in those more refined manufactures even for their own consumption; but insists upon their purchasing of her merchants and manufacturers all goods of this kind which they have occasion for.

She prohibits the exportation from one province to another by water, and even the carriage by land upon horseback or in a cart, of hats, of wools and woollen goods, of the produce of America; a regulation which effectually prevents the establishment of any manufacture of such commodities for distant sale, and confines the industry of her colonists in this way to such coarse and household manufactures, as a private family commonly makes for its own use, or for that of some of its neighbours in the same province.

To prohibit a great people, however, from making all that they can of every part of their own produce, or from employing their stock and industry in the way that they judge most advantageous to themselves, is a manifest violation of the most sacred rights of mankind. Unjust, however, as such prohibitions may be, they have not hitherto been very hurtful to the colonies. Land is still so cheap, and, consequently, labour so dear among them, that they can import from the mother country, almost all the more refined or more advanced manufactures cheaper than they could make them for themselves. Though they had not, therefore, been prohibited from establishing such manufactures, yet in their present state of improvement, a regard to their own interest would, probably, have prevented them from doing so. In their present state of improvement, those prohibitions, perhaps without cramping their industry, or restraining it from any employment to which it would have gone of its own accord, are only impertinent badges of slavery imposed upon them, without any sufficient reason, by the groundless jealousy of the merchants and manufacturers of the mother country. In a more advanced state they might be really oppressive and insupportable.

Great Britain too, as she confines to her own market some of the most important productions of the colonies, so in compensation she gives to some of them an advantage in that market; sometimes by imposing higher duties upon the like productions when imported from other countries, and sometimes by giving bounties upon their importation from the colonies. In the first way she gives an advantage in the home-market to the sugar, tobacco, and iron of her own colonies, and in the second to their raw silk, to their hemp and flax, to their indigo, to their naval-stores, and to their building-timber. This second way of encouraging the colony produce by bounties upon importation, is, so far as I have been able to learn, peculiar to Great Britain. The first is not. Portugal does not content herself with imposing higher duties upon the importation of tobacco from any other country, but prohibits it under the severest penalties.

With regard to the importation of goods from Europe, England has likewise dealt more liberally with her colonies than any other nation.

Great Britain allows a part, almost always the half, generally a larger portion, and sometimes the whole of the duty which is paid upon the importation of foreign goods, to be drawn back upon their exportation to any foreign country. No independent foreign country, it was easy to foresee, would receive them if they came to it loaded with the heavy duties to which almost all foreign goods are subjected on their importation into Great Britain. Unless, therefore, some part of those duties was drawn back upon exportation, there was an end of the carrying trade: a trade so much favoured by the mercantile system.

Our colonies, however, are by no means independent foreign countries; and Great Britain having assumed to herself the exclusive right of supplying them with all goods from Europe, might have forced them (in the same manner as other countries have done their colonies) to receive such goods, loaded with all the same duties which they paid in the mother country. But, on the contrary, till 1763, the same drawbacks were paid upon the exportation of the greater part of foreign goods to our colonies as to any independent foreign country. In 1763, indeed, by the 4th of Geo. III. c. 15. this indulgence was a good deal abated, and it was enacted, "That no part of the duty called the old subsidy should be drawn back for any goods of the growth, production, or manufacture of Europe or the East Indies, which should be exported from this kingdom to any British colony or plantation in America; wines, white callicoes and muslins excepted." Before this law, many different sorts of foreign goods might have been bought cheaper in the plantations than in the mother country and some may still.

Of the greater part of the regulations concerning the colony trade, the merchants who carry it on, it must be observed, have been the principal advisers. We must not wonder, therefore, if, in the greater part of them, their interest has been more considered than either that of the colonies or that of the mother country. In their exclusive privilege of supplying the colonies with all the goods which they wanted from Europe, and of purchasing all such parts of their surplus produce as could not interfere with any of the trades which they themselves carried on at home, the interest of the colonies was sacrificed to the interest of those merchants. In allowing the same drawbacks upon the re-exportation of the greater part of European and East India goods to the colonies, as upon their re-exportation to any independent country, the interest of the mother country was sacrificed to it, even according to the mercantile ideas of that interest. It was for the interest of the merchants to pay as little as possible for the foreign goods which they sent to the colonies, and consequently, to get back as much as possible of the duties which they advanced upon their importation into Great Britain. They might thereby be enabled to sell in the colonies, either the same quantity of goods with a greater profit, or a greater quantity with the same profit, and, consequently, to gain something either in the one way or the other. It was, likewise, for the interest of the colonies to get all such goods as cheap and in as great abundance as possible. But this might not always be for the interest of the mother country. She might frequently suffer both in her revenue, by giving back a great part of the duties which had been paid upon the importation of such goods; and in her manufactures, by being undersold in the colony market, in consequence of the easy terms upon which foreign manufactures could be carried thither by means of those drawbacks. The progress of the linen manufacture of Great Britain, it is commonly said, has been a good deal retarded by the drawbacks upon the re-exportation of German linen to the American colonies.

But though the policy of Great Britain with regard to the trade of her colonies has been dictated by the same mercantile spirit as that of other nations, it has, however, upon the whole, been less illiberal and oppressive than that of any of them.

11. The State of the Colonial Economy

in the 1720's

In 1650, when the imperial government began to impose regulations upon the colonial economies, slightly more than 50,000 people inhabited the British North American colonies. Thereafter the colonial population expanded at a rapid rate; by 1720, when the following report was written, over 460,000 colonists lived in North America. Mainly responsible for the spectacular growth of the economy that this increase in population suggests was the international and intercolonial trade developed by these colonies, which took advantage of the vast natural resources of the New World. The export of staple products—such as sugar from the West Indies, tobacco from Virginia and Maryland, and rice from the Carolinas—was the backbone of the colonial trade. The extensive growth of New England and the beginnings of development in the Middle Colonies were mainly tied to trade with these Atlantic Colonies, especially the West Indies. New England provided forest products, fish, and shipping services, and the Middle Colonies provided breadstuffs to feed the labor force engaged in producing export staples in the West Indies. This pattern of colonial development had become established by 1720, as the following document suggests, and it provided a foundation for the even more rapid extensive development that occurred between 1720 and the outbreak of the American Revolution. It is possible to identify three major colonial economic regions. One, composed of those colonies which had established a large direct trade with the mother country, included the Southern Colonies with their exports of tobacco, rice, and indigo, as well as the West Indies with their major export, sugar. A second region comprised the Middle Colonies, producing foodstuffs whose primary market was the staple-producing colonies. Basically this region was made up of the colonies of New York, New Jersey, and Pennsylvania. The third region was composed of the New England Colonies which engaged in fishing to produce foodstuffs (also mainly for the staple-producing colonies) and in an extensive intracolonial carrying trade. It was this system of interdependence through trade which governed the extensive economic growth of the British Atlantic colonies.

SOURCE: "Copy of a Representation of the Lords Commissioners for Trade and Plantations to the King upon the State of His Majesty's Colonies & Plantations on the Continent of North America, dated September the 8th 1721," in E. B. O'Callaghan (ed.), *Documents Relative to the Colonial History of the State of New York* (Albany, 1855), V, 591, 595, 597–8, 600–6, 608–10, 613–17, 630.

To the KING's MOST EXCELLENT MAJESTY.

May it please your Majesty.

In obedience to your Majesty's commands, we have prepared the following state of your Majesty's Plantations on the Continent of America; wherein we have distinguished their respective situations, Governments, strengths and Trade, and have observed of what importance their Commerce is to Great Britain, . . .

Your Majesty's Plantations on the Continent of America, beginning from the North, are Nova Scotia, New Hampshire, Massachusetts, Rhode Island, Connecticut, New York, New Jersey, Pensylvania, Maryland, Virginia, and Carolina.

· · ·

NEW HAMPSHIRE

Lumber, Fish, Masts for the Royal Navy, and Turpentine are the chief produce of this Province; they build some ships, but not so many since the last war as before; they have some mines, which produce very good Iron, tho' but little of it hath been hitherto forged; there are likewise great quantities of Stone, in which 'tis believed there may be silver. The annual produce of these commodities is very uncertain, the price falling and rising according to the demand there is for them, seldom exceeding £50,000 per Annum of New England money.

This Province would produce hemp and flax if proper encouragement were given for it, and the people had good seed for the first sowing.

They export their Lumber, and some part of their fish to the neighbouring Governments of the West Indies, and to the Western Islands, from whence they get their Wines. They likewise have sent some Lumber, tar and Turpentine of late to this Kingdom, in exchange for linnen and woolen manufactures; but they have some supplies of this kind from Ireland also, either directly or by way of other plantations. Their best and most merchantable fish is exported to Portugal and Italy and the produce of it generally remitted to this Kingdom except what is returned in Salt for the fishery.

Their fishing is much increased since the Peace with France, but the Lumber trade decreased, by reason of the low price it bears in the West Indies, and the little encouragement there is to send it to this Kingdom, because of the duties on that commodity here.

The Ships, trading directly from this Province to foreign parts, are now very few, not exceeding 20 in number, but they have about 100 fishing vessels, and the number of sea faring men is near 400, tho' many of them not settled Inhabitants there; and there are no manufactures carried on in this Province.

. . .

MASSACHUSETTS BAY

The products of this Country proper for the consumption of this Kingdom, are timber, turpentine, tar and pitch, masts, pipe and hogshead staves, whale fins and oil, and some furs. They supply Spain, Portugal, and the West Indies with considerable quantities of fish and Lumber. We are likewise informed, that they have mines of several kinds, which might be wrought upon proper encouragement.

Their Trade to the foreign plantations in America consists chiefly in the Exportation of Horses to Surinam, and (as we are informed) to Martinico, and the other french Islands, which is a very great discouragement to the Sugar planters in the British Islands; for without these supplies, neither the french nor the Dutch could carry on their sugar works to any great degree; and in return for their Horses, they receive Sugar, molasses and rum.

In this Province there are all sorts of Common Manufactures. The Inhabitants have always worked up their own wool into coarse Cloths, druggets, and serges; but these, as well as their homespun linnen, which is generally half cotton, serve only for the use of the meanest sort of people. A great part of the Leather used in the Country is also manufactured among themselves; some hatters have lately set up their trade in the principal Towns; and several Irish families, not long since arrived, and settled, to the Eastward, make good Linnen and diaper; however, the excessive price of labour enhances the value of all their manufactures.

It is therefore to be presumed that necessity, and not choice, has put them upon erecting manufactures; not having sufficient commodities of their own to give in exchange for those they do receive already from Great Britain; and the most natural method of curing this evil would be to allow them all proper encouragement for the importation of Naval Stores, and minerals of all kinds.

The branch of Trade which is of the greatest importance to them, and which they are best enabled to carry on, is the building of Ships, Sloops, &c. And according to our advices from thence, they have annually launched from 140 to 160 vessels of all sorts, which at 40 tons one with another, amount to 6000 Tons; and altho' the greatest part are built for account of, or sold to the Merchants of this Kingdom, and in the plantations, nevertheless there belongs to this Province about 190 sail, which may contain 8,000 tons, and are navigated with about 1,100 men, besides 150 boats, with 600 men, employed in the fisheries on their own Coast.

Their Iron works which were erected many years past, furnish them with small quantities of iron for common use, but the iron imported from this Kingdom, being esteemed much better, is generally used in their shipping.

• • •

RHODE ISLAND

As to the number of inhabitants in this Colony their trade and state of their Government, we have but very imperfect accounts; and indeed the Misfeazances of this and most of the other propri-etary Governments are so numerous, that we shall not trouble your Majesty with them in this place, but will take leave to give our humble opinion concerning them in the concluding part of this representation.

• • •

CONNECTICUT

This government is upon the same foot as Rhode Island, under the same regulations of Government, and liable to the same inconveniences.

• • •

NEW YORK

The natural produce of this Country consists in provisions, which are sent to the British Islands in the West Indies; in Horses sent to Surinam, Curaçoa, and St. Thomas, and in Whale-oil, and peltry to this Kingdom; besides some Naval stores, which this Country is capable of producing in very great quantities, if proper measures were taken for this purpose.

• • •

This province could likewise furnish iron in great quantities. It has some Copper and lead, but at a great distance from the British, and amongst the Indian Settlements. There are Coal Mines in Long Island, which has not yet been wrought.

The several Commodities, exported from this Kingdom to New York, have at a medium of three years, commonly amounted to about £50,000 a year. The imports from thence have not, upon the same medium, risen higher than £16,000 a year; so that the balance in favour of this Kingdom, as far as can be judged of it by the Custom house accounts, has been upwards of £25,000 a year.

The Vessels belonging to this province are small, and not considerable in number; being employed only in carrying provisions to the Southern Islands, and in the coasting trade to the Neighbouring colonies on the Continent.

The number of the inhabitants in this province increases daily; chiefly from New England, and from the North of Ireland. . . .

·   ·   ·

NEW JERSEY

This province produces all sorts of grain or corn, the inhabitants likewise breed all sorts of Cattle, in great quantities, with which they supply the Merchants of New York and Philadelphia, to carry on their trade, to all the American Islands; but were they a distinct Government, (having very good harbours) merchants would be encouraged to settle amongst them, and they might become a considerable trading people; whereas, at present, they have few or no ships, but coasting vessels, and they are supplied from New York and Philadelphia with English Manufactures having none of their own.

The Inhabitants daily increase in great numbers from New England and Ireland; . . .

·   ·   ·

PENNSYLVANIA

The natural produce of this Country is wheat, beef, pork, and lumber. Their Trade consequently consists chiefly in the exportation of these to the several parts of the west Indies, and Madieras; from whence; in return, they take rum, sugar, Cotton, Spanish money, and wine. They likewise build many Brigantines and Sloops for sale; but having few or no manufactures of their own, they are supplied therewith from Great Britain, to the yearly value of about 20,000£. And as this province does greatly abound in iron, so we have good grounds to believe, that, if proper encouragement was given in Great Britain, to take off that, and their timber, the people would thereby be diverted from the thoughts of setting up any manufactures of their own, and consequently the consumption of those of Great Britain considerably advanced. For it must be observed, that this Plantation is in a very flourishing condition; greatly increased in its inhabitants; and altho' the informations we have received touching their numbers, differ extremely, some computing them at about 60,000 whites and 5,000 blacks, and others not above half that number; yet they all agree in their opinion, concerning the flourishing state of this Colony, and that the produce of their commodities may well be reckoned at 100,000£ per Annum.

·   ·   ·

MARYLAND

The number of Inhabitants was computed in the year 1704. to be 30,537 men, women and children, and 4,475 slaves young and old, in all 35,012.

In the year 1710. was computed 34,796, whites, and 7,935 negroes, in all 42,741.

And in the year 1719. was computed 55,000 white inhabitants, and 25,000 blacks, in all 80,000.

From whence it appears, that the Inhabitants of this province have increased to above double the number in 15 years, and altho' some part of this increase may have been occasioned by the transportation of the rebels from Preston, by the purchase of slaves, as well as by the arrival of several convict persons, and of many poor families, who have transported themselves from Ireland; yet it must be allowed, that Maryland is one of the most flourishing provinces upon the Continent of America.

·   ·   ·

Tobacco is the staple commodity of this province of which about 30. or 35,000 hogsheads are yearly exported to Great Britain. The inhabitants export some tobacco to the other plantations, as also grain, beef, pork, and lumber, for which they have in return rum and sugar.

They likewise send some corn to the Madeiras for wine, but the most part of the wine they have from thence is purchased by bills of Exchange.

Whilst tobacco answers, in its price, the planter's labour, all manufactures, and all other trade, that might arise from the product of the Country are laid aside.

The Inhabitants wear the like cloathing, and have the same furniture within their houses with those in this Kingdom. The Slaves are cloathed with Cottons, Kerseys, flannel, and coarse linnens, all imported; and it is computed that this province consumes of British Manufactures to the value of £20,000 per annum.

No mines are yet discovered here, except iron, which are very common, but not wrought, for want of a sufficient stock, and persons of skill to engage in such an undertaking.

The number of ships belonging to this province, are only four small Brigantines, and not more than 20 Sloops for the Sea; the inhabitants not being inclined to navigation, but depending upon British bottoms for the exportation and importation of the bulk of their trade; and there has been employed of late years above 100 sail of ships from Great Britain.

·   ·   ·

VIRGINIA

The principal product of Virginia is tobacco; and in general it's of a better quality than that of Maryland. Before the conclusion of the last peace with France, the Virginia planters exported to this Kingdom at least 30,000 hogsheads per Annum; but about that time, the trade declining, for want of foreign consumption, an Act was passed in the 12th of Her late Majesty's reign for encouraging the tobacco trade, and your Majesty hath been since graciously pleased to give your Royal Assent to an Act for continuing the same.

·   ·   ·

The other branches of the trade between this kingdom and Virginia consist in pitch and tar, pipe and hogshead staves, skins and furrs, and a few drugs. They also export to the other Plantations some small quantities of tobacco, provisions, and lumber; but their dependence is almost wholly on the produce of tobacco.

·   ·   ·

NORTH CAROLINA

There are great tracts of good land in this Province, and it is a very healthy country; but the situation renders it forever incapable of being a place of considerable trade, by reason of a great Sound near sixty miles over, that lies between the Coast and the Sea, barred by a vast Chain of Sand-banks, so very shallow and shifting, that sloops, drawing only five foot water, run great risk in crossing them.

The little Commerce therefore driven to this Colony, is carried on by very small Sloops, chiefly from New England; who bring them Clothing and Iron ware, in exchange for their pork and Corn: but of late, they have made small quantities of pitch and tar, which are first exported to New England, and thence to Great Britain.

We are not thoroughly informed of the number of inhabitants; but according to the best accounts we could get, the number of persons in their tythables, or poll-tax, were not long since above 1600, of which about one third were blacks.

· · ·

SOUTH CAROLINA

The trade of this Province, with respect to their own shipping is not hitherto very considerable; the inhabitants not having above 20 sail of their own, amounting to about 1500 ton; and as they chiefly apply themselves to the plantation work, they have not many sea faring men, but their trade is carried on by the Merchants of Great Britain, who reap a considerable advantage thereby.

The commodities the people of Carolina take from Great Britain, are all manner of Cloathing, woollen linnen, iron ware, brass and pewter, and all sorts of household goods, having no manufactures of their own; and their southerly situation will make them always dependent on Great Britain for a supply of these commodities, whose consumption may be computed at about £23,000 per Annum; besides the cost of a considerable number of Negroes, with which the British Merchants have for some time furnished them yearly, taking their returns in rice, and naval stores.

There is a small trade carried on between Carolina and the Madeiras for wine; and the Commissioners of the Customs have a Surveyor General, a Collector, a Comptroller, a Searcher, a Waiter, and a Naval Officer, to put the laws of trade and Navigation in execution here: But daily experience shews, that illegal trade is not to be prevented in a proprietary Government.

The natural produce of this Country is Rice, pitch, tar, turpentine, buck-skins, furs, corn, beef, pork, soap, myrtle-wax, candles, various sorts of lumber, as Masts, cedar-boards, staves, shingles, and hoop-poles; but the soil is thought capable of producing wine, oil, silk, indigo, pot-ashes, iron, hemp, and flax.

The number of white inhabitants in this province has some time since been computed at 9000; and the blacks at 12,000, But the frequent massacres committed of late years by the neighbouring Indians, at the instigation of the French and Spaniards, have diminished the white men, whilest the manufacture of pitch and tar has given occasion to increase the number of black slaves, who have lately attempted, and were very near succeeding in a new revolution, which would probably have been attended by the utter extirpation of all your Majesty's subjects in this province; and therefore it may be necessary for your Majesty's service, that the Governor should be instructed to propose some law to the Assembly there, for encouraging the entertainment of more white servants for the future.

.   .   .

THE CONSEQUENCE OF THE PLANTATION TRADE

Thus having gone through the several Colonies on the Continent, in order to demonstrate the consequence their trade is of to Great Britain; we have drawn out from the Custom House books an Account No. 1. containing the total amount or value of all goods imported from, and exported to the said Colonies, communibus Annis, on a medium of three years from Christmas 1714 to Christmas 1717.

.   .   .

From this Account it will appear, that the plantations in America take from hence yearly to the value of one million sterling, in British products and Manufactures, and foreign goods.

And although the exports charged in this account to the several Colonies on the continent, amount to no more than £431,027. 16s. 5d yet as the Continent has undoubtedly a great share in the General article of entry to the West Indies, as well as in the articles of entry to Africa and the Madeiras, the exports to the Continent may well be computed at £500,000.

But before we enter into the particular circumstances of the plantation trade on the Continent, it will be necessary to ascertain the principal commodities, wherein their trade consists, and how much they respectively amount to; which will appear, Account No. 2.

It may be observed from this Account, that the exports to the Continent of America exceed the imports from thence about £200,- 000 per annum; which debt falls upon the provinces to the Northward of Maryland; who probably are enabled to discharge the same, by the trade they are permitted to carry on in America, and to Europe, in commodities not enumerated in the Acts of Trade, . . .

.   .   .

There still remains to be considered another great advantage that arises to this Kingdom from the plantation trade, which is, the constant employment it gives to our British Shipping.

. . .

It is very probable, that the trade which is carried on between England and the American plantations employs at least one fourth part of the Shipping annually cleared from this kingdom.

And upon casting up the tonnage of the plantation products re-exported in the year 1717, it appears there was employed near half as much Shipping, in transporting these goods from hence to Germany, Holland, and other foreign countries, as was employed in the trade directly from the British Colonies in America.

Consequently therefore it may be concluded, that about one third part of the Shipping employed in the foreign trade of this Kingdom is maintained by the plantation trade.

But notwithstanding the advantages, at present arising from the Plantation trade, are so very considerable, it is not to be doubted, but that they might still be rendered much more useful, if sufficient encouragement were given to induce them to turn their industry to the production of Naval Stores, of all kinds, and of such other commodities as our necessities require, and which are purchased by us with great disadvantage from foreign Countries; from whence this convenience, amongst many others, would naturally result,— That the more Northern Colonies would be thereby enabled to pay their balance to England, without lying under the necessity of carrying on a trade to foreign parts, in some respects detrimental to their mother Kingdom.

No. 1

The total value of the Imports from				The total value of the Exports to		
£	s	d		£	s	d
65,016	7	2	New England	139,269	14	6
22,607	16	4	New York	50,314	6	6
5,051	7	00	Pennsylvania	20,176	14	2
92,675	10	6		209,760	15	2
250,994	10	6	Virginia & Maryland	198,276	4	9
38,906	16	1	Carolina	22,987	16	6

No. 2

The principal imports from New England, New York, Pennsylvania, Virginia, Maryland, and Carolina, are as follows.

	£	s	d	
In skins & furrs	17,340	14	10	Products of the Indian Trade
Turpentine	12,082	19	5	
Pitch and tar	34,990	00	00	
Train oil	7,680	18	7	of the sd Plantations
Whalefins	3,679	14	3	
Tobacco	236,588	18	1	
Rice	19,206	18	4	
Sugar, brown	9,834	7	3	of foreign Plantations
Logwood	21,060	6	4	of Campeche
	362,464	17	1	
In all other Goods	20,112	00	00	
The total import according to the aforesd Genl account	382,576	17	1	per annum
But the Tobacco being over-valued about	80,000	00	00	
The said import cannot amount to more than	302,576	17	1	per annum

No. 3

And the principal exports to the said provinces are as follows.

In British Manufacture & Products,	£	s	d
Woollen Manufactures	147,438	11	7
Silk wrought & thrown	18,468	7	1
Linnens & sail cloth	11,464	9	00
Cordage	11,284	5	9
Gunpowder	2,392	15	5
Leather wrought, & saddles	15,161	12	6
Brass & copper wrought	2,565	6	7
Iron wrought & nails	35,631	13	6
Lead & shot	2,850	9	3
Pewter	3,687	6	11
In many other goods	43,941	5	6
	294,886	3	1

In Foreign Goods.			
Linnens	86,413	00	00
Callicoes	10,102	4	00
Prohibited East India Goods	10,523	12	9
Wrought Silks	1,189	11	1

Iron & Hemp	6,152	5	11
In other foreign goods	21,760	19	9
Foreign Goods	136,141	13	6
British Goods	294,886	3	1
The said Exports amounts to according to the aforesaid general account (per annum)	431,027	16	7
But as it has been always mentioned, the total export might probably amount to at least (per annum)	500,000	00	00

.   .   .

All which is most humbly submitted.

J. Chetwynd
P. Doeminique

Whitehall   M. Bladen
Sepr. 8. 1721   E. Ashe

12. Official Trade Statistics between the American Colonies and England, 1697-1775

Statistics in the English Inspector General's ledgers, which comprise the original source for the following table, are frequently misrepresented as a measure of the value of trade between the American colonies and Great Britain. However, they are a measure not of the value of trade but rather of the volume, comprising an index of the physical quantity of trade between the American colonies and England. Furthermore, the statistics measure the volume of trade between the American colonies and England alone—the trade with Scotland, for example, is not included. These statistics were gathered by applying the prices of commodities as they existed between 1705 and 1728, and then using the quantities of the goods shipped during each subsequent year. If the prices of commodities varied between years, as they most certainly did, then the true value of trade would differ from the figures presented in the following tables.

Besides revealing the obvious increase in the total volume of trade these statistics show the dependence of the American colonies upon England as a source of imports. They also indicate that only the staple-producing colonies found a large market for their exports in the mother country. By implication then, New England and the Middle Colonies must have earned the means of paying for their English imports by trading with other areas.

SOURCE: U. S. Bureau of the Census, *Historical Statistics of the United States, Colonial Times to 1957* (Washington, D.C.: U. S. Government Printing Office, 1960), 757.

An Index of the Volume of Exports to and Imports from England to the American Colonies, 1697–1776

Year	Total		New England		New York		Pennsylvania		Virginia and Maryland		Carolina		Georgia	
	Exports	Imports	Exports	Imports	Exports	Imports	Exports	Imports	Exports	Imports	Exports	Imports	Exports	Imports
1775	1,920,950	196,162	116,588	71,625	187,018	1,228	175,962	1,366	758,356	1,921	579,549	6,245	103,477	113,777
1774	1,373,846	2,590,437	112,248	562,476	80,008	437,937	69,611	625,652	612,030	528,738	432,302	378,116	67,647	57,518
1773	1,369,229	1,979,412	124,624	527,055	76,246	289,214	36,652	426,448	589,803	328,904	456,513	344,859	85,391	62,932
1772	1,258,515	3,012,635	126,265	824,830	82,707	343,970	29,133	507,909	528,404	793,910	425,923	449,610	66,083	92,406
1771	1,339,840	4,202,472	150,381	1,420,119	95,875	653,621	31,615	728,744	577,848	920,326	420,311	409,169	63,810	70,493
1770	1,015,535	1,925,571	148,011	394,451	69,882	475,991	28,109	134,881	435,094	717,782	278,907	146,273	55,532	56,193
1769	1,060,206	1,336,122	129,353	207,993	73,466	74,918	26,111	199,909	361,892	488,362	387,114	306,600	82,270	58,340
1768	1,251,454	2,157,218	148,375	419,797	87,115	482,930	59,406	432,107	406,048	475,954	508,108	289,868	42,402	56,562
1767	1,096,079	1,900,923	128,207	406,081	61,422	417,957	37,641	371,830	437,926	437,628	395,027	244,093	35,856	23,334
1766	1,043,958	1,804,333	141,733	409,642	67,020	330,829	26,851	327,314	461,693	372,548	293,587	296,732	53,074	67,268
1765	1,151,698	1,944,114	145,819	451,299	54,959	382,349	25,148	363,368	505,671	383,224	385,918	334,709	34,183	29,165
1764	1,110,572	2,249,710	88,157	459,765	53,697	515,416	36,258	435,191	559,408	515,192	341,727	305,808	31,325	18,338
1763	1,106,170	1,631,997	74,815	258,854	53,998	238,560	38,228	284,152	642,294	555,391	282,366	250,132	14,469	44,908
1762	742,632	1,377,160	41,733	247,385	58,882	288,046	38,091	206,199	415,709	417,599	181,695	194,170	6,522	23,761
1761	847,892	1,652,078	46,225	334,225	48,648	289,570	39,170	204,057	455,083	545,350	253,002	254,587	5,764	24,279
1760	761,099	2,611,764	37,802	599,647	21,125	480,106	22,754	707,998	504,451	605,882	162,769	218,131	12,198	
1759	639,909	2,345,453	25,985	527,067	21,684	630,785	22,404	498,161	357,228	459,007	206,534	215,255	6,074	15,178
1758	670,720	1,712,887	30,204	465,694	14,260	356,555	21,383	260,953	454,362	438,471	150,511	181,002		10,212
1757	610,684	1,628,348	27,556	363,404	19,168	353,311	14,190	268,426	418,881	426,687	130,889	213,949		2,571
1756	659,356	1,352,178	47,359	384,371	24,073	250,425	20,095	200,169	337,759	334,897	222,915	181,780	7,155	536
1755	939,553	1,112,997	59,533	341,796	28,054	151,071	32,336	144,456	489,668	285,157	325,525	187,887	4,437	2,630
1754	1,007,759	1,176,279	66,538	329,433	26,663	127,497	30,649	244,647	573,435	323,513	307,238	149,215	3,236	1,974
1753	972,740	1,452,944	83,395	345,523	50,553	277,864	38,527	245,644	632,574	356,776	164,634	213,009	3,057	14,128
1752	1,004,182	1,148,127	74,313	273,340	40,648	194,030	29,978	201,666	569,453	325,151	288,264	150,777	1,526	3,163

Year														
1751	835,651	1,233,168	63,287	305,974	42,363	248,941	23,870	190,917	460,085	347,027	245,491	138,244	555	2,065
1750	814,768	1,313,083	48,455	343,659	35,634	267,130	28,191	217,713	508,939	349,419	191,607	133,037	1,942	2,125
1749	663,524	1,230,386	39,999	238,286	23,413	265,773	14,944	238,637	434,618	323,600	150,499	164,085	51	5
1748	716,626	830,433	29,748	197,682	12,358	143,311	12,363	75,330	494,852	252,624	167,305	160,172		1,314
1747	660,715	726,669	41,771	210,640	14,992	137,984	3,832	82,404	492,619	200,088	107,500	95,529		24
1746	559,500	755,926	38,612	209,177	8,841	86,712	15,779	73,699	419,371	282,545	76,897	102,809		984
1745	554,431	535,253	38,948	140,463	14,083	54,957	10,130	54,280	399,423	197,799	91,847	86,815		939
1744	667,524	640,881	50,248	143,982	14,527	119,920	7,446	62,214	402,709	234,855	192,594	79,141		769
1743	880,807	829,273	63,185	172,461	15,067	135,487	9,596	79,340	557,821	328,195	235,136	111,499	2	2,291
1742	659,227	800,052	53,166	148,899	13,536	167,591	8,527	75,295	427,769	264,186	154,607	127,063	1,622	17,018
1741	912,291	885,492	60,052	198,147	21,142	140,430	17,158	91,010	577,109	248,582	236,830	204,770		2,553
1740	718,416	813,382	72,389	171,081	21,498	118,777	15,048	56,751	341,997	281,428	266,560	181,821	924	3,524
1739	754,276	695,869	46,604	220,378	18,459	106,070	8,134	54,452	444,654	217,200	236,192	94,445	233	3,324
1738	620,212	751,270	59,116	203,233	16,228	133,438	11,918	61,450	391,814	258,860	141,119	87,793	17	6,496
1737	775,382	682,434	63,347	223,923	16,833	125,833	15,198	56,690	492,246	211,301	187,758	58,986		5,701
1736	699,764	677,624	66,788	222,158	17,944	86,000	20,786	61,513	380,163	204,794	214,083	101,147		2,012
1735	652,326	668,664	72,899	189,125	14,155	80,405	21,919	48,804	394,995	220,381	145,348	117,837	3,010	12,112
1734	611,350	556,275	82,252	146,460	15,307	81,758	20,217	54,392	373,090	172,086	120,466	99,658	18	1,921
1733	669,633	548,890	61,983	184,570	11,626	65,417	14,776	40,565	403,198	186,177	177,845	70,466	203	1,695
1732	519,036	531,253	64,095	216,600	9,411	65,540	8,524	41,698	310,799	148,289	126,207	58,298		828
1731	650,863	536,266	49,048	183,467	20,756	66,116	12,786	44,260	408,502	171,278	159,771	71,145		
1730	572,585	536,860	54,701	208,196	8,740	64,356	10,582	48,592	346,823	150,931	151,739	64,785		
1729	575,282	422,958	52,512	161,102	15,833	64,760	7,434	29,799	386,174	108,931	113,329	58,366		
1728	605,324	517,861	64,689	194,590	21,141	81,634	15,230	37,478	413,089	171,092	91,175	33,067		
1727	637,135	502,927	75,052	187,277	31,617	67,452	12,823	31,979	421,588	192,965	96,055	23,254		
1726	526,303	553,297	63,816	200,882	38,307	84,866	5,960	37,634	324,767	185,981	93,453	43,934		
1725	415,650	549,693	72,021	201,768	24,976	70,650	11,981	42,209	214,730	195,884	91,942	39,182		
1724	462,681	461,584	69,585	168,507	21,191	63,020	4,057	30,324	277,344	161,894	90,504	37,839		
1723	461,761	411,590	59,337	176,486	27,992	53,013	8,332	15,992	287,997	123,853	78,103	42,246		
1722	437,696	424,725	47,955	133,722	20,118	57,478	6,882	26,397	283,091	172,754	79,650	34,374		

An Index of the Volume of Exports to and Imports from England to the American Colonies, 1697–1776 (continued)

Year	Total Exports	Total Imports	New England Exports	New England Imports	New York Exports	New York Imports	Pennsylvania Exports	Pennsylvania Imports	Virginia and Maryland Exports	Virginia and Maryland Imports	Carolina Exports	Carolina Imports	Georgia Exports	Georgia Imports
1721	493,871	331,905	50,483	114,524	15,681	50,754	8,037	21,548	357,812	127,376	61,858	17,703		
1720	468,188	319,702	49,206	128,767	16,836	37,397	7,928	24,531	331,482	110,717	62,736	18,290		
1719	463,054	393,000	54,452	125,317	19,596	56,355	6,564	27,068	332,069	164,630	50,373	19,630		
1718	457,471	425,333	61,591	131,885	27,331	62,966	5,588	22,716	316,576	191,925	46,385	15,841		
1717	426,090	439,666	58,898	132,001	24,534	44,140	4,499	22,505	296,884	215,962	41,275	25,058		
1716	424,389	402,042	69,595	121,156	21,971	52,173	5,193	21,842	281,343	179,599	46,287	27,272		
1715	297,246	452,366	66,555	164,650	21,316	54,629	5,461	17,182	174,756	199,274	29,158	16,631		
1714	395,774	333,443	51,541	121,288	29,810	44,643	2,663	14,927	280,470	128,873	31,290	23,712		
1713	303,222	284,556	49,904	120,778	14,428	46,470	178	17,037	206,263	76,304	32,449	23,967		
1712	365,971	309,691	24,699	128,105	12,466	18,524	1,471	8,464	297,941	134,583	29,394	20,015		
1711	324,698	297,626	26,415	137,421	12,193	28,856	38	19,408	273,181	91,535	12,871	20,406		
1710	249,814	293,659	31,112	106,338	8,203	31,475	1,277	8,594	188,429	127,639	20,793	19,613		
1709	324,534	269,596	29,559	120,349	12,259	34,577	617	5,881	261,668	80,268	20,431	28,521		
1708	286,435	240,183	49,635	115,505	10,847	26,899	2,120	6,722	213,493	79,061	10,340	11,996		
1707	284,798	413,244	38,793	120,631	14,283	29,855	786	14,365	207,625	237,901	23,311	10,492		
1706	187,073	161,691	22,210	57,050	2,849	31,588	4,210	11,037	149,152	58,015	8,652	4,001		
1705	150,961	291,722	22,793	62,504	7,393	27,902	1,309	7,206	116,768	174,322	2,698	19,788		
1704	321,972	176,088	30,823	74,896	10,540	22,294	2,430	11,819	264,112	60,458	14,057	6,621		
1703	204,295	296,210	33,539	59,608	7,471	17,562	5,160	9,899	144,928	196,713	13,197	12,428		
1702	335,788	186,809	37,026	64,625	7,965	29,991	4,145	9,342	274,782	72,391	11,870	10,460		
1701	309,134	343,826	32,656	86,322	18,547	31,910	5,220	12,003	235,738	199,683	16,973	13,908		
1700	395,021	344,341	41,486	91,918	17,567	49,410	4,608	18,529	317,302	173,481	14,058	11,003		
1699	255,397	403,614	26,660	127,279	16,818	42,792	1,477	17,064	198,115	205,078	12,327	11,401		
1698	226,055	458,097	31,254	93,517	8,763	25,279	2,720	10,704	174,053	310,135	9,265	18,462		
1697	279,852	140,129	26,282	68,468	10,093	4,579	3,347	2,997	227,756	58,796	12,374	5,289		

13. Exports from the British West Indies

The single most important commodity produced in the West Indies was sugar, the major portion of which was exported directly to the mother country. The official values of West Indian exports, like those for the trade between England and the North American colonies, are not a measure of the value of trade but rather an index of the volume of trade. The reader should note that in terms of total exports to the mother country as measured by the official values, the West Indies were more important than the continental colonies throughout the colonial period.

Official Statistics of West Indian
Exports to Great Britain, 1698–1773

Years	Value	Years	Value	Years	Value
1698	£629,533	1724	£1,160,568	1749	£1,478,075
1699	586,255	1725	1,359,185	1750	1,514,452
1700	824,246	1726	1,222,511	1751	1,444,775
1701	738,601	1727	1,089,513	1752	1,428,824
1702	476,168	1728	1,498,023	1753	1,838,137
1703	626,488	1729	1,515,421	1754	1,462,601
1704	489,906	1730	1,571,603	1755	1,867,256
1705	706,574	1731	1,310,580	1756	1,687,177
1706	537,744	1732	1,315,458	1757	1,906,147
1707	604,889	1733	1,618,013	1758	1,858,425
1708	592,750	1734	1,141,068	1759	1,833,646
1709	645,689	1735	1,460,609	1760	1,861,668
1710	730,505	1736	1,423,039	1761	1,953,622
1711	556,198	1737	946,423	1762	1,762,406
1712	648,190	1738	1,475,910	1763	2,254,231
1713	762,248	1739	1,566,838	1764	2,391,552
1714	843,390	1740	1,185,107	1765	2,196,549
1715	999,412	1741	1,402,986	1766	2,705,114
1716	1,104,188	1742	1,309,886	1767	2,690,673
1717	1,204,057	1743	1,401,610	1768	2,942,717
1718	896,031	1744	1,156,952	1769	2,686,714
1719	875,358	1745	1,024,097	1770	2,110,026
1720	1,117,576	1746	1,148,124	1771	2,979,378
1721	852,529	1747	941,116	1772	3,530,082
1722	1,015,617	1748	£1,615,122	1773	£2,902,407
1723	£1,087,254				

SOURCE: Brian Edwards, The History, Civil and Commercial, of the British West Indies (London, 1819), II, 595–8.

Quantity of Sugar Annually Exported from the
West Indies to Great Britain: 1699–1775

Years	Quantity cwt.	qrs.	lbs.	Years	Quantity cwt.	qrs.	lbs.	Years	Quantity cwt.	qrs.	lbs.
1699	427,573	2	25	1725	851,952	2	25	1751	825,936	2	0
1700	489,326	1	7	1726	668,346	1	9	1752	825,121	1	16
1701	435,465	1	21	1727	645,158	0	1	1753	1,114,084	3	26
1702	259,062	3	6	1728	972,240	0	1	1754	859,131	2	12
1703	408,914	0	1	1729	994,761	3	24	1755	1,202,679	3	14
1704	315,837	2	12	1730	1,024,078	2	3	1756	1,051,265	3	6
1705	370,157	1	7	1731	818,277	1	12	1757	1,230,843	0	20
1706	335,873	3	3	1732	822,844	3	15	1758	1,145,628	2	3
1707	388,267	3	26	1733	1,001,784	2	0	1759	1,199,682	2	26
1708	377,107	2	11	1734	695,679	3	9	1760	1,374,720	2	5
1709	397,570	3	12	1735	903,634	2	22	1761	1,491,317	3	16
1710	507,662	1	21	1736	877,591	0	24	1762	1,441,581	1	4
1711	366,394	1	26	1737	550,900	1	10	1763	1,732,174	1	5
1712	423,541	0	1	1738	864,252	1	0	1764	1,488,079	0	15
1713	503,528	1	8	1739	951,073	3	4	1765	1,227,159	3	18
1714	512,221	3	0	1740	706,947	0	8	1766	1,522,732	2	19
1715	617,414	3	11	1741	886,124	1	0	1767	1,538,834	1	8
1716	684,759	2	16	1742	731,410	3	11	1768	1,651,512	2	14
1717	763,175	3	14	1743	895,134	1	26	1769	1,525,070	0	5
1718	566,885	0	1	1744	724,411	2	14	1770	1,818,229	1	23
1719	544,634	0	25	1745	655,190	3	0	1771	1,492,096	2	24
1720	706,385	3	20	1746	753,472	1	19	1772	1,786,045	0	1
1721	497,611	0	21	1747	806,458	2	14	1773	1,762,387	3	15
1722	616,941	0	9	1748	932,588	2	13	1774	2,015,911	1	15
1723	660,766	2	9	1749	933,271	3	9	1775	2,002,224	3	8
1724	729,133	2	13	1750	915,344	2	5				

14. The Importance of the Staple Colonies to the Mother Country

The staple-exporting regions, composed of the West Indies, the middle South, and the lower South, were considered by the mother country to be the most valuable colonies in the empire. Each produced a commodity highly valued in Europe and exchanged directly with the merchants of Great Britain for goods of British manufacture or for slaves obtained by British merchants in the African trade. The West Indies in particular, and also to some extent the lower and middle South, also provided a market for the produce of the northern colonies which were unable to produce goods acceptable to Great Britain in sufficient quantities to pay for all the British imports they desired. By exchanging foodstuffs and provisions with staple-producing colonies, the northern colonies gained the requisite foreign exchange.

The staple-producing colonies had two things in common: they all produced semi-tropical commodities, and they all used slave labor in this production. The following document describing the importance of Jamaica to the mother country shows how these staple-producing colonies fitted into the mercantilistic British Atlantic Empire.

That we may take a comprehensive view of the trade of this island, it is proper to begin with the Negroe trade, which is the groundwork of all. The Negroe slaves are purchased in Africa, by the British merchants, with a great variety of woollen goods; a cheap sort of fire-arms from Birmingham, Sheffield, and other places; powder, bullets, iron bars, copper bars, brass pans, malt spirits, tallow, tobacco-pipes, Manchester goods, glass beads; some particular kind of linens, ironmongery and cutlery ware; certain toys, some East India goods; but, in the main, with very little that is not of British growth, or manufacture. Besides these slaves (which make up the greatest part of their cargo), our African traders also purchase gold dust, elephants teeth, and dying woods, with some valuable drugs; and in the West Indies also, when they have any surplus of slaves, they dispose of them at a good price to foreign nations. All the incidental profits, exclusive of what is produced by the sale of slaves, whether obtained by the purchase of other articles upon the African coasts, or from the sale of their commodities to foreigners in the West Indies, find their way into Great Britain; on the winding-up of the account therefore, as the sale of the Negroes centers in the West Indies, so the profit arising upon them, and every other accession of gain, from whatever article of our African commerce it is produced, centers ultimately with, and becomes the property of, the inhabitants of Britain. When these Negroes are sold to the British planters, they cannot be employed in, or furnished with, instruments proper for their daily labour, but with fresh advantage to the British nation. For, in his field work, the planter must supply his Negroes with bills, hoes, and axes; his Negroe tradesmen require instruments and tools of various sorts, which, in consequence of their being used continually, makes it necessary to have yearly supplies, for the making good wear and tear, which, in so moist and warm a climate, must rise to a very considerable amount. To this we may add, that these people, selling no small part of the provisions they raise, lay out the product which thus arises from their private industry, chiefly for Birmingham, Sheffield, and Manchester wares; so that all this, which, their numbers considered, amounts to no despicable sum, is likewise returned to Great Britain. But

SOURCE: Edward Long, "Trade," in The History of Jamaica (London, 1774), Vol. I, Bk. II, ch. v, 491–4.

the field expences are trifling, in comparison of the utensils necessary in sugar works; such as coppers, stills, mill-cases, and other mill-
work of iron; ladles, skimmers, lamps, and almost innumerable other
articles; to which may be added nails, locks, staples, hinges, bolts,
bars, and lead, employed by the planter in his other buildings, and
the numberless kinds of iron-work that are used in waggons, carts,
and other things, not only exceedingly expensive at the first setting
out, but which, from their being in constant use, require frequent
supplies. All these (at whatsoever price) must be had from Britain.
Even the value of the lumber, provisions, and other commodities,
which are imported from the Northern colonies, and paid for by
the sugar planters, goes in discharge of the balances respectively due
from those colonies to the mother country; or, at least, a very great
part of them are this way discharged. To this catalogue we must
add many of the materials necessary for building their houses; by
far the greatest part of their furniture: and it is not only by their industry, and the success attending it, that Great Britain is enriched,
but also by their luxuries, whenever they are in a condition to have
more than the conveniencies of life, such as chaises, coaches, chari-
ots, and the like, together with all sorts of wearing apparel, but
chiefly of the finest and costliest fabricks; no small part likewise of
their provisions, such as cheese, hams, bacon, tongues, salmon, on-
ions, refined sugars, confectionary, and grocery wares, spices, pickles,
beer, porter, ale, and cyder, in vast quantities; and flour, and biscuit,
when they are cheap. Their Negroes also are in this respect very
beneficial, for they annually consume a large abundance of cheque
linens, striped hollands, fustian, blanketting, long ells, and baize,
Kendal cottons, Oznabrugs, canvas, coarse hats, woollen caps, cotton
and silk handkerchiefs, knives, scissars, razors, buckles, buttons, tobacco-pipes, fishing tackle, small glasses, ribbons, beads, thread,
needles, pins, and various other articles, all or most of them of British growth or manufacture. Further, as sugar, rum, and melasses; so
likewise cotton, indigo, pimento, mahogany, fustic; and, in a word,
every thing that comes from these plantations are bulky commodities; they require and employ an immense quantity of shipping, the
freights of which, outward and homeward, insurance, commissions,
and petit charges, are all paid by the inhabitants of these islands,
and are all received by British merchants and factors. We must
also take into this account the very large revenue which annually
arises from this commerce to the crown. If, upon the whole, we re-
volve in our minds, what an amazing variety of trades receive their

daily support, as many of them did originally their being, from the calls of the African and West India markets; if we reflect on the numerous families of those mechanics and artisans which are thus maintained, and contemplate that ease and plenty, which is the constant as well as just reward of their incessant labours; if we combine with these the several tribes of active and busy people, who are continually employed in the building, repairing, rigging, victualling, and equipping, the multitudes of seamen who earn their wages by navigating, and the prodigious crowds who likewise obtain their bread by loading, unloading, and other necessary attendances upon ships; if we remember, that the subsistance of all these ranks and degrees of men, thus usefully employed, constitutes a new fund of support to the landed and trading interests of this country; that their various consumptions contribute to raise the value of land, to cause a regular and constant demand for immense quantities of our native commodities, as well as to procure a vent for our numberless manufactures; and that all this is equally regular, permanent, and certain; we may from thence form a competent idea of the prodigious value of our sugar colonies, and a just conception of their immense importance to the grandeur and prosperity of their mother country, to whom, from the circumstance of this relation, they pay without repining such vast and multifarious tributes. . . .

15. The Expansion of the Colonial Tobacco Industry

Since no statistical series exists which measures the annual colonial output of tobacco, we must use in its place a series which measures the importation of tobacco into the mother country. The first such series, for the years 1616 to 1693, may significantly understate the true production of tobacco by the colonists, since before 1660 tobacco was not an enumerated product, and a significant volume of direct trade with the Dutch purportedly existed. In addition, a certain amount of smuggling must have occurred after 1660 and before the turn of the century. The second series is probably more accurate than the first because tobacco was an enumerated product during the whole period which this series covers, and little smuggling of tobacco took place during the eighteenth century. It should be noted that Great Britain did not consume all the tobacco imported but re-exported increasing amounts to the Continent throughout the colonial period.

SOURCE: U. S. Bureau of the Census, *Historical Statistics of the United*

American Tobacco Imported by England: 1616 to 1693
(In thousands of pounds. For years ending September 28 except 1637–1640,
unknown; 1672–1682, December 24; 1690–1693, November. Leaders denote
no satisfactory data available. Outports are English ports other than London.)

Year	Total	London	Outports
1693	..	19,866.0	..
1692	..	13,423.5	..
1691	..	14,830.5	..
1690	..	12,638.0	..
1689	..	14,392.6	..
1688	28,385.5	14,890.5	13,495.0
1687	27,567.0	14,072.0	13,495.0
1686	28,036.5	14,541.5	13,495.0
1684	..	..	13,495.0
1683	..	..	13,495.0
1682	21,399.0	12,592.0	8,807.0
1681	..	14,472.0	..
1680	..	11,943.0	..
1679	..	12,983.0	..
1678	..	14,455.0	..
1677	..	11,735.0	..
1676	..	11,127.0	..
1672	17,559.0	10,539.0	7,020.0
1669	..	9,037.3	..
1663	..	7,371.1	..
1640	..	1,257.0	..
1639	..	1,345.0	..
1638	..	3,134.0	..
1637	..	1,537.0	..
1631	272.3	209.7	62.5
1630	458.2	360.6	97.5
1629	178.7	89.0	89.7
1628	552.9	420.1	132.8
1627	376.9	335.3	41.6
1626	333.1	213.3	119.8
1625	131.8	111.1	20.7
1624	203.0	187.3	15.6
1623	134.6	119.4	15.2
1622	61.6	59.4	2.2
1621	73.8	73.8	..
1620	119.0	118.0	1.0
1619	45.8	45.8	..
1618	49.7	49.5	0.2
1617	18.8	18.8	..
1616	2.5	2.3	0.2

States, Colonial Times to 1957 (Washington, D.C.: U. S. Government
Printing Office, 1960), 766.

American Tobacco Imported and Reexported by
Great Britain: 1697 to 1775

(In millions of pounds. For years ending December 24 unless otherwise
noted. Leaders denote no satisfactory data available. Outports are English
ports other than London.)

		Imports				Reexports	
		England		Scot-			Scot-
Year	Total	Total	London	Outports	land[1]	Total	England	land[1]
---	---	---	---	---	---	---	---	---
1775	102	56	..	..	46	74	44	30
1774	97	56	..	..	41	79	45	34
1773	100	56	38	18	45	97	50	46
1772	97	51	36	15	45	94	50	44
1771	105	58	43	15	47	87	41	46
1770	78	39	27	12	39	73	33	40
1769	70	34	24	9	36	59	24	35
1768	69	36	23	12	33	67	31	36
1767	68	39	26	14	29	63	36	26
1766	73	43	27	16	29	63	33	30
1765	81	48	29	20	33	68	39	29
1764	81	54	37	17	26	85	54	31
1763	98	65	47	18	33	65	41	24
1762	71	44	22	22	27	62	36	25
1761	73	47	27	20	26	66	37	29
1760	85	52	28	24	32	64	40	25
1759	50	35	18	16	15	50	32	19
1758	70	44	24	20	26	43	26	17
1757	60	42	22	20	18	46	28	18
1756	46	33	19	14	12	38	26	12
1755	64	49	27	22	15	45	34	10
1754	79	59	33	26	20	73	53	20
1753	87	63	37	25	24	74	50	23
1752	78	57	33	24	21	69	49	20
1751	..	46	26	20	..	..	39	..
1750	..	51	26	26	..	..	33	..
1749	..	45	21	23	..	..	44	..
1748	..	51	28	23	..	..	43	..
1747	64	51	29	23	13	52	39	13
1746	52	40	19	21	12	49	32	16
1745	55	41	22	19	14	43	33	10
1744	52	41	24	17	11	51	42	10
1743	67	57	33	24	11	58	47	11
1742	53	43	24	19	10	52	44	8
1741	68	59	41	19	9	54	46	8
1740	41	36	19	17	5	42	35	7
1739	53	47	31	16	7	43	38	5
1738	45	40	25	15	5	37	33	4
1737	..	50	32	19	..	..	41	..
1736	..	38	25	13	..	..	32	..

[1] For 1721–1731 and 1752–1754, for years ending Sept. 28; 1755–1775, years
ending Jan. 4 of following year.

American Tobacco Imported and Reexported by Great Britain: 1697 to 1775

(In millions of pounds. For years ending December 24 unless otherwise noted. Leaders denote no satisfactory data available. Outports are English ports other than London.)

Year	Total	Imports England Total	London	Outports	Scot- land[1]	Reexports Total	England	Scot- land[1]
1735	..	40	26	14	..	..	33	..
1734	..	36	24	12	..	..	27	..
1733	..	40	27	13	..	..	26	..
1732	..	31	20	11	..	..	31	..
1731	46	42	29	13	4	34	29	5
1730	41	35	24	11	6	33	27	5
1729	47	40	27	13	7	38	31	7
1728	50	43	29	14	7	35	29	6
1727	50	43	28	16	7	32	26	5
1726	36	32	20	12	4	31	28	3
1725	25	21	14	7	4	16	13	3
1724	32	27	18	8	6	28	18	11
1723	34	29	21	9	5	24	22	1
1722	35	29	19	9	7	25	21	4
1721	41	37	..	..	4	30	26	4
1720	..	35	..	..	..	..	23	..
1719	..	34	..	..	..	..	20	..
1718	..	32	..	..	..	..	19	..
1717	32	30	..	..	2	21	19	2
1716	31	28	..	..	2	19	17	2
1715	20	18	..	..	2	15	13	2
1714	..	29	..	..	..	..	20	..
1713	..	22	..	..	..	..	17	..
1712	..	31	..	..	..	..	19	..
1711	30	28	..	..	1	16	15	1
1710	25	23	..	..	1	16	15	1
1709	36	35	..	..	1	22	21	1
1708	30	29	..	..	1	18	17	1
1707	..	28	15	13	..	..	21	..
1706	..	20	12	8	..	..	11	..
1705	..	16	..	..	..	..	11	..
1704	..	35	25	10	..	..	20	..
1703	..	20	..	11	..	..	17	..
1702	..	37	25	12	..	..	14	..
1701	..	32	21	11	..	..	21	..
1700	..	38	25	12	..	..	25	..
1699	..	31	18	13	..	..	22	..
1698[2]	..	23	10	13	..	..	18	..
1697[2]	..	36	26	10	..	..	18	..

[1] For 1721–1731 and 1752–1754, for years ending Sept. 28; 1755–1775, years ending Jan. 4 of following year.
[2] For years ending Sept. 28.

16. A Description of the
Tobacco-Growing Economy

The following account provides an excellent description of the colonial tobacco industry. The many navigable streams and rivers of Virginia and Maryland allowed the planters easy access to the tobacco centers of Great Britain; the establishment of warehouses by the colonial legislatures aided the marketing process by maintaining quality controls; and the issuance of warehouse receipts provided a form of paper money which, by circulating from hand to hand, encouraged the exchange of other commodities within the tobacco colonies.

This plant [tobacco] is cultivated in all parts of North America, from Quebec to Carolina, and even the West Indies; but, except in Maryland, Virginia, and North Carolina, they plant no more than for private use, making it an object of exportation only in these provinces, where it is of such immense consequence. . . .

One of the greatest advantages attending the culture of tobacco, is the quick, easy, and certain method of sale. This was effected by the inspection law, which took place in Virginia in the year 1730, but not in Maryland till 1748. The planter, by virtue of this, may go to any place and sell his tobacco, without carrying a sample of it along with him, and the merchant may buy it, though lying a hundred miles, or at any distance from his store, and yet be morally sure both with respect to quantity and quality. For this purpose, upon all the rivers and bays of both provinces, at a distance of about twelve or fourteen miles from each other, are erected warehouses, to which all the tobacco in the country must be brought, and there lodged, before the planters can offer it for sale; and inspectors are appointed to examine all the tobacco brought in, receive such as is good and merchantable, condemn and burn what appears damnified or insufficient. The greatest part of the tobacco is prized, or put up into hogsheads by the planters themselves, before it is carried to the warehouses. Each hogshead, by an act of assembly, must be 950 lb. neat, or upwards; some of them weigh 14 cwt. and even 18 cwt. and the heavier they are the merchants like them the better; be-

SOURCE: *American Husbandry* (London, 1775), I, 222 passim; reprinted in Guy Stevens Callender (ed.), *Selections from the Economic History of the United States, 1765–1860* (Boston: Ginn and Company, 1909), 22–5.

cause four hogsheads, whatsoever their weight be, are esteemed a tun, and pay the same freight. The inspectors give notes of receipt for the tobacco, and the merchants take them in payment for their goods, passing current indeed over the whole colonies; a most admirable invention, which operates so greatly, that in Virginia they have no paper currency.

The merchants generally purchase the tobacco in the country, by sending persons to open stores for them; that is, warehouses in which they lay in a great assortment of British commodities and manufactures, to these, as to shops, the planters resort, and supply themselves with what they want, paying, in inspection receipts, or taking on credit according to what will be given them; and as they are in general a very luxurious set of people, they buy too much upon credit; the consequence of which is, their getting in debt to the London merchants, who take mortgages on their plantations, ruinous enough, with the usury of eight per cent. But this is apparently the effect of their imprudence in living upon trust. . . .

There is no plant in the world that requires richer land, or more manure than tobacco; it will grow on poorer soils, but not to yield crops that are sufficiently profitable to pay the expences of negroes, &c. The land they found to answer best is fresh woodlands, where many ages have formed a stratum of rich black mould. Such land will, after clearing, bear tobacco many years, without any change, prove more profitable to the planter than the power of dung can do on worse lands: this makes the tobacco planters more solicitous for new land than any other people in America, they wanting it much more. Many of them have very handsome houses, gardens, and improvements about them, which fixes them to one spot; but others, when they have exhausted their grounds, will sell them to new settlers for corn-fields, and move backwards with their negroes, cattle, and tools, to take up fresh land for tobacco; this is common, and will continue so as long as good land is to be had upon navigable rivers: this is the system of business which made some, so long ago as 1750, move over the Allegany mountains, and settle not far from the Ohio, where their tobacco was to be carried by land some distance, which is a heavy burthen on so bulky a commodity, but answered by the superior crops they gained: the French encroachments drove these people all back again; but upon the peace, many more went, and the number increasing, became the occasion of the new colony which has been settled in that country.

A very considerable tract of land is necessary for a tobacco plantation; first, that the planter may have a sure prospect of increasing his culture on fresh land; secondly, that the lumber may be a winter employment for his slaves, and afford casks for his crops. Thirdly, that he may be able to keep vast flocks of cattle for raising provisions in plenty, by ranging in the woods; and where the lands are not fresh, the necessity is yet greater, as they must yield much manure for replenishing the worn-out fields. This want of land is such, that they reckon a planter should have 50 acres of land for every working hand; with less than this they will find themselves distressed for want of room. . . .

The tobacco planters live more like country gentlemen of fortune than any other settlers in America; all of them are spread about the country, their labour being mostly by slaves, who are left to overseers; and the masters live in a state of emulation with one another in buildings, (many of their houses would make no slight figure in the English counties) furniture, wines, dress, diversions, &c. and this to such a degree, that it is rather amazing they should be able to go on with their plantations at all, than they should not make additions to them: such a country life as they lead, in the midst of a profusion of rural sports and diversions, with little to do themselves, and in a climate that seems to create rather than check pleasure, must almost naturally have a strong effect in bringing them to be just such planters, as foxhunters in England make farmers. . . .

The poverty of the planters here, many of them at least, is much talked of, and from thence there has arisen a notion that their husbandry is not profitable: this false idea I have endeavoured to obviate, and to shew that the cause of it has little or no reference to their culture, but to the general luxury, and extravagant way of living which obtains among the planters—a circumstance which ought rather to occasion a contrary conclusion;—a supposition that their agriculture was very valuable; for men without some rich article of product cannot afford, even with the assistance of credit, to live in such a manner: it must be upon the face of it a profitable culture, that will support such luxury, and pay eight per cent. interest on their debts. What common culture in Europe will do this? . . .

17. The Expansion of Colonial Rice and Indigo Industries

Beginning in South Carolina before the turn of the century, the colonial rice industry expanded rapidly during the eighteenth century, as the following table indicates. Statistics on the export of indigo are incomplete, but some idea of the rate of growth of the industry is afforded by figures showing its export out of the lower South.

Rice Exported from Producing Areas: 1698 to 1774

Year	Total, pounds	Year	Total, pounds	Year	Total, pounds
1774	76,265,700	1749	21,381,030	1724	8,654,447
1773	81,476,325	1748	28,368,550	1723	8,797,304
1772	69,218,625	1747	27,643,060	1722	9,732,377
1771	81,755,100	1746	27,335,040	1721	7,963,615
1770	83,708,625	1745	29,813,375	1720	6,485,662
1769	73,078,950	1744	39,963,630	1719	4,001,210
1768	77,284,200	1743	35,935,200	1718	2,956,727
1767	63,465,150	1742	22,706,060	1717	2,881,335
1766	48,396,600	1741	38,720,955	1716	4,584,927
1765	65,710,575	1740	43,326,000	1715	2,367,605
1764	55,907,250	1739	32,167,800	1714	3,139,361
1763	61,959,450	1738	16,327,350	1713	3,850,533
1762	47,435,325	1737	20,201,400	1711	1,181,430
1761	58,480,275	1736	24,804,000	1710	1,600,983
1760	35,327,250	1735	21,259,800	1709	1,510,679
1759	30,472,575	1734	13,991,850	1708	675,327
1758	38,527,650	1733	23,245,200	1707	561,185
1757	33,976,950	1732	16,866,000	1706	267,309
1756	45,344,250	1731	21,753,450	1704	759,536
1755	59,057,775	1730	18,774,900	1703	694,493
1754	49,179,520	1729	14,248,960	1702	612,646
1753	19,747,675	1728	12,884,950	1701	194,618
1752	42,245,850	1727	11,291,280	1700	394,130
1751	32,751,270	1726	9,442,710	1699	131,207
1750	27,372,500	1725	7,093,600	1698[1]	10,407

[1] Year ending September 28; exports from September 29 to December 24, 1698 were 1,599 pounds.

SOURCE: U. S. Bureau of the Census, *Historical Statistics of the United States, Colonial Times to 1957* (Washington, D.C.: U. S. Government Printing Office, 1960), 762, 767-8.

Indigo Exported from South Carolina
and Georgia: 1747 to 1775

Year	Indigo (1,000 pounds) Total	Year	Indigo (1,000 pounds) Total	Year	Indigo (1,000 pounds) Total
1775	n.a.	1765	351.9	1755	308.0
1774	n.a.	1764	543.2	1754	129.6
1773	n.a.	1763	447.7	1753	28.5
1772	759.8	1762	264.4	1752	3.8
1771	454.1	1761	385.6	1751	19.9
1770	573.1	1760	519.3	1750	63.1
1769	416.6	1759	696.2	1749	138.3
1768	517.7	1758	572.6	1748	62.2
1767	n.a.	1757	894.5	1747	138.3
1766	506.2	1756	232.1		

18. The Growing of Rice and Indigo
in South Carolina

Rice and indigo were the two chief agricultural products of the lower South during the colonial period. The following description of the growing of these two staple exports was written by the governor of South Carolina in 1749. Seasonal labor requirements of each crop were sufficiently staggered so that in this region the same slave labor could be fully employed throughout the year.

The land of South Carolina for a hundred or a hundred and fifty miles back is flat and woody; intersected with many large rivers, some of which rise out of the Cherokee Mountains, and after a winding course of some hundreds of miles, discharge themselves into the sea.

It is remarkable for the diversity of its soil; that near the coast is generally sandy, but not therefore unfruitful; in other parts there is

SOURCE: James Glen, "A Description of South Carolina," in Chapman J. Milling (ed.), Colonial South Carolina: Two Contemporary Descriptions by Governor James Glen and Doctor George Milligen-Johnston (South Carolina Sesquicentennial Series, No. 1 [Columbia, S.C.: 1951]), Section II; reprinted in Merrill Jensen (ed.), English Historical Documents: American Colonial Documents to 1776 (New York: Oxford University Press, 1955), IX, 332–4.

clay, loam, and marl; I have seen of the soil of some high bluffs, near the sides of rivers, that exactly resembles castile soap, and is not less variegated with red and blue veins, nor less clammy.

There are dispersed up and down the country several large Indian old fields, which are lands that have been cleared by the Indians, and now remain just as they left them.

There arise in many places fine savannahs, or wide extended plains, which do not produce any trees; these are a kind of natural lawns, and some of them as beautiful as those made by art.

The country abounds everywhere with large swamps, which, when cleared, opened, and sweetened by culture, yield plentiful crops of rice. Along the banks of our rivers and creeks there are also swamps and marshes, fit either for rice, or, by the hardness of their bottoms, for pasturage.

It would open too large a field to enter very minutely into the nature of the soil; and I think that this will sufficiently appear by the following account of what the labour of one Negro employed on our best lands will annually produce in rice, corn, and indigo.

The best land for rice is a wet, deep, miry soil such as is generally to be found in cypress swamps; or a black, greasy mould with a clay foundation; but the very best lands may be meliorated by laying them under water at proper seasons.

Good crops are produced even the first year when the surface of the earth appears in some degree covered with the trunks and branches of trees. The proper months for sowing rice are March, April, and May. The method is to plant it in trenches or rows made with a hoe, about three inches deep. The land must be kept pretty clear from weeds and at the latter end of August or the beginning of September it will be fit to be reaped.

Rice is not the worse for being a little green when cut. They let it remain on the stubble till dry, which will be in about two or three days, if the weather be favourable, and then they house or put it in large stacks.

Afterwards it is threshed with a flail, and then winnowed, which was formerly a very tedious operation, but it is now performed with great ease by a very simple machine, a wind-fan, but lately used here and a prodigious improvement.

The next part of the process is grinding, which is done in small mills made of wood of about two feet in diameter. It is then winnowed again, and afterwards put into a mortar made of wood, sufficient to contain from half a bushel to a bushel, where it is beat with a pestle of a size suitable to the mortar and to the strength of the person who is to pound it. This is done to free the rice from a thick skin, and is the most laborious part of the work.

It is then sifted from the flour and dust, made by the pounding, and afterwards by a wire sieve called a market sieve it is separated from the broken and small rice, which fits it for the barrels in which it is carried to market.

They reckon thirty slaves a proper number for a rice plantation, and to be tended with one overseer. These in favourable seasons and on good land will produce a surprising quantity of rice; but that I may not be blamed by those who being induced to come here upon such favourable accounts and may not reap so great a harvest; and that I may not mislead any person whatever, I choose rather to mention the common computation throughout the province, *communibus Annis*; which is, that each good working hand employed in a rice plantation makes four barrels and a half of rice, each barrel weighing five hundred pounds weight, neat; besides a sufficient quantity of provisions of all kinds, for the slaves, horses, cattle, and poultry of the plantation, for the ensuing year.

Rice last year bore a good price, being at a medium about forty-five shillings of our currency per hundred weight; and all this year it hath been fifty-five shillings [to] three pounds; though not many years ago it was sold at such low prices as ten or twelve shillings per hundred.

Indian corn delights in high loose land. It does not agree with clay, and is killed by much wet. It is generally planted in ridges made by the plough or hoe, and in holes about six or eight feet from each other. It requires to be kept free from weeds, and will produce, according to the goodness of the land, from fifteen to fifty bushels an acre; some extraordinary rich land in good seasons will yield eighty bushels, but the common computation is that a Negro will tend six acres and that each acre will produce from ten to thirty-five bushels. It sells generally for about ten shillings currency a bushel, but is at present fifteen.

Indigo is of several sorts. What we have gone mostly upon is the sort generally cultivated in the Sugar Islands, which requires a high loose soil, tolerably rich, and is an annual plant; but the wild sort, which is common in this country, is much more hardy and luxuriant, and is perennial. Its stalk dies every year, but it shoots up again next spring. The indigo made from it is of as good a quality as the other, and it will grow on very indifferent land, provided it be dry and loose.

An acre of good land may produce about eighty pounds weight of good indigo, and one slave may manage two acres and upwards, and raise provisions besides, and have all the winter months to saw lumber and be otherwise employed in. But as much of the land hitherto used for indigo is improper, I am persuaded that not above thirty pounds weight of good indigo per acre can be expected from the land at present cultivated. Perhaps we are not conversant enough in this commodity, either in the culture of the plant or in the method of managing or manufacturing it, to write with certainty.

I am afraid that the limewater which some use to make the particles subside, contrary as I have been informed to the practice of the French, is prejudicial to it by precipitating different kinds of particles, and consequently incorporating them with the indigo.

But I cannot leave this subject without observing how conveniently and profitably, as to the charge of labour, both indigo and rice may be managed by the same persons; for the labour attending indigo being over in the summer months, those who were employed in it may afterwards manufacture rice in the ensuing part of the year, when it becomes most laborious; and after doing all this they will have some time to spare for sawing lumber, and making hogshead and other staves to supply the Sugar Colonies.

19. The Trade of the Middle Colonies

Denied a market for their foodstuffs in Great Britain by the Corn Laws but still required by the Navigation Acts to purchase their manufactures from that country, the Middle Colonies (New York, Pennsylvania, and New Jersey) were forced to obtain the foreign exchange needed to pay for British imports by trading with other areas. The following document, written by a traveler to North America in the middle of the eighteenth century, describes the manner in which the Middle Colonies carried on this enterprise.

SOURCE: Peter Kalm, *Travels into North America* (1749), I, 253–8; 243–5; reprinted in Guy Stevens Callender (ed.), *Selections from the Economic History of the United States, 1765–1860* (Boston: Ginn and Co., 1909), 16–20.

New York probably carries on a more extensive commerce, than any town in the English North American provinces; at least it may be said to equal them: Boston and Philadelphia however come very near up to it. The trade of New York extends to many places, and it is said they send more ships from thence to London, than they do from Philadelphia. They export to that capital all the various sorts of skins which they buy of the Indians, sugar, logwood, and other dying woods, rum, mahogany, and many other goods which are the produce of the West Indies; together with all the specie which they get in the course of trade. Every year they build several ships here, which are sent to London, and there sold; and of late years they have shipped a quantity of iron to England. In return for these, they import from London stuffs and every other article of English growth or manufacture, together with all sorts of foreign goods. England, and especially London, profits immensely by its trade with the American colonies; for not only New York, but like-wise all the other English towns on the continent, import so many articles from England, that all their specie, together with the goods which they get in other countries, must altogether go to Old England, in order to pay the amount, to which they are however insufficient. From hence it appears how much a well regulated colony contributes to the increase and welfare of its mother country.

New York sends many ships to the West Indies, with flour, corn, biscuit, timber, tuns, boards, flesh, fish, butter, and other provisions; together with some of the few fruits that grow here. Many ships go to Boston in New England, with corn and flour, and take in exchange, flesh, butter, timber, different sorts of fish, and other articles, which they carry further to the West Indies. They now and then take rum from thence, which is distilled there in great quantities, and sell it here with a considerable advantage. Sometimes they send yachts with goods from New York to Philadelphia, and at other times yachts are sent from Philadelphia to New York; which is only done, as appears from the gazettes, because certain articles are cheaper at one place than at the other. They send ships to Ireland every year, laden with all kinds of West India goods; but especially with linseed, which is reaped in this province. I have been assured, that in some years no less than ten ships have been sent to Ireland, laden with nothing but linseed; because it is said the flax in Ireland does not afford good seed. But probably the true reason is this: the people of Ireland, in order to have the better flax, make use of the plant before the seed is ripe, and therefore are obliged to send for foreign seed; and hence it becomes one of the chief articles in trade.

At this time a bushel of linseed is sold for eight shillings of New York currency, or exactly a piece of eight.

The goods which are shipped to the West Indies, are sometimes paid for with ready money, and sometimes with West India goods, which are either first brought to New York, or immediately sent to England or Holland. If a ship does not chuse to take in West India goods in its return to New York, or if no body will freight it, it often goes to Newcastle in England, to take in coals for ballast, which when brought home sell for a pretty good price. In many parts of the town coals are made use of, both for kitchen fires, and in rooms, because they are reckoned cheaper than wood, which at present costs thirty shillings of New York currency per fathom; of which measure I have before made mention. New York has likewise some intercourse with South Carolina; to which it sends corn, flour, sugar, rum, and other goods, and takes rice in return, which is almost the only commodity exported from South Carolina.

The goods with which the province of New York trades are not very numerous. They chiefly export the skins of animals, which are bought of the Indians about Oswego; great quantities of boards, coming for the most part from Albany; timber and ready made lumber, from that part of the country which lies about the river Hudson; and lastly wheat, flour, barley, oats and other kinds of corn, which are brought from New Jersey and the cultivated parts of this province. I have seen yachts from New Brunswick, laden with wheat which lay loose on board, and with flour packed up into tuns; and also with great quantities of linseed. New York likewise exports some flesh and other provisions out of its own province, but they are very few; nor is the quantity of pease which the people about Albany bring much greater. Iron however may be had more plentifully, as it is found in several parts of this province, and is of a considerable goodness; but all the other products of this country are of little account.

Most of the wine, which is drank here and in the other colonies is brought from the Isle of Madeira and is very strong and fiery.

No manufactures of note have as yet been established here; at present they get all manufactured goods, such as woollen and linen cloth, &c. from England, and especially from London. . . .

· · ·

Philadelphia, the capital of Pensylvania, a province which makes part of what formerly was called New Sweden is one of the principal towns in North-America; and next to Boston the greatest. . . .

Several ships are annually built of American oak, in the docks which are made in several parts of the town and about it, yet they can by no means be put in comparison with those built of European oak, in point of goodness and duration.

The town carries on a great trade, both with the inhabitants of the country, and to other parts of the world, especially to the West Indies, South America, and the Antilles; to England, Ireland, Portugal, and to several English colonies in North America. Yet none but English ships are allowed to come into this port.

Philadelphia reaps the greatest profits from its trade to the West Indies. For thither the inhabitants ship almost every day a quantity of flour, butter, flesh and other victuals; timber, plank and the like. In return they receive either sugar, molasses, rum, indigo, mahogany, and other goods, or ready money. The true mahogany, which grows in Jamaica, is at present almost all cut down.

They send both West India goods, and their own productions to England; the latter are all sorts of woods, especially black walnut, and oak planks for ships; ships ready built, iron, hides and tar. Yet this latter is properly bought in New Jersey, the forests of which province are consequently more ruined than any others. Ready money is likewise sent over to England, from whence in return they get all sorts of goods there manufactured, viz. fine and coarse cloth, linen, iron ware, and other wrought metals, and East India goods. For it is to be observed that England supplies Philadelphia with almost all stuffs and manufactured goods which are wanted here.

A great quantity of linseed goes annually to Ireland, together with many of the ships which are built here. Portugal gets wheat, corn, flour, and maize which is not ground. Spain sometimes takes some corn. But all the money, which is got in these several countries, must immediately be sent to England, in payment for the goods which are got from thence, and yet those sums are not sufficient to pay all the debts. . . .

20. A Description of Agriculture
in the Middle Colonies

The Middle Colonies, like their neighbors to the south, were favored by extensive areas of arable lands and so, naturally, turned to the production of agricultural products. The types of crops most suitable to the area were, however, quite different from those in the South, and as a result the methods of organizing production also differed significantly. Since the region was suited mainly to general farming, especially the production of grains, small family farms, each producing a wide range of cash crops, became the rule—in sharp contrast to the specialization characteristic of the South. The following document, dealing with New York, is equally descriptive of the other Middle Colonies.

Wheat in many parts of the province [New York] yields a larger produce than is common in England: upon good lands about Albany, where the climate is the coldest in the country, they sow two bushels and better upon one acre, and reap from 20 to 40: the latter quantity, however, is not often had; but from 20 to 30 bushels are common, and this with such bad husbandry as would not yield the like in England, and much less in Scotland. This is owing to the richness and freshness of the soil. In other parts of the province, particularly adjoining to New Jersey and Pensylvania, the culture is better and the country more generally settled. Though there are large tracts of waste land within twenty miles of the city of New York.

Rye is a common crop upon the inferior lands, and the sort they produce is pretty good, though not equal to the rye of England. The crops of it are not so great in produce as those of wheat on the better lands.

Maize is sown generally throughout the province, and they get vast crops of it. . . . It is also of great advantage in affording a vast produce of food for cattle in the winter, which in this country is a matter of great consequence, where they are obliged to keep all their cattle housed from November till the end of March, with exception

SOURCE: *American Husbandry* (London, 1775), I, 98–103; reprinted in Ernest Ludlow Bogart and Charles Manfred Thompson (eds.), *Readings in the Economic History of the United States* (New York: Longmans, Green and Co., 1927), 32–4.

indeed of unprovident farmers, who trust some out the chief of the winter, to their great hazard.

Barley is much sown in all the southern parts of the province; and the crops they sometimes get of it are very great, but the grain is not of a quality equal to that of Europe. They make much malt and brew large quantities of beer from it at New York, which serves the home consumption, and affords some also for exportation. Pease are a common article of culture here, and though uncertain in their produce, yet are they reckoned very profitable; and the straw is valued as winter food. Thirty bushels per acre they consider as a large crop, but some times they get scarcely a third of that. Oats they sow in common, and the products are generally large; sixty bushels an acre have been known on land of but moderate fertility. Buckwheat is everywhere sown, and a few crops are supposed to pay the farmer better, at the same time that they find it does very little prejudice to the ground, in which it resembles pease.

Potatoes are not common in New England, but in New York many are planted; and upon the black, loose, fresh woodland they get very great crops, nor does any pay them better if so well, for at the city of New York there is a constant and ready market for them; I have been assured that from five to eight hundred bushels have been often gained on an acre.

There are many very rich meadows and pastures in all parts of the province; and upon the brooks and rivers, the watered ones (for they are well acquainted with that branch of husbandry) are mown twice and yield large crops of hay. In their marshes they get large crops also, but it is a coarse bad sort; not however to a degree, as to make cattle refuse it, on the contrary, the farmers find it of great use in the winter support of their lean cattle, young stock, and cows. . . . The fruits in this province are much superior to those in New England; and they have some, as peaches and nectarines, which will not thrive there. Immense quantities of melons, and water melons are cultivated in the fields near New York, where they come to as great perfection as in Spain and Italy; nor can it well be conceived how much of these fruits and peaches, &c. all ranks of people eat here, and without receiving any ill consequence from the practice. This is an agreeableness far superior to any thing we have in England; and indeed, the same superiority runs through all their fruits, and several articles of the kitchen garden, which are here raised without trouble, and in profusion. Every planter and even the smallest farmers have all an orchard near their house of some acres, by means of which they command a great quantity of cyder, and export apples by ship loads to the West Indies. Nor is this an improper place to observe that the rivers in this province and the sea upon the coast are richly furnished with excellent fish; oysters and lobsters are no where in greater plenty than in New York. I am of opinion they are more plentiful than at any other place on the globe; for very many poor families have no other subsistence than oysters and bread. Nor is this the only instance of the natural plenty that distinguishes this country: the woods are full of game, and wild turkies are very plentiful; in these particulars New York much exceeds New England.

21. A Description of the New England Economy

The New England colonies were not favored with large areas suitable to agriculture, for the climate was harsh and the soil less fertile than in the other regions. However, the area possessed large amounts of timber, and the forest-products industry became important in this region. Like the fishing industry, which had been established in the area even before permanent colonization, the building and operating of ships was a natural outgrowth of the physical endowments of the area, and New Englanders soon became the merchants and carriers of the American colonies.

The province of Rhode Island is divided into counties and townships; of the former there are four or five, but they are exceedingly small; of the latter between twenty and thirty; the towns themselves are inconsiderable villages: however they send members to the assembly, in the whole about seventy. The number of inhabitants, with Negroes, and Indians, of which in this province there are several hundreds, amounts to 35,000. As the province affords but few commodities for exportation; horses, provisions, and an inconsiderable quantity of grain, with spermaceti candles, being the chief articles; they are obliged to Connecticut, and the neighbouring colonies, for most of their traffic; and by their means they carry on an extensive trade. Their mode of commerce is this; they trade to Great Britain, Holland, Africa, the West Indies, and the neighbouring

SOURCE: Rev. Andrew Burnaby, *Travels through the Middle Settlements in North America in the Years 1759–1760* (New York: Cornell University Press, 1960), 86–7, 96–8, 107–8.

colonies; from each of which places they import the following articles; from Great Britain, dry goods; from Holland, money; from Africa, slaves; from the West Indies, sugars, coffee, and molasses; and from the neighbouring colonies, lumber and provisions: and with what they purchase in one place they make their returns in another. Thus with the money they get in Holland, they pay their merchants in London; the sugars they procure in the West Indies, they carry to Holland; the slaves they fetch from Africa they send to the West Indies, together with lumber and provisions, which they get from the neighbouring colonies: the rum that they distil they export to Africa; and with the dry goods, which they purchase in London, they traffick in the neighbouring colonies. By this kind of circular commerce they subsist and grow rich. They have besides these some other inconsiderable branches of trade, but nothing worth mentioning. They have very few manufactures; they distil rum and make spermaceti candles; but in the article of dry goods, they are far behind the people of New York and Pensylvania.

·   ·   ·

The number of souls in this province (Massachusetts) is supposed to amount to 200,000; and 40,000 of them to be capable of bearing arms. They carry on a considerable traffick, chiefly in the manner of the Rhode-Islanders; but have some material articles for exportation, which the Rhode-Islanders have not, except in a very trifling degree: these are salt fish, and vessels. Of the latter they build annually a great number, and send them, laden with cargoes of the former to Great Britain, where they sell them. They clear out from Boston, Salem, Marblehead, and the different ports in this province, yearly, about 70,284 ton of shipping. Exclusive of these articles, their manufactures are not large; those of spirits, fish-oil, and iron, are, I believe, the most considerable. They fabricate beaver-hats, which they sell for a moidore a-piece; and some years ago they erected a manufactory, with a design to encourage the Irish settlers to make linens; but at the breaking out of the war the price of labour was inhanced so much, that it was impossible to carry it on. Like the rest of the colonies they also endeavour to make woollens; but they have not yet been able to bring them to any degree of perfection; indeed it is an article in which I think they will not easily succeed; for the American wool is not only coarse, but in comparison of the English, exceedingly short. Upon the best inquiry I could make, I was not able to discover that any one had ever seen a staple of American wool longer than seven inches; whereas in the counties of Lincoln and Leicester, they are frequently twenty-two inches long. In the southern colonies, at least in those parts where I travelled, there is scarcely any herbage; and whether it is owing to this, or to the excessive heats, I am ignorant, the wool is short and hairy. The northern colonies have indeed greater plenty of herbage, but are for some months covered with snow; and without a degree of attention and care in housing the sheep, and guarding them against accidents, and wild beasts, which would not easily be compensated, it would be very difficult to increase their numbers to any great amount. The Americans seem conscious of this fact, and, notwithstanding a very severe prohibition, contrive to procure from England, every year a considerable number of rams, in order to improve and multiply the breed. What the lands beyond the Alleghenny and upon the banks of the Ohio may be, I do not know; they are said to be very rich: but the climate I believe is not less severe; and I think, upon collating different accounts, that the severity of heat and cold is not much abated by cultivation. The air becomes dryer and more wholesome, in proportion as the woods are cut down, and the ground is cleared and cultivated; but the cold is not less piercing, nor the snow less frequent. I think therefore upon the whole, that America, though it may with particular care and attention, produce small quantities of tolerably good wool, will yet never be able to produce it in such plenty and of such a quality as to serve for the necessary consumption of its inhabitants.

•   •   •

The capital of this province . . . is Portsmouth, which is situated upon the river: it is an inconsiderable place, and chiefly built of wood. Very little can be said of the province of New Hampshire, materially different from what has been said of Massachusetts Bay. — The climate, produce, trade, government, religion, and manners of it are much the same.— There are supposed to be about 40,000 inhabitants, 8,000 militia, and 6 or 700 provincial troops.— There are only two missionaries of the church of England, and one of these has lately applied to be removed to Rhode Island.— The chief articles for exportation are fish, cattle, ships, of which they annually build near 200, and masts for the royal navy. These are made of the white pine, and are, I believe, the finest in the world, many of them being forty yards long, and as many inches in diameter. They never cut them down but in times of deep snow, as it would be impossible in any other season to get them down to the river. When the trees are fallen, they yoke seventy or eighty pair of oxen, and drag them along the snow. It is exceedingly difficult to put them first into motion, which they call raising them; and when they have once effected this, they never stop upon any account whatsoever till they arrive at the waters side. Frequently some of the oxen are taken ill; upon which they immediately cut them out of the gears; and are sometimes obliged, I was told, to destroy five or six pair of them.— The forests, where these masts grow, are reserved to the crown, which appoints a surveyor of them; who is commonly the governor of this province. This is not the only expedient employed by government for the preservation of such trees as may be of use for the royal navy; for there is an act of parliament, I believe, which prohibits, under pain of certain fines and penalties, the cutting down, or destroying of any white pine-tree, of specified dimensions, not growing within the boundaries of any township, without his majesty's licence, in any of the provinces of New England, New York, or New Jersey: a restriction absolutely necessary, whether considered as securing a provision for the navy, or as a check upon that very destructive practice, taken from the Indians, of fire-hunting. . . .

22. An Overall View of the North American Colonies in 1763

The following description of the North American colonies allows the determination of the relative size of the export sector for three colonial regions near the end of the colonial period. The values for the exports of each colony as presented in the document are probably fairly accurate.

To shew the vast importance of these colonies [Virginia and Maryland] to Great Britain, it will be necessary to lay before the reader the last accounts of their exports [1763?], from which we shall also see what proportion their common husbandry bears to their tobacco.

SOURCE: *American Husbandry* (London, 1775), I, 256–7, 124–5, 181–2, 89–91; reprinted in Ernest Ludlow Bogart and Charles Manfred Thompson (eds.), *Readings in the Economic History of the United States* (New York: Longmans, Green and Co., 1927), 80–1, 77–8, 73–4.

Tobacco, 96,000 hogsheads, at £8	£768,000
Indian corn, beans, pease, &c	30,000
Wheat, 40,000 quarters, at 20s	40,000
Deer and other skins	25,000
Iron in bars and pigs	35,000
Sassafras, snake-root, ginseng, &c	7,000
Masts, plank, staves, turpentine, and tar	55,000
Flax-seed, 7000 hogsheads, at 40 s	14,000
Pickled pork, beef, hams, and bacon	15,000
Ships built for sale, 30 at 1000 l.	30,000
Hemp 1000 tons at £21 (besides 4000 tons more and 2000 of flax worked up for their own use)	21,000
Total	1,040,000

Upon this table I must observe once more, how extremely important these colonies are to the mother country. To raise above a million sterling, the greatest part of which are true staples, and the rest necessary for the West Indies, with no fish, whale bone, oil, &c. commodities which some of the colonies have run away with from Britain, by rivalling her in her fishery—possessing no manufactures, even to such a degree that all attempts to bring the people into towns have proved vain. By manufactures, I mean those for sale; for as to private families working wool, hemp, and flax for their own use, it is what many do all over America, and are necessitated to do, for want of money and commodities to buy them. A colony so truly important, I say, deserves every attention from the mother country, and every encouragement to induce settlers to fix in it. . . .

•   •   •

I shall next lay before the reader the exports of this province [New York] as taken on an average of three years since the peace [of 1763].

Flour and biscuit 250,000 barrels, at 20s	£250,000
Wheat 70,000 qrs.	70,000
Beans, pease, oats, Indian corn and other grains	40,000
Salt beef, pork, hams, bacon, and venison,	18,000
Bees wax, 30,000 lb. at 1s	1,500
Tongues, butter, and cheese,	8,000
Flax seed, 7000 hhds. at 40s	14,000
Horses and live stock	17,000
Product of cultivated lands,	418,500
Timber planks, masts, boards, staves, and shingles	25,000
Pot ash, 7000 hhds.	14,000
Ships built for sale, 20, at £700	14,000
Copper ore, and iron in bars and pigs	20,000
	£526,000
	[491,500]*

* Correct total. Ed. note.

Let me upon this table observe, that far the greater part of this export is the produce of the lands including timber; and even the metals may be reckoned in the same class; this shews us that agriculture in New York is of such importance as to support the most considerable part of the province without the assistance of either the fishery or of commerce; not that the city of New York has not traded largely, perhaps equal to Boston, but the effects of that trade have been chiefly the introduction of money by the means of barter, besides the exportation of their own products: whereas New England's exports consist five parts in six of fish, and the other products of the fishery; a strong proof that agriculture is far more profitable in one country, than in the other; for settlers in colonies will never take to the sea, in a country whose agriculture yields well; but in very bad climates, and such as destroy instead of cherishing the products of the earth, any branch of industry pays better than cultivating the earth. . . .

Before I conclude this chapter, I shall insert a table of the exports of the province [Pennsylvania].

Biscuit flour, 350,000 barrels, at 20s	£350,000
Wheat, 100,000 qrs. at 20s	100,000
Beans, pease, oats, Indian corn, and other grain,	12,000
Salt beef, pork, hams, bacon, and venison,	45,000
Bees wax, 20,000 lb. at 1s	1,000
Tongues, butter, and cheese,	10,000
Deer, and sundry other sorts of skins,	50,000
Live stock and horses,	20,000
Flax seed, 15,000 hhds. at 40s	30,000
Timber plank, masts, boards, staves, and shingles	35,000
Ships built for sale, 25, at £700	17,500
Copper ore, and iron in pigs and bars,	35,000
Total	£705,500

Upon this account I must observe, that far the greatest part is the cultivated produce of the land; which is the very contrary to New England, whose lands yield nothing to export. In proportion to this circumstance, is the value of a colony, for it is the nature of colonization, that the people ought, on first principles, to support themselves by agriculture alone. Wheat appears to be the grand export of this province: that, and other articles of food, amount to above half a million, which is a vast sum of money to export regularly, besides feeding every rank of people in the utmost plenty; but of late years this has risen to much more, for wheat, instead of being at 20s. a quarter, is at above 30s. No circumstance in the world can be more strong, in proof of the temperature, moderation and health-iness of the climate, than this of exporting such quantities of wheat, which throughout the globe, thrives nowhere in climates insalubri-ous to mankind: . . .

•   •   •

I shall conclude this account, with a table of the exports of this province [Massachusetts] since the peace [of 1763].

Cod-fish dried, 10,000 tons, at £10	£100,000
Whale and cod-oil, 8500 tons, at £15	127,500
Whale-bone, 28 tons, at £300	8,400
Pickled mackerel and shads, 15,000 barrels at 20s	15,000
Masts, boards, staves, shingles, &c	75,000
Ships about 70 sail, at £700	49,000
Turpentine, tar, and pitch, 1500 barrels, at 8s	600
Horses, and live stock,	37,000
Pot-ash, 14,000 barrels, at 50s	35,000
Pickled beef and pork, 19,000 barrels, at 30s	28,500
Bees-wax, and sundries,	9,000
Total	£485,000

Upon this table I must observe, that the fishery amounts to £250,-900 of it; or rather more than half the total, which shews what a great proportion of the people of this colony are employed in it. The other half is the produce of their lands, for so both ships and pot-ash must be esteemed; Cattle and beef, pork, &c. came to £65,-500 all the rest is timber or what is made of timber; this is a pro-portion that gives us at once a tolerable idea of the colony. We are not from hence to suppose, that the great body of the landed inter-ests in this country has, like Canada, no other resource to purchase foreign commodities with, than this small export. The case is very different, New England enjoys a vast fishery, and a great trade, which brings in no slight portion of wealth. The most considerable commercial town in all America is in this province; and another circumstance is the increase of population. These causes operate so as to keep up a considerable circulation within the colony. Boston and the shipping are a market which enriches the country interest far more than the above mentioned export, which, for so numerous a people, is very inconsiderable. By means of this internal circula-tion, the farmers and country gentlemen are enabled very amply to purchase whatever they want from abroad.

IV

Growth of the Factors of Production

The preceding sections dealt with the extensive growth in output occurring during the colonial period. The following sections deal with two ways in which the increase in output could come about: first, through substantial increases in the quantity of the factors of production, and second, through increases in the productivity of the factors of production. That is, output could be increased by extensive growth—bringing more land, labor, and capital into the production process—or by intensive growth—making each acre of land, each man, and each unit of capital more efficient. During the colonial period most of the increase in output was due probably to increases in the quantities of the factors of production, or to extensive rather than intensive growth. The following documents have been selected to illuminate such extensive growth of the American colonies.

23. The Growth in Population of
the American Colonies

The following population statistics are decade estimates by colony. They are, by and large, built up from scattered fragments and not from a decade census, and are therefore less reliable than later population statistics. Nevertheless, they are probably as accurate an indication of the growth in population, and of the supply of labor, as we are likely to possess. The increases reflected in these tables are consistent with the astonishment expressed by contemporary observers over the rate of expansion of the colonial population. When compared with increases in trade, this rapid growth in population forms the basis for the assertion that the acceleration in conial output came about mainly from increases in the quantity of the factors of production.

SOURCE: U. S. Bureau of the Census, *Historical Statistics of the United States, Colonial Times to 1957* (Washington, D.C.: U. S. Government Printing Office, 1960), 756.

Estimated Population of American Colonies: 1630 to 1780

Colony	1630	1640	1650	1660	1670	1680	1690	1700	1710	1720	1730	1740	1750	1760	1770	1780
White and Negro Total	4,646	26,634	50,368	75,058	111,935	151,507	210,372	250,888	331,711	466,185	629,445	905,563	1,170,760	1,593,625	2,148,076	2,780,369
Maine (counties)[1]															31,257	49,133
New Hampshire	400	900	1,000	1,555	1,805	2,047	4,164	4,958	5,681	9,375	10,755	23,256	27,505	39,093	62,396	87,802
Vermont															10,000	47,620
Plymouth[2]	390	1,020	1,566	1,980	5,333	6,400	7,424									
Massachusetts[1] [2]	506	8,932	14,037	20,082	30,000	39,752	49,504	55,941	62,390	91,008	114,116	151,613	188,000	222,600	235,308	268,627
Rhode Island		300	785	1,539	2,155	3,017	4,224	5,894	7,573	11,680	16,950	25,255	33,226	45,471	58,196	52,946
Connecticut		1,472	4,139	7,980	12,603	17,246	21,645	25,970	39,450	58,830	75,530	89,580	111,280	142,470	183,881	206,701
New York	350	1,930	4,116	4,936	5,754	9,830	13,909	19,107	21,625	36,919	48,594	63,665	76,696	117,138	162,920	210,541
New Jersey					1,000	3,400	8,000	14,010	19,872	29,818	37,510	51,373	71,393	93,813	117,431	139,627
Pennsylvania						680	11,450	17,950	24,450	30,962	51,707	85,637	119,666	183,703	240,057	327,305
Delaware				540	700	1,005	1,482	2,470	3,645	5,385	9,170	19,870	28,704	33,250	35,496	45,385
Maryland		583	4,504	8,426	13,226	17,904	24,024	29,604	42,741	66,133	91,113	116,093	141,073	162,267	202,599	245,474
Virginia	2,500	10,442	18,731	27,020	35,309	43,596	53,046	58,560	78,281	87,757	114,000	180,440	231,033	339,726	447,016	538,004
North Carolina				1,000	3,850	5,430	7,600	10,720	15,120	21,270	30,000	51,760	72,984	110,442	197,200	270,133
South Carolina					200	1,200	3,900	5,704	10,883	17,048	30,000	45,000	64,000	94,074	124,244	180,000
Georgia												2,021	5,200	9,578	23,375	56,071
Kentucky															15,700	45,000
Tennessee															1,000	10,000

112

Negro

Total	575,420	459,822	325,806	236,420	150,024	91,021	68,839	44,866	27,817	16,729	6,971	4,535	2,920	1,600	597	60
Maine (counties)[1]	458	475			500											
New Hampshire	541	654	600	550	500	200	170	150	130	100	75	65	50	40	30	
Vermont	50	25														
Massachusetts[1]	4,822	4,754	4,866	4,075	3,035	2,780	2,150	1,310	800	400	170	160	422	295	150	
Rhode Island	[3]2,671	3,761	3,468	3,347	2,408	1,648	543	375	300	250	175	115	65	25	15	
Connecticut	[3]5,885	5,698	3,783	3,010	2,598	1,490	1,093	750	450	200	50	35	25	20		
New York	21,054	19,112	16,340	11,014	8,996	6,956	5,740	2,811	2,256	1,670	1,200	690	600	500	232	10
New Jersey	10,460	8,220	6,567	5,354	4,366	3,008	2,385	1,332	840	450	200	60				
Pennsylvania	7,855	5,761	4,409	2,872	2,055	1,241	2,000	1,575	430	270	25					
Delaware	2,996	1,836	1,733	1,496	1,035	478	700	500	135	82	55	40	30	15		
Maryland	80,515	63,818	49,004	43,450	24,031	17,220	12,499	7,945	3,227	2,162	1,611	1,190	758	300	20	
Virginia	220,582	187,605	140,570	101,452	60,000	30,000	26,559	23,118	16,390	9,345	3,000	2,000	950	405	150	50
North Carolina	91,000	69,600	33,554	19,800	11,000	6,000	3,000	900	415	300	210	150	20			
South Carolina	97,000	75,178	57,334	39,000	30,000	20,000	12,000	4,100	2,444	1,500	200	30				
Georgia	20,831	10,625	3,578	1,000												
Kentucky	7,200	2,500														
Tennessee	1,500	200														

[1] For 1660–1760, Maine Counties included with Massachusetts.
[2] Plymouth became a part of the Province of Massachusetts in 1691.

24. Causes for the Increase in Colonial Population

In the following passage dealing with colonial population, Adam Smith provides an economic explanation for the continued growth of colonial population. This classical economist argues that in America the availability of good land in almost limitless amounts kept wages from falling to the subsistence level, thereby allowing population to continue to increase throughout the period.

The colony of a civilized nation which takes possession either of a waste country, or of one so thinly inhabited, that the natives easily give place to the new settlers, advances more rapidly to wealth and greatness than any other human society.

The colonists carry out with them a knowledge of agriculture and of other useful arts, superior to what can grow up of its own accord in the course of many centuries among savage and barbarous nations. They carry out with them too the habit of subordination, some notion of the regular government which takes place in their own country, of the system of laws which supports it, and of a regular administration of justice; and they naturally establish something of the same kind in the new settlement. But among savage and barbarous nations, the natural progress of law and government is still slower than the natural progress of arts, after law and government have been so far established, as is necessary for their protection. Every colonist gets more land than he can possibly cultivate. He has no rent, and scarce any taxes to pay. No landlord shares with him in its produce, and the share of the sovereign is commonly but a trifle. He has every motive to render as great as possible a produce, which is thus to be almost entirely his own. But his land is commonly so extensive, that with all his own industry, and with all the industry of other people whom he can get to employ, he can seldom make it produce the tenth part of what it is capable of producing. He is eager, therefore, to collect labourers from all quarters, and to reward them with the most liberal wages. But those liberal wages, joined to the plenty and cheapness of land, soon make those labourers leave him, in order to become landlords themselves, and to reward, with equal liberality, other labourers, who soon leave

SOURCE: Adam Smith, "Causes of the Prosperity of New Colonies," *An Inquiry Into the Nature and Causes of the Wealth of Nations* (New York: Random House Modern Library, 1937), Bk. III, vii, 531–3.

them for the same reason that they left their first master. The liberal reward of labour encourages marriage. The children, during the tender years of infancy, are well fed and properly taken care of, and when they are grown up, the value of their labour greatly overpays their maintenance. When arrived at maturity, the high price of labour, and the low price of land, enable them to establish themselves in the same manner as their fathers did before them.

In other countries, rent and profit eat up wages, and the two superior orders of people oppress the inferior one. But in new colonies, the interest of the two superior orders obliges them to treat the inferior one with more generosity and humanity; at least, where that inferior one is not in a state of slavery. Waste lands of the greatest natural fertility, are to be had for a trifle. The increase of revenue which the proprietor, who is always the undertaker, expects from their improvement constitutes his profit; which in these circumstances is commonly very great. But this great profit cannot be made without employing the labour of other people in clearing and cultivating the land; and the disproportion between the great extent of the land and the small number of the people, which commonly takes place in new colonies, makes it difficult for him to get this labour. He does not, therefore, dispute about wages, but is willing to employ labour at any price. The high wages of labour encourage population. The cheapness and plenty of good land encourage improvement, and enable the proprietor to pay those high wages. In those wages consists almost the whole price of the land; and though they are high, considered as the wages of labour, they are low, considered as the price of what is so very valuable. What encourages the progress of population and improvement, encourages that of real wealth and greatness.

25. The Labor System in the Colonies

The persistent shortage of labor in the American colonies was met in several ways. Although the high wages paid to labor attracted immigrants to the colonies, the high cost of passage to the New World often provided a significant obstacle to individuals. To overcome this problem, a system of indentured servitude developed, under which an immigrant exchanged several years of labor in return for his passage and, often, some land at the end of the term. The high value of labor in the New World was also responsible for the development of a slave trade. The following document describes the various labor systems that existed in the colonies.

The servants which are made use of in the English American colonies are either free persons, or slaves, and the former are again of two different sorts.

First, Those who are quite free serve by the year; they are not only allowed to leave their service at the expiration of their year, but may leave it at any time when they do not agree with their masters. However, in that case they are in danger of losing their wages, which are very considerable. A man-servant who has some abilities, gets between sixteen and twenty pounds in Pennsylvania currency, but those in the country do not get so much. A servant-maid gets eight or ten pounds a year: these servants have their food besides their wages, but must buy their own clothes, and what they get of these, they must thank their master's goodness for.

Second, The second kind of free servants consist of such persons as annually come from Germany, England, and other countries, in order to settle here. These new comers are very numerous every year: there are old and young ones, and of both sexes; some of them have fled from oppression, under which they supposed themselves to have laboured. Others have been driven from their country by persecution on account of religion; but most of them are poor, and have not money enough to pay their passage, which is between six and eight pounds sterling for each person; therefore they agree with the captain that they will suffer themselves to be sold for a few years, on their arrival. In that case the person who buys them, pays the freight for them; but frequently very old people come over, who cannot pay their passage, they therefore sell their children, so that they serve both for themselves and for their parents: there are likewise some who pay part of their passage, and they are sold only for a short time. From these circumstances, it appears, that the price of the poor foreigners who come over to North America is not equal, and that some of them serve longer than others: when their time is expired, they get a new suit of clothes from their master, and some other things: he is likewise obliged to feed and clothe them during the years of their servitude. Many of the Germans who come hither, bring money enough with them to pay their passage,

SOURCE: Peter Kalm, *Travels Into North America* (London, 1770), in Pinkerton, *Voyages and Travels*, XIII, 499–502; reprinted in Ernest Ludlow Bogart and Charles Manfred Thompson (eds.), *Readings in the Economic History of the United States* (New York: Longmans, Green and Co., 1927), 84–7.

but rather suffer themselves to be sold, with a view, that during their servitude they may get some knowledge of the language and quality of the country, and the like, that they may the better be able to consider what they shall do when they have got their liberty. Such servants are taken preferable to all others, because they are not so dear; for to buy a negroe or black slave requires too much money at once; and men or maids who get yearly wages, are likewise too dear; but this kind of servants may be got for half the money, and even for less; for they commonly pay fourteen pounds, Pensylvania currency, for a person who is to serve four years, and so on in proportion. Their wages therefore are not above three pounds Pensylvania currency, per annum. This kind of servants, the English call servings. When a person has bought such a servant for a certain number of years, and has an intention to sell him again, he is at liberty to do so; but he is obliged, at the expiration of the term of servitude, to provide the usual suit of cloaths for the servant, unless he has made that part of the bargain with the purchaser. The English and Irish commonly sell themselves for four years, but the Germans frequently agree with the captain before they set out, to pay him a certain sum of money, for a certain number of persons; as soon as they arrive in America, they go about and try to get a man who will pay the passage for them: in return they give according to the circumstances, one or several of their children, to serve a certain number of years: at last they make their bargain with the highest bidder.

Third, The negroes or blacks make the third kind. They are in a manner slaves; for when a negro is once bought, he is the purchaser's servant as long as he lives, unless he gives him to another, or makes him free. However, it is not in the power of the master to kill his negro for a fault, but he must leave it to the magistrates to proceed according to the laws. Formerly the negroes were brought over from Africa, and bought by almost every one who could afford it. The quakers alone scrupled to have slaves; but they are no longer so nice, and they have as many negroes as other people. However, many people cannot conquer the idea of its being contrary to the laws of Christianity to keep slaves. There are likewise several free negroes in town, who have been lucky enough to get a very zealous quaker for their master, who gave them their liberty, after they had faithfully served him for some time. . . .

At present they seldom bring over any negroes to the English colonies, for those which were formerly brought thither, have multiplied considerably. . . .

The negroes were formerly brought from Africa, as I mentioned before, but now this seldom happens, for they are bought in the West Indies, or American Islands, whither they were originally brought from their own country: for it has been found that on transporting the negroes from Africa, immediately into these northern countries, they have not such a good state of health, as when they gradually change places, and are first carried from Africa to the West Indies, and from thence to North America. . . .

The price of negroes differs according to their age, health, and abilities. A full-grown negro costs from forty pounds and upwards to a hundred, of Pensylvania currency. A negro boy or girl of two or three years old, can hardly be got for less than eight or fourteen pounds in Pensylvania currency.

26. The Availability of Land

The abundance of land in the colonies afforded the colonial legislatures an opportunity to attract immigrants by offering a "headright," usually amounting to fifty acres, to each settler or to each man who brought a settler into the colony. Such an inducement often led one man to import a number of persons to claim the headrights. It has been claimed that the system led to abuses and the concentration of large amounts of land in the hands of a few men. However, land existed in such abundance that it is doubtful that these abuses posed a significant obstacle to colonial economic growth. The willingness of legislatures actually to give away land, reserving only a small annual quitrent, testifies to the ease with which land could be obtained in the American colonies.

Anne, by the Grace of God, of Great Britain, France, and Ireland, Queen, Defender of the Faith, etc.

To all to whom these presents shall come, Greeting.

Know ye that for divers good causes and considerations, but more especially for and in consideration of the importation of one person to dwell within this our colony of Virginia, whose name is William Shoreman,

We have given, granted, and confirmed, and by these presents for us, our heirs and successors, do give, grant, and confirm unto

SOURCE: Fairfax Harrison, *Virginia Land Grants* (Richmond: Old Dominion Press, 1925), 39–40.

John Wade of the county of James City one certain tract or parcel of land in same, containing 47 acres, and bounded as follows, to wit: [Description of boundaries]

With all woods, underwoods, swamps, marshes, low grounds, meadows, feedings, and his due share of all veins, mines, and quarries, as well discovered as not discovered, within the bounds aforesaid, same being part of the said quantity of 47 acres of land and also the rivers, waters, and watercourses therein contained, together with the privileges of hunting, hawking, fishing, fowling, and all other profits, commodities, and hereditaments whatsoever to the same or any part thereof belonging or in any wise appertaining.

To have, hold, possess, and enjoy the said tract or parcel of land, and all other the before-mentioned and granted premises and every part thereof, with their and every of their appurtenances unto the said John Wade and to his heirs and assigns for ever, to the only use and behoof of him, the said John Wade, his heirs and assigns for ever.

To be held of us, our heirs and successors, as of our manor of East Greenwich in the county of Kent, in free and common socage and not *in capite* or by knight's service.

Yielding and paying unto us, our heirs and successors, for every fifty acres of land (and so proportionably for a lesser or greater quantity than fifty acres) the fee rent of one shilling yearly, to be paid upon the Feast of Saint Michael the Archangel.

And also cultivating and improving three acres part of every fifty of the tract above-mentioned within three years after the date of these presents.

Provided always that if three years of the said fee rent shall at any time be in arrear and unpaid, or if the said John Wade, his heirs or assigns do not within the space of three years next coming after the date of these presents, cultivate and improve three acres part of every fifty of the tract above-mentioned, then the estate hereby granted shall cease and be utterly determined; and thereafter it shall and may be lawful to and for us, our heirs and successors, to grant the same lands and premises with the appurtenances unto such other person or persons as we, our heirs and successors, shall think fit.

In witness whereof we have caused these our letters patent to be made.

Witness our trusty and well-beloved Alexander Spotswood, esquire, our lieutenant-governor and commander-in-chief of our said colony and dominion at Williamsburg, under the seal of our said colony the 12th day of December, one thousand seven hundred and ten, in the ninth year of our reign.

27. The Natural Increase of the Population

While immigration was naturally important to the settlement of the New World, the high rate of natural increase among the settlers was at the very least equally important. The following document by Benjamin Franklin reveals his belief that natural increase accounted for almost all of the expansion in colonial population. His assertion may well be correct, although he apparently had no sound statistical basis for this contention.

2. For people increase in proportion to the number of marriages, and that is greater in proportion to the ease and convenience of supporting a family. When families can be easily supported, more persons marry, and earlier in life.

· · ·

6. Land being thus plenty in America, and so cheap as that a laboring man, that understands husbandry, can in a short time save money enough to purchase a piece of new land sufficient for a plantation, whereon he may subsist a family, such are not afraid to marry; for, if they even look far enough forward to consider how their children, when grown up, are to be provided for, they see that more land is to be had at rates equally easy, all circumstances considered.

7. Hence marriages in America are more general, and more generally early than in Europe. And if it is reckoned there, that there is but one marriage per annum among one hundred persons, perhaps we may here reckon two; and if in Europe they have but four births to a marriage (many of their marriages being late), we may here reckon eight, of which, if one half grow up, and our marriages are made, reckoning one with another, at twenty years of age, our people must at least be doubled every twenty years.

8. But notwithstanding this increase, so vast is the territory of

SOURCE: Benjamin Franklin, "Observations Concerning the Increase of Mankind and the Peopling of Countries," in Jared Sparks (ed.), *The Works of Benjamin Franklin* (Boston: Hilliard, Gray and Company, 1840), II, 312–4, 318–9.

North America, that it will require many ages to settle it fully; and, till it is fully settled, labor will never be cheap here, where no man continues long a laborer for others, but gets a plantation of his own, no man continues long a journeyman to a trade, but goes among those new settlers, and sets up for himself, &c. Hence labor is no cheaper now in Pennsylvania, than it was thirty years ago, though so many thousand laboring people have been imported.

. . .

19. The great increase of offspring in particular families is not always owing to greater fecundity of nature, but sometimes to examples of industry in the heads, and industrious education; by which the children are enabled to provide better for themselves, and their marrying early is encouraged from the prospect of good subsistence.

. . .

22. There is, in short, no bound to the prolific nature of plants or animals, but what is made by their crowding and interfering with each other's means of subsistence. . . . Thus, there are supposed to be now upwards of one million English souls in North America, (though it is thought scarce eighty thousand has been brought over sea,) and yet perhaps there is not one the fewer in Britain, but rather many more, on account of the employment the colonies afford to manufacturers at home. This million doubling, suppose but once in twenty-five years, will, in another century, be more than the people of England, and the greatest number of Englishmen will be on this side the water.

28. The Accumulation of Capital

Although no estimates exist on the extent or rate of capital accumulation in the colonies, historical evidence suggests that capital accumulation kept pace with the growth of the economy. Benjamin Franklin suggested in the preceding document that the combination of inexpensive land and high wages allowed a worker to accumulate quickly sufficient funds to establish a farm. Besides such indigenous sources, the mother country also supplied capital to the colonies. The following document, if read closely, outlines the operations of a London tobacco factor as he went about his business of advancing working capital to the colonial planter, handling his produce, and shipping goods to the colonies. The factor often dealt directly with the planter through a resident agent (in this case the son of the firm's senior partner). This was one of several *possible arrangements—in New England and the Middle Colonies, for example, a group of local merchants developed which made arrangements with English merchants, often entailing the advancement of goods on credit. Through these various institutional channels the mother country provided substantial amounts of capital to the American colonies.*

[To John Hatley Norton, Virginia]

London the 21st April 1770

Dr. Hatley.

I wrote you a few lines 12 inst. pr. the *Harrietta* Capt. Clarke advising the arrival of the *Thomas,* and *Molly* Barron, by the former I have 43 hhds. Tobo. besides Ginseng and Bar Iron there is none of the tobo yet landed, therefore can't say what condition the Cargo is in, the Ginseng must be stored till the Fall, at prest. it is not above 1/6; I am now to acknoledge the receipt of your sevl. letters of 2d and 6th Sepr. pr. the *Thomas* 24th Decr. pr. Necks and 27th Feby. pr. Barron: Capt. Esten, Junr. has been paid for inspection of Jones and Clarks 30hhd Tobo. pr. *Farmer* and tis charg'd in their Sales. In your long letter of 27th Feby. you say the share I have allow'd you in the Capital, as well as proportion of the annual profits in Trade you are pleas'd with, that it might serve every earthly purpose so long as you should remain single, but—and there you stop by which I should suppose you are not well satisfied. I must confess I am a little surpris'd at it; I was willing to allow you as large a share of the Profits as I could consistent with Justice to my other children. Tis double what my Uncle Hatley allow'd me on my first setting out, on a much smaller business, besides I paid Interest for my part of the Stock in Trade and during the time of my partnership with Mr. Flowerdewe my proportion of the yearly profits divided seldom exceeded £ 400 Ann. on an average you seem amaz'd that the dividend is not more than £ 1600, and desire to know if that is the whole amot. to which I answer you it is not, the balla. of the accot, of P. and L. remaining in Sepr. after allowing for interest of money which was then due, Chas. of Merchandize and other incident charges on trade was about £ 400 wch. was not divided, but left as usual and call'd by Traders a Nest Egg, in case of any losses by Debts and which might happen. This method is al-

SOURCE: Frances Norton Mason (ed.), *John Norton & Sons Merchants of London and Virginia, Being the Papers from their Counting House for the Years 1750 to 1795* (Richmond: Dietz Press, 1937), 129–33.

ways pursued by prudent persons and by those I have been conected with, you will be entitled to your share thereof at a future day if no disaster happens to deprive us of it. The Importn. of Tobo. that year was 741 hhds. The reason the profits do not rise in proportion is obvious as I have said formerly we have too much money in advance for our trade, for besides our Capital of £ 6000, we have upwards of £ 12,000 more borrow'd here from Mr. Turner Williamson, Fludger and myself, for which a yearly interest is going out at 5 pct. and besides this many times we are oblig'd to borrow money of the Banker to pay down dutys at the custom house on an emergency, as also for paymt. of Tradesmens Bills and Bills drawn on us exclusive of the money left in our hands by sevl. correspts. who have the advantage in paymt. either of dutys on their Tobo. or Interest allow'd them. I am sorry you should set out and assume a way of living somewhat inadequate to your Circumstances, a conduct you must condemn in another, you formerly told me how happy you cou'd live in Virga. for about £ 500 Sterlg. yearly when married, now tis only a bare maintenance for you as a single man, tho' in a cheap country. I am sorry to find you so inconsistent with yourself and doubt not but a little more experience in life will cause you to view things in a proper light. . . .

I have been so hurried lately in settling the books, delivg. Tobo. giving out the orders to go by Goosley, Accot. Sales &c that tis impossible for me to send you a List of Debts, as also the Accots. prov'd by this opportuy. Indeed some can't be prov'd till their Tobo. is Credited which will I hope be soon, having not above 25 hhds. unsold and imagine I shall send them pr. Necks next month. Inclos'd you have a list of what Sales now go, which hope will please or the greater part, think I can safely say I have sold on as good terms as any of my neighbors. . . .

. . . The Cargo Invoice of P. W. C. which only just came to hand by Barron and after I had ship'd the goods pr. Goosley shall be sent by first good conveyce, which will probably be Necks or Barron, you have a List of those ship'd in Goosley. Geo, Thomas has taken his passage with him, his debt with me is £ 12.3.11. he is not able to pay it here being oblig'd I believe to borrow money to pay his passage. I have denied him any Credit. You talk of my sending in accots. proved of every Debtor; such a step unless practis'd by Merchts. in general if it took wind might entirely put an end to our trade. I have charg'd an interest up to "Xmas" to all our correspts.

where it was justice so to do. The Ozenbgs. now ship'd Capt. Wm. Anderson and John Lewis I observe far exceeds the price order'd occasioned by that article starting greatly, indeed scarce is any to be had at any price, upon talking with Jones and Clarke they agree that if Capt. Anderson does not approve of the highest numbers sent him, he may sell them for their Accot. and Mr. Lewis if he should not approve of what sent him, 'tis to be deliver'd to you and to be sold for their accot. which their Letters to you and to those Gent. will explain properly. Mr. Russell and many others have substituted Scotch instead of German Linnen for want of the latter tho' I did not care to do so. I shall write Mr. John Tucker concerning the settlemt. of his Mother's accot. I find there will be many thousand hhds. Tobo. made more than you expected the last year. I had like to have suffer'd greatly by strictly adhering to your first accot, of the disaster and refusing prices I can't now obtain. This last importation which is 943 hhds. to this time will be more profitable to us than the year before having sold upwards of 500 hhds. for Town Trade. You mistake my meaning in my letter to you of 21st Nov. I did not blame you or think you was accessary to Dr. J. Walkers sending his son home. I only said for the future, if any application was made to you, the best way is to be plain and not give them any reason to expect me to comply with their requests of that sort as I am scituated, however the Boy is a smart little fellow and shall not suffer. Mr. R. S. Taylor is answerable for his annual Expense, and your Mother is very fond of him. Your Cozen Baylor is at Cambridge. I hope it may answer tho' I think he has not capacity to make a scholar and had better contented himself with learning the grammar in his Mother tongue properly, and reading history instead of attempting Greek Authors. This is intended you pr. Capt. Goosley in the *Golden Fleece*, believe she will stow upwards of 300 hhds may be 350. Have charter'd her to lay 90 runing days at her moorings (if required) to pay £ 7.5. p ton and 2/3d Port charges, we to pay the Masters expences in the country. The Ship stands well on the Insurers books and has brot. home dry cargoes. All Putney Suffolk and Bedford Row friends are well, and join those of this Place in best wishes to you and all friends in Virga. I wish you a happy meeting with G. G. and remain,

Dr. Hatley

Yours Affectionately

John Norton

P.S. Have insured Young Morlands Goods agreeable to order, tho' the Ship was Sail'd before your letter got to hand. The Affair of Saml. Meredith's was transacted in T.F.'s time therefore don't know where to look for the Original Bill. We propose when at leisure to hunt for it, tho' have little hope of success. I omitted telling you I have accepted the followg. drats. on accot. of Garland Anderson.

To J.H.N. dated	6th July 1769	£ 200	
3 to Do	30th Oct.	300	
1 to Do	do	50	700 £
1 to Starke Cross & Co. 6 Sepr.		160	

besides these heavy drats. another has lately appear'd drawn by him to Jno. Ellis & Co. dated 19th Dec. 1769 for £ 80, which has been ptested for want of advice—

V

Increases in Colonial Per Capita Income

Although there is no doubt that the extensive growth of the American colonies was more impressive than the growth in per capita income, the latter should not be ignored. Since the American colonial period for the most part preceded the English Industrial Revolution, the performance of the colonial economy should not be judged by comparison with that of the nineteenth-century American economy. The rate of increase in colonial per capita income, at a guess, probably did not exceed one half of 1 per cent annually; that is, it doubled approximately every century. While this rate of increase is not spectacular when compared to the almost 2 per cent rate of increase of the following century, it was probably excellent for its time.

Little concrete evidence is available on the actual rate of increase in colonial per capita income. However, the conditions then prevalent naturally favored some increase. One such contributing cause was the significant extensive growth of the economy in general, which resulted, for example, in the growth of urban areas. This led in turn to some specialization of economic functions, with resultant gains in productivity through the division of labor. Also the interest in education on the part of the American colonists (to a degree extraordinary for the eighteenth century) created a highly educated population, inquisitive by nature. This combination produced limited technological improvements, which followed from observation of trial-and-error procedures. The dissemination of improved techniques throughout the colonies was then made possible via the printed word. Although such technological improvements were modest compared to those occurring during the Industrial Revolution, they did exist, as attested by documents from the period.

29. A Description of Philadelphia in 1685

The rise of Philadelphia provides a good example of the growth of cities in the New World. The following description is of a small town vigorously extending itself only a few years after its founding.

II. Philadelphia, and our intended Metropolis, as I formerly Writ, is two Miles long, and a Mile broad, and at each end it lies that mile upon a Navigable River. The scituation high and dry, yet replenished with running streams. Besides the High Street, that runs in the middle from River to River, and is an hundred foot broad, it has Eight streets more that run the same course, the least of which is fifty foot in bredth. And besides Broad Street, which crosseth the Town in the middle, and is also an hundred foot wide, there are twenty streets more, that run the same course, and are also fifty foot broad. The names of those Streets are mostly taken from the things that Spontaneously grow in the Country, As Vine Street, Mulberry Street, Chesnut Street, Wallnut Street, Strawberry Street, Cranberry Street, Plumb Street, Hickery Street, Pine Street, Oake Street, Beach Street, Ash Street, Popler Street, Sassafrax Street, and the like.

III. I mentioned in my last Account that from my Arrival, in Eighty-two, to the Date thereof, being ten Moneths, we had got up Fourscore Houses at our Town, and that some Villages were settled about it. From that time to my coming away, which was a Year within a few Weeks, the Town advanced to Three hundred and fifty-seven Houses; divers of them large, well built, with good Cellars, three stories, and some with Balconies.

IV. There is also a fair Key of about three hundred foot square, Built by Samuel Carpenter, to which a ship of five hundred Tuns may lay her broadside, and others intend to follow his example. We have also a Ropewalk made by B. Wilcox, and cordage for shipping already spun at it.

V. There inhabits most sorts of useful Tradesmen, As Carpenters, Joyners, Bricklayers, Masons, Plasterers, Plumers, Smiths, Glasiers, Taylers, Shoemakers, Butchers, Bakers, Brewers, Glovers, Tanners, Felmongers, Wheelrights, Millrights, Shiprights, Boatrights, Ropemakers, Saylmakers, Blockmakers, Turners, &c.

VI. There are Two Markets every Week, and Two Fairs every year. In other places Markets also, as at Chester and New-Castle.

VII. Seven Ordinaries for the Intertainment of Strangers and

SOURCE: William Penn, A Further Account of the Province of Pennsylvania and its Improvements, for the Satisfaction of those that are Adventurers, and enclined to be so (1685); reprinted in Pennsylvania Magazine of History and Biography (Philadelphia, 1885), IX, 65–7.

Workmen, that are not Housekeepers, and a good Meal to be had for sixpence, sterl.

VIII. The hours for Work and Meals to *Labourers* are fixt, and known by Ring of *Bell.*

IX. After nine at Night the *Officers* go the Rounds, and no Person, without very good cause, suffered to be at any Publick House that is not a Lodger.

X. Tho this *Town* seemed at first contrived for the Purchasers of the *first hundred shares,* each share consisting of 5000 Acres, yet few going, and that their absence might not Check the Improvement of the Place, and *Strangers* that flockt to us be thereby Excluded, I added that half of the Town, which lies on the *Skulkill,* that we might have Room for present and after Commers, that were not of that number, and it hath already had great success to the Improvement of the Place.

XI. Some *Vessels* have been here Built, and many *Boats;* and by that means a ready Conveniency for Passage of People and Goods.

XII. Divers *Brickerys* going on, many Cellars already Ston'd or Brick'd and some Brick Houses going up.

XIII. The *Town* is well furnish'd with convenient *Mills;* and what with their *Garden Plats* (the least half an Acre), the *Fish* of the River, and their labour, to the *Countryman,* who begins to pay with the provisions of his own growth, they live Comfortably.

XIV. The Improvement of the place is best measur'd by the *advance* of Value upon every man's Lot. I will venture to say that the worst Lot in the Town, without any Improvement upon it, is worth *four times* more than it was when it was lay'd out, and the best *forty.* And though it seems unequal that the Absent should be thus benefited by the Improvements of those that are upon the place, especially when they have serv'd no Office, run no hazard, nor as yet defray'd any Publick charge, yet this advantage does certainly redound to them, and whoever they are they are great Debtors to the Country; of which I shall now speak more at large.

30. Philadelphia in 1760

A comparison of this description of Philadelphia with that in the previous document illustrates the growth of the city that occurred in roughly seventy-five years. Population increased from less than 2,000 to around 20,000, public buildings were erected, and the value of land increased markedly—in short, Philadelphia was transformed from a town into a small city.

The next day I set out for Philadelphia, distant about thirty-six miles, and arrived there in the evening. The country all the way bore a different aspect from any thing I had hitherto seen in America. It was much better cultivated, and beautifully laid out into fields of clover, grain, and flax. I passed by a very pretty village called Wilmington; and rode through two others, viz. Chester and Derby. The Delaware river is in sight great part of the way, and is three miles broad. Upon the whole nothing could be more pleasing than the ride which I had this day. I ferried over the Schuilkill, about three miles below Philadelphia; from whence to the city the whole country is covered with villas, gardens, and luxuriant orchards.

Philadelphia, if we consider that not eighty years ago the place where it now stands was a wild and uncultivated desert, inhabited by nothing but ravenous beasts, and a savage people, must certainly be the object of every one's wonder and admiration. It is situated upon a tongue of land, a few miles above the confluence of the Delaware and Schuilkill; and contains about 3000 houses, and 18 or 20,000 inhabitants. It is built north and south upon the banks of the Delaware; and is nearly two miles in length, and three quarters of one in breadth. The streets are laid out with great regularity in parallel lines, intersected by others at right angles, and are handsomely built: on each side there is a pavement of broad stones for foot passengers; and in most of them a causeway in the middle for carriages. Upon dark nights it is well lighted, and watched by a patrole: there are many fair houses, and public edifices in it. The stadthouse is a large, handsome, though heavy building; in this are held the councils, the assemblies, and supreme courts; there are apartments in it also for the accommodation of Indian chiefs or sachems; likewise two libraries; one belonging to the province; the other to a society, which was incorporated about ten years ago, and consists of sixty members. . . .

At a small distance from the stadt-house, there is another fine library, consisting of a very valuable and chosen collection of books,

SOURCE: Rev. Andrew Burnaby, "Philadelphia," *Travels through the Middle Settlements in North-America in the Years 1759 and 1760* (New York: Cornell University Press, 1960), 53–6.

left by a Mr. Logan; they are chiefly in the learned languages. Near this there is also a noble hospital for lunatics, and other sick persons. Besides these buildings, there are spacious barracks for 17 or 1800 men; a good assembly-room belonging to the society of free-masons; and eight or ten places of religious worship; . . . There is also an academy or college, originally built for a tabernacle for Mr. Whitefield. . . . These, with a few alms houses, and a school-house belonging to the quakers, are the chief public buildings in Philadelphia. The city is in a very flourishing state, and inhabited by merchants, artists, tradesmen, and persons of all occupations. There is a public market held twice a week, upon Wednesday and Saturday, almost equal to that of Leadenhall; and a tolerable one every day besides. The streets are crowded with people, and the river with vessels. Houses are so dear, that they will let for £100 currency per annum; and lots, not above thirty feet in breadth, and a hundred in length, in advantageous situations, will sell for £1000 sterling. There are several docks upon the river, and about twenty-five vessels are built there annually. I counted upon the stocks at one time no less than seventeen, many of them three-masted vessels.

Can the mind have a greater pleasure than in contemplating the rise and progress of cities and kingdoms? Than in perceiving a rich and opulent state arising out of a small settlement or colony? This pleasure every one must feel who considers Pensylvania.

31. The Frontier Economy

The specialization existing in urban areas along the eastern coast and near navigable streams and rivers was in marked contrast with the primitive economic organization away from these areas. The following document describes a frontier economy which functioned largely outside the market economy. Here, every man was a "jack-of-all-trades" and probably master of none.

Workmen are dear and scarce. I have about a dozen acres of clear ground, and the rest woods, in all, three hundred acres. Had I servants and money, I might live very comfortably upon it, raise

SOURCE: Reverend John Urmstone, letter written in North Carolina, July 7, 1711 to the Secretary of the Society for Propagating the Gospel, in F. L. Hawks, *History of North Carolina* (Fayetteville, 1857–1858); reprinted in Ulrich B. Phillips (ed.), *A Documentary History of American Industrial Society* (Cleveland: Arthur H. Clark Company, 1910), II, 271–2.

good corn of all sorts, and cattle without any great labor or charges, could it once be stocked; but for want thereof shall not make any advantage of my land. I have bought a horse some time ago; since that, three cows and calves, five sheep, and some fowls of all sorts, but most of them unpaid for, together with fourteen bushels of wheat, for all which I must give English goods. At this rate I might have had any thing that either this government or any of the neighboring colonies afford; but had I stock, I need not fear wanting either butter, cheese, beef, or mutton, of my own raising, or good grain of all sorts. I am forced to work hard with axe, hoe, and spade. I have not a stick to burn for any use, but what I cut down with my own hands. I am forced to dig a garden, raise beans, peas, etc., with the assistance of a sorry wench my wife brought with her from England.

Men are generally of all trades, and women the like within their spheres, except some who are the posterity of old planters, and have great numbers of slaves, who understand most handicraft. Men are generally carpenters, joiners, wheelwrights, coopers, butchers, tanners, shoemakers, tallow-chandlers, watermen, and what not; women, soap-makers, starch-makers, dyers, etc. He or she that cannot do all these things, or hath not slaves that can, over and above all the common occupations of both sexes, will have but a bad time of it; for help is not to be had at any rate, every one having business enough of his own. This makes tradesmen turn planters, and these become tradesmen. No society one with another, with all study to live by their own hands, of their own produce; and what they can spare, goes for foreign goods. Nay, many live on a slender diet to buy rum, sugar, and molasses, with other such like necessaries, which are sold at such a rate that the planter here is but a slave to raise a provision for other colonies, and dare not allow himself to partake of his own creatures, except it be the corn of the country in hominy bread.

32. The Value of Education

It has been estimated that more than 50 per cent of American colonists could write their own names. This was an extremely high rate of literacy for the time, probably surpassing even that which existed in Great Britain; if reliable, the figure serves to illustrate the high regard that the colonists in general must have had for education. The investment of the populace with the ability to read and write was consistent with the relatively high standard of living enjoyed in colonial America and perhaps even one of its causes. In the following document Benjamin Franklin points out the usefulness of education to society, not the smallest part being its contribution to the growth of the economy.

PROPOSALS

The good Education of Youth has been esteemed by wise Men in all Ages, as the surest Foundation of the Happiness both of private Families and of Commonwealths. Almost all Governments have therefore made it a principal Object of their Attention, to establish and endow with proper Revenues, such Seminaries of Learning, as might supply the succeeding Age with Men qualified to serve the Publick with Honour to themselves, and to their Country.

Many of the first Settlers of these Provinces were Men who had received a good Education in Europe, and to their Wisdom and good Management we owe much of our present Prosperity. But their Hands were full, and they could not do all Things. The present Race are not thought to be generally of equal Ability: For though the American Youth are allow'd not to want Capacity; yet the best Capacities require Cultivation, it being truly with them, as with the best Ground, which unless well tilled and sowed with profitable Seed, produces only ranker Weeds.

That we may obtain the Advantages arising from an Increase of Knowledge, and prevent as much as may be the mischievous Consequences that would attend a general Ignorance among us, the following *Hints* are offered towards forming a Plan for the Education of the Youth of *Pennsylvania*, viz.

It is propos'd,

That some Persons of Leisure and publick Spirit apply for a CHARTER, by which they may be incorporated, with Power to erect an ACADEMY for the Education of Youth, to govern the same, provide Masters, make Rules, receive Donations, purchase Lands, etc., and to add to their Number, from Time to Time such other Persons as they shall judge suitable.

That the Members of the Corporation make it their Pleasure, and in some Degree their Business, to visit the Academy often, en-

SOURCE: Benjamin Franklin, "Proposals relating to the education of youth in Pennsylvania" (1749), in Albert Henry Smyth (ed.), *The Writings of Benjamin Franklin* (New York: Macmillan Company, 1905), II, 388–96.

courage and countenance the Youth, countenance and assist the Masters, and by all Means in their Power advance the Usefulness and Reputation of the Design; that they look on the Students as in some Sort their Children, treat them with Familiarity and Affection, and, when they have behav'd well, and gone through their Studies, and are to enter the World, zealously unite, and make all the Interest that can be made to establish them, whether in Business, Offices, Marriages, or any other Thing for their Advantage, preferably to all other Persons whatsoever even of equal Merit.

And if Men may, and frequently do, catch such a Taste for cultivating Flowers, for Planting, Grafting, Inoculating, and the like, as to despise all other Amusements for their Sake, why may not we expect they should acquire a Relish for that *more useful* Culture of young Minds. *Thompson says,*

> 'T is Joy to see the human Blossoms blow,
> When infant Reason grows apace, and calls
> For the kind Hand of an assiduous Care.
> Delightful Task! to rear the tender Thought,
> To teach the young Idea how to shoot;
> To pour the fresh Instruction o'er the Mind,
> To breathe th' enliv'ning Spirit, and to fix
> The generous Purpose in the glowing Breast.

That a House be provided for the ACADEMY, if not in the Town, not many Miles from it; the Situation high and dry, and if it may be, not far from a River, having a Garden, Orchard, Meadow, and a Field or two.

That the House be furnished with a Library (if in the Country, if in the Town, the Town Libraries may serve) with Maps of all Countries, Globes, some mathematical Instruments, an Apparatus for Experiments in Natural Philosophy, and for Mechanics; Prints, of all Kinds, Prospects, Buildings, Machines, &c.

That the Rector be a Man of good Understanding, good Morals, diligent and patient, learn'd in the Languages and Sciences, and a correct pure Speaker and Writer of the *English* Tongue; to have such Tutors under him as shall be necessary.

That the boarding Scholars diet together, plainly, temperately, and frugally.

That, to keep them in Health, and to strengthen and render active their Bodies, they be frequently exercis'd in Running, Leaping, Wrestling, and Swimming, &c.

That they have peculiar Habits to distinguish them from other Youth, if the Academy be in or near the Town; for this, among other Reasons, that their Behaviour may be the better observed.

As to their STUDIES, it would be well if they could be taught *every Thing* that is useful, and *every Thing* that is ornamental: But Art is long, and their Time is short. It is therefore propos'd that they learn those Things that are likely to be *most useful* and *most ornamental*. Regard being had to the several Professions for which they are intended.

All should be taught to write a *fair Hand*, and swift, as that is useful to All. And with it may be learnt something of *Drawing*, by Imitation of Prints, and some of the first Principles of Perspective.

Arithmetick, Accounts, and some of the first Principles of *Geometry* and *Astronomy.*

The *English* Language might be taught by Grammar; in which some of our best Writers, as *Tillotson, Addison, Pope, Algernoon Sidney, Cato's Letters,* &c., should be Classicks: the *Stiles* principally to be cultivated, being the *clear* and the *concise.* Reading should also be taught, and pronouncing, properly, distinctly, emphatically; not with an even Tone, which *under-does,* nor a theatrical, which *over-does* Nature.

To form their Stile they should be put on Writing Letters to each other, making Abstracts of what they read; or writing the same Things in their own Words; telling or writing Stories lately read, in their own Expressions. All to be revis'd and corrected by the Tutor, who should give his Reasons, and explain the Force and Import of Words, &c.

To form their Pronunciation, they may be put on making Declamations, repeating Speeches, delivering Orations &c.; The Tutor assisting at the Rehearsals, teaching, advising, correcting their Accent, &c.

But if History be made a constant Part of their Reading, such as the Translations of the *Greek* and *Roman* Historians, and the modern Histories of ancient *Greece* and *Rome,* &c. may not almost all Kinds of useful Knowledge be that Way introduc'd to Advantage, and with Pleasure to the Student? As

GEOGRAPHY, by reading with Maps, and being required to point out the Places *where* the greatest Actions were done, to give their old and new Names, with the Bounds, Situation, Extent of the Countries concern'd, &c.

CHRONOLOGY, by the Help of *Helvicus* or some other Writer of the Kind, who will enable them to tell *when* those Events happened; what Princes were Cotemporaries, what States or famous Men flourish'd about that Time, &c. The several principal Epochas to be first well fix'd in their Memories.

ANTIENT CUSTOMS, religious and civil, being frequently mentioned in History, will give Occasion for explaining them; in which the Prints of Medals, Basso-Relievos, and antient Monuments will greatly assist.

MORALITY, by descanting and making continual Observations on the Causes of the Rise or Fall of any Man's Character, Fortune, Power &c. mention'd in History; the Advantages of Temperance, Order, Frugality, Industry, Perseverance &c. &c. Indeed the general natural Tendency of Reading good History must be, to fix in the Minds of Youth deep Impressions of the Beauty and Usefulness of Virtue of all Kinds, Publick Spirit, Fortitude, &c.

History will show the wonderful Effects of ORATORY, in governing, turning and leading great Bodies of Mankind, Armies, Cities, Nations. When the Minds of Youth are struck with Admiration at this, then is the Time to give them the Principles of that Art, which they will study with Taste and Application. Then they may be made acquainted with the best Models among the antients, their Beauties being particularly pointed out to them. Modern Political Oratory being chiefly performed by the Pen and Press, its Advantages over the Antient in some Respects are to be shown; as that its Effects are more extensive, more lasting, &c.

History will also afford frequent Opportunities of showing the Necessity of a *Publick Religion*, from its Usefulness to the Publick; the Advantage of a Religious Character among private Persons; the Mischiefs of Superstition, &c. and the Excellency of the CHRISTIAN RELIGION above all others antient or modern.

History will also give Occasion to expatiate on the Advantage of Civil Orders and Constitutions; how Men and their Properties are protected by joining in Societies and establishing Government; their Industry encouraged and rewarded, Arts invented, and Life made more comfortable: The Advantages of *Liberty*, Mischiefs of *Licentiousness*, Benefits arising from good Laws and a due Execution of Justice, &c. Thus may the first Principles of sound *Politicks* be fix'd in the Minds of Youth.

On *Historical* Occasions, Questions of Right and Wrong, Justice and Injustice, will naturally arise, and may be put to Youth, which they may debate in Conversation and in Writing. When they ardently desire Victory, for the Sake of the Praise attending it, they will begin to feel the Want, and be sensible of the Use of *Logic*, or the Art of Reasoning to *discover* Truth, and of Arguing to *defend* it, and *convince* Adversaries. This would be the Time to acquaint them with the Principles of that Art. Grotius, Puffendorff, and some other Writers of the same Kind, may be used on these Occasions to decide their Disputes. Publick Disputes warm the Imagination, whet the Industry, and strengthen the natural Abilities.

When Youth are told, that the Great Men whose Lives and Actions they read in History, spoke two of the best Languages that ever were, the most expressive, copious, beautiful; and that the finest Writings, the most correct Compositions, the most perfect Productions of human Wit and Wisdom, are in those Languages, which have endured Ages, and will endure while there are Men; that no Translation can do them Justice, or give the Pleasure found in Reading the Originals; that those Languages contain all Science; that one of them is become almost universal, being the Language of Learned Men in all Countries; that to understand them is a distinguishing Ornament, &c. they may be thereby made desirous of learning those Languages, and their Industry sharpen'd in the Acquisition of them. All intended for Divinity, should be taught the *Latin* and *Greek*; for Physick, the *Latin, Greek,* and *French*; for Law, the *Latin* and *French*; Merchants, the *French, German,* and *Spanish:* And though all should not be compell'd to learn *Latin, Greek,* or the modern foreign Languages; yet none that have an ardent Desire to learn them should be refused; their *English,* Arithmetick and other Studies absolutely necessary, being at the same Time not neglected.

If the new *Universal History* were also read, it would give a connected Idea of human Affairs, so far as it goes, which should be follow'd by the best modern Histories, particularly of our Mother Country; then of these Colonies; which should be accompanied with Observations on their Rise, Encrease, Use to *Great Britain,* Encouragements, Discouragements, etc. the Means to make them flourish, secure their Liberties, &c.

With the History of Men, Times, and Nations, should be read at proper Hours or Days, some of the best *Histories of Nature,* which would not only be delightful to Youth, and furnish them with Matter for their Letters, &c. as well as other History; but afterwards of great Use to them, whether they are Merchants, Handicrafts, or Divines; enabling the first the better to understand many Commodities, Drugs, &c.; the second to improve his Trade or Handicraft by new Mixtures, Materials, &c., and the last to adorn his Discourses by beautiful Comparisons, and strengthen them by new Proofs of Divine Providence. The Conversation of all will be improved by it, as Occasions frequently occur of making Natural Observations, which are instructive, agreeable, and entertaining in almost all Companies. *Natural History* will also afford Opportunities of introducing many Observations, relating to the Preservation of Health, which may be afterwards of great Use. *Arbuthnot* on Air and Aliment, *Sanctorius* on Perspiration, *Lemery* on Foods, and some others, may now be read, and a very little Explanation will make them sufficiently intelligible to Youth.

While they are reading Natural History, might not a little *Gardening, Planting, Grafting, Inoculating,* etc., be taught and practised; and now and then Excursions made to the neighbouring Plantations of the best Farmers, their Methods observ'd and reason'd upon for the Information of Youth? The Improvement of Agriculture being useful to all, and Skill in it no Disparagement to any.

The History of *Commerce*, of the Invention of Arts, Rise of Manufactures, Progress of Trade, Change of its Seats, with the Reasons, Causes, &c., may also be made entertaining to Youth, and will be useful to all. And this, with the Accounts in other History of the prodigious Force and Effect of Engines and Machines used in War, will naturally introduce a Desire to be instructed in *Mechanicks,* and to be inform'd of the Principles of that Art by which weak Men perform such Wonders, Labour is sav'd, Manufactures expedited, &c. This will be the Time to show them Prints of antient and modern Machines, to explain them, to let them be copied, and to give Lectures in Mechanical Philosophy.

With the whole should be constantly inculcated and cultivated, that *Benignity of Mind,* which shows itself in *searching for* and *seizing* every Opportunity *to serve* and *to oblige;* and is the Foundation of what is called GOOD BREEDING; highly useful to the Possessor, and most agreeable to all.

The Idea of what is *true Merit* should also be often presented to Youth, explain'd and impress'd on their Minds, as consisting in an *Inclination* join'd with an *Ability* to serve Mankind, one's Country,

Friends and Family; which *Ability* is (with the Blessing of God) to be acquir'd or greatly encreas'd by *true Learning*; and should indeed be the great *Aim* and *End* of all Learning.

33. The Establishment of a Rudimentary Technical Journal

In the 1740's Jared Eliot began to write annually a series of essays recounting the progress of experiments that he and others had undertaken to improve the productivity of various industries in the colonies. The printed word thus was used as the means of disseminating useful knowledge, and the ability to read became a necessary tool for profiting from it. Whether this was actually an important force for increasing productivity throughout the economy remains unknown. The fact is that the combination of a high level of literacy and at least one technical journal did facilitate the acquiring of new knowledge.

It is not an Hundred and Thirty Years since the first Settlement of *New-England*, and much less than that since the greater Part hath been Planted.

When we consider the small Number of the first Settlers, and coming from an old Cultivated Country, to thick Woods, rough unimproved Lands; where all their former Experience and Knowledge was now of very little service to them: They were destitute of Beasts of Burthen or Carriage; Unskill'd in every Part of Service to be done: It may be said, That in a Sort, *they began the World a New.*

Their unacquaintedness with the Country, led them to make choice of the worst Land for their Improvement, and the most expensive and chargeable Methods of Cultivation: They tho't themselves obliged to stubb all Staddle, and cut down or lop all great Trees; in which they expended much Cost and Time, to the prejudice of the Crop and impoverishing the Land.

When we consider these things, the Progress that hath been made in so short a Time is very wonderful.

There hath been great Improvements in *Husbandry* far and wide;

SOURCE: Jared Eliot, *Essays Upon Field Husbandry In New England And Other Papers, 1748–1762* (New York: Columbia University Press, 1934), 7–9, 23.

besides various *Trades* and *Manufactures*, which are Yearly increasing.

Particularly,

1. There are considerable Advances made in the *Linnen* and *Woollen Trades*. There are many alive at this Day, who remember since the *Linnen* was Course, and what we call *Tow Cloth*; the other Cloth for *outer Garments, Linsy Woolsy*; and for some time was worn without Fulling or any kind of Dressing; After they began to Full Cloth, for a Time they used neither Tentering or Pressing; they only stretched and wound the Cloth hard upon a smooth log of Wood.

2. We have Improved in *the Iron-mongers Trade*. In the early Times of the Country, the most of the Iron made and in use, was *Taunton* Iron, made of Bog Oar, and so course and brittle as to break in the working, and when it was wrought, to the loss and vexation of the Smith and the Farmer.

This Metal, such as it was, was all the Iron then in use among us, except a little *Spanish* and *Sweeds* Iron for some special Uses; so that it is wonderful to think how that Generation did to subsist.

After a while Bog Oar of a better sort and of a more kindly nature and temper was found, after that Mountain Oar was discovered, which being melted and refined makes excellent Iron.

We have further Improved upon it by converting it into *Steel*; which was entered upon without previous Skill, and wrought and beat out by frequent Experiments and by continued Practice.

3. We have also Increased in our *Stocks of Cattle*, and Improved our *Breed of Horses*. For some time after the Country was settled, they had no Cattle at all; when some were brought over, what with the bad Hay they provided, it being cut upon Bog Meadow, the multitude of Wolves and other Beasts of Prey, for sundry Years they were kept so low and had so few Cattle, that the common Price for a grown Bullock was *Twenty Pounds* Sterling, which is Equal to *Two-Hundred Pounds* Old Tenor.

I remember when I was a Boy, I heard a very ancient Woman of good Credit say, That she had seen Twenty broad Pieces paid down for a Two Year old Heifer, which is now Equal to *Two Hundred and Fifty Pounds* Old Tenor.

Although the Progress we have made be very Considerable, our Country yet needs and is capable of greater Improvement in the management of our Lands; of which I design to consider in several Sorts.

· · ·

It might serve to increase useful Knowledge, if something of this Nature were Published every Year, giving a faithful Account of the Success of all the Experiments and Trials that may be made on various Sorts of Land, and of divers Sorts of Grains, Roots, Grass and Fruits, not only such as we have in Use, as also what we have not as yet introduced among us.

There are few Men of Business, Ingenuity and Observation, but what have found out Things valuable and useful, but for Want of some proper Method to communicate them, they die with the Discoveries, and are lost to Mankind.

Therefore whoever has made any Observations or Discoveries, althô it be but a Hint, and looks like a small Matter, yet if pursued and improved, may be of publick Service. If they see Cause to favour me with such Discoveries and Experiments as they have or shall Make, I shall Receive it with Thankfulness, and publish it either with or without their Names to it, as they shall see fit: For if this Essay should be tho't useful, if God give Life and Health I purpose next Year to furnish you with another Winter's Evening Entertainment: For I would be glad to do Good as far as lies in my power.

34. The Standard of Living

The colonial economy provided a relatively high standard of living for its inhabitants, as the following document describes. Although the passages deal explicitly with New England and Pennsylvania, the description is probably accurate for the white population of the southern colonies as well. The standard of living of the slaves was certainly not equal to that of free men; whether it was higher than that currently prevailing in their native lands remains an open question.

There is in many respects a great resemblance between New England and Great Britain. In the best cultivated parts of it, you would not in travelling through the country, know, from its appearance, that you were from home. The face of the country has in general

SOURCE: Anon., *American Husbandry* (London, 1775), I, 61–2, 70–1, 184–5, 187–8.

a cultivated, inclosed, and chearful prospect; the farm-houses are well and substantially built, and stand thick; gentlemen's houses appear every where, and have an air of a wealthy and contented people. Poor, strolling and ragged beggars are scarcely ever to be seen; all the inhabitants of the country appear to be well fed, cloathed, and lodged, nor is any where a greater degree of independency, and liberty to be met with: nor is that distinction of the ranks and classes to be found which we see in Britain, but which is infinitely more apparent in France and other arbitrary countries. . . .

Respecting the lower classes in New England, there is scarcely any part of the world in which they are better off. The price of labour is very high, and they have with this advantage another no less valuable, of being able to take up a tract of land whenever they are able to settle it. In Britain a servant or labourer may be master of thirty or forty pounds without having it in their power to lay it out in one useful or advantageous purpose; it must be a much larger sum to enable them to hire a farm, but in New England there is no such thing as a man procuring such a sum of money by his industry without his taking a farm and settling upon it. The daily instances of this give an emulation to all the lower classes and make them point their endeavours with peculiar industry to gain an end which they all esteem so particularly flattering.

This great ease of gaining a farm, renders the lower class of people very industrious; which, with the high price of labour, banishes everything that has the least appearance of begging, or that wandering, destitute state of poverty, which we see so common in England. A traveller might pass half through the colony without finding, from the appearance of the people, that there was such a thing as a want of money among them. . . .

This country [Pennsylvania] is peopled by as happy and free a set of men as any in America. Out of trade there is not much wealth to be found, but at the same time there is very little poverty, and hardly such a thing as a beggar in the province. This is not only a consequence of the plenty of land and the rate of labour, but also of the principles of the Quakers, who have a considerable share in the government of the country. It is much to the honour of this sect that they support their own poor in all countries, in a manner much more respectable than known in any other religion. . . .

Their meals are three times a day, and served quite in the English taste: coffee, tea, and chocolate, are of the best sorts, cheap enough to be commanded in plenty by every planter, especially coffee and chocolate; sugar also is cheaper than in England; these, with good bread and good butter, give a breakfast superior to what gentlemen of small estates usually make in England. For dinner and supper they are much better supplied, as may easily be supposed, when the plenty is considered that abounds in an American plantation: game, variety of fish, venison almost every where, poultry in prodigious plenty and variety, meat of all kinds, very good, and killed on every plantation of any size; several sorts of fruits, in a plenty surpassing any thing known in the best climates of Europe, such as melons, water-melons, and cucumbers, in the open field; apples, pears, cherries, peaches, nectarines, goose-berries, currants, strawberries, and rasberries, gathering some every month from May till October. Their grapes, though plentiful to excess, are inferior. These are circumstances that make it neither difficult nor expensive to keep an excellent table. The wine commonly drank is Madeira, at not more than half the price of England; freight is cheaper, and there is none, or a very trifling duty. French and Spanish wines are also drank; rum is very cheap; and good beer is brewed by those who are attentive to the operation.

From hence it is sufficiently clear, that the time passed at the table need not be a barren entertainment.

VI

The Economic Problems of
a New Nation

The period between the end of the French and Indian War and the end
of the War of 1812 was a time of disruption and readjustment for the
American economy. The rapid extensive growth of the American economy
had probably made independence inevitable. However, the timing of separation was decidedly influenced by the cession of Canada to England by
France and the vigorous administration of various restrictions of trade
which the colonists found intolerable. As a result of successful revolution,
the new nation found itself beset by serious economic problems, both internal and external. A solution to the internal problems was found in the
Constitution, which established a legal framework consistent with economic growth. The external problems proved more stubborn, and a second
war with England intervened before they could be controlled.

35. Prophecy of Independence

*Peter Kalm, a Swedish traveler in the American colonies, foresaw as
early as 1748 a possibility of independence for the American colonies
within thirty to fifty years. He asserted that it was only the protection
provided by the mother country which kept the colonies within the empire and suggested that the rapid economic growth of the colonies would
allow them to dispense with this shelter in a few decades. The implication of this document is that economic growth made independence
probable, if not inevitable.*

It is however of great advantage to the crown of England that the
North American colonies are near a country under the government
of the French, like Canada. There is reason to believe that the

SOURCE: Peter Kalm, *Travels into North America* (London, 1770), in Pinkerton, *Voyages and Travels*, XIII, 401: reprinted in Ernest Ludlow Bogart
and Charles Manfred Thompson (eds.), *Readings in the Economic History
of the United States* (New York: Longmans, Green and Co., 1927), 143–4.

King never was earnest in his attempts to expel the French from their possessions there; though it might have been done with little difficulty: for the English colonies in this part of the world have increased so much in their number of inhabitants, and in their riches, that they almost vie with Old England. Now in order to keep up the authority and trade of their mother country, and to answer several other purposes, they are forbid to establish new manufactures, which would turn to the disadvantage of the British commerce: they are not allowed to dig for any gold or silver, unless they send them to England immediately; they have not the liberty of trading to any parts that do not belong to the British dominions, excepting some settled places; and foreign traders are not allowed to send their ships to them. These and some other restrictions, occasion the inhabitants of the English colonies to grow less tender for their mother country. This coldness is kept up by the many foreigners, such as Germans, Dutch, and French, settled here, and living among the English, who commonly have no particular attachment to Old England; add to this likewise, that many people can never be contented with their possessions, though they be ever so great, and will always be desirous of getting more, and of enjoying the pleasure which arises from changing; and their over great liberty, and their luxury, often lead them to licentiousness.

I have been told by Englishmen, and not only by such as were born in America, but even by such as came from Europe, that the English colonies in North America, in the space of thirty or fifty years, would be able to form a state by themselves, entirely independent on Old England: but as the whole country which lies along the sea-shore is unguarded, and on the land side is harrassed by the French in times of war, these dangerous neighbours are sufficient to prevent the connection of the colonies with their mother country from being quite broken off. The English government has therefore sufficient reason to consider the French in North America as the best means of keeping the colonies in their due submission.

36. Causes of the Revolution

The following document, commenting on the causes of the American Revolution, lists revival of the acts of trade and the administration of

SOURCE: Josiah Tucker, *Four Tracts on Political and Commercial Subjects* (Gloucester, 1776), 132–7.

these acts as the primary grievance of the colonists. The prohibition of paper money is alleged to be the second cause, and the third, that the economic growth of the colonies had made political independence possible and, indeed, desirable.

Upon the Whole therefore, what is the Cause of such an amazing Outcry as you raise at present?—Not the Stamp Duty itself; all the World are agreed on that Head; and none can be so ignorant, or so stupid, as not to see, that this is a mere Sham and Pretence. What then are the real Grievances, seeing that the Things which you alledge are only the pretended ones? Why, some of you are exasperated against the Mother Country, on account of the Revival of certain Restrictions laid upon their Trade:—I say, a *Revival;* for the same Restriction have been the standing Rules of Government from the Beginning; though not enforced at all Times with equal Strictness. During the late War, you *Americans* could not import the Manufactures of other Nations (which it is your constant Aim to do, and the Mother Country always to prevent) so conveniently as you can in Times of Peace; and therefore, there was no Need of watching you so narrowly, as far as that Branch of Trade was concerned. But immediately upon the Peace, the various Manufactures of *Europe*, particularly those of *France*, which could not find Vent before, were spread, as it were, over all your Colonies, to the prodigious Detriment of your Mother Country; and therefore our late Set of Ministers acted certainly right, in putting in Force the Laws of their Country, in order to check this growing Evil. If in so doing, they committed any Error; or, if the Persons to whom the Execution of these Laws were intrusted, exceeded their Instructions; there is no Doubt to be made, but that all this will be rectified by the present Administration. And having done that, they will have done all that in Reason you can expect from them. But alas! the Expectations of an *American* carry him much further: For he will ever complain and smuggle, and smuggle and complain, 'till all Restraints are removed, and 'till he can both buy and sell, whenever, and wheresoever he pleases. Any thing short of this, is still a Grievance, a Badge of Slavery, an Usurpation on the natural Rights and Liberties of a free People, and I know not how many bad Things besides.

But, my good Friend, be assured, that these are Restraints, which neither the present, nor any future Ministry can exempt you from.

They are the standing Laws of the Kingdom; and God forbid, that
we should allow that dispensing Power to our Ministers, which we
so justly deny to our Kings. In short while you are a Colony, you
must be subordinate to the Mother Country. These are the Terms
and Conditions, on which you were permitted to make your first
Settlements: They are the Terms and Conditions on which you
alone can be entitled to the Assistance and Protection of *Great-
Britain;*— . . .

So much as to your first Grievance; and as to your second, it is,
beyond Doubt, of a Nature still worse. For many among you are
sorely concerned, That they cannot pay their *British* Debts with an
American Sponge. This is an intolerable Grievance; and they long
for the Day when they shall be freed from this galling Chain. Our
Merchants in *London, Bristol, Liverpool, Glasgow, &c. &c.* perfectly understand your many Hints and Inuendoes to us, on this
Head. But indeed, lest we should be so dull as not to comprehend
your Meaning, you have spoken out, and proposed on open Association against paying your just Debts. Had our Debtors in any other
Part of the Globe, had the *French* or *Spaniards* proposed the like
(and surely they have all at least an equal Right) what Name would
you have given to such Proceedings? But I forget: You are not the
faithless *French* or *Spaniards:* You are ourselves: You are honest
Englishmen.

Your third Grievance is the Sovereignty of *Great-Britain:* For you
want to be independent: You wish to be an Empire by itself, and
to be no longer the Province of another. This Spirit is uppermost;
and this Principle is visible in all your Speeches, and all your Writings, even when you take some Pains to disguise it.—

"What! an Island! A Spot such as this to command the great and
mighty Continent of *North-America!* Preposterous! A Continent,
whose Inhabitants double every five and twenty Years! Who therefore, within a Century and an Half will be upwards of an hundred and
twenty Millions of Souls!—Forbid it Patriotism, forbid it Politics, that
such a great and mighty Empire as this, should be held in Subjection
by the paltry Kingdom of *Great-Britain!* Rather let the Seat of Empire be transferred; and let it be fixt, where it ought to be, viz. in
Great America!"

37. The Disposal of Public Lands

One of the extraordinary accomplishments of the period of confederation was the establishment of a plan for the disposal of the public lands. The Land Ordinance of May 20, 1785, laid the basic, initial groundwork for such a dispersal: it determined that the lands would be shifted from public into private hands and that their development should take place as part of a market economy, and it set up an orderly system for such an undertaking. The following selection is from the original bill as introduced into the Continental Congress in 1785. While some modifications were made in the bill, and while innumerable changes in specific provisions were later adopted, the basic outlines of land disposal as here described were preserved throughout the nineteenth century.

An Ordinance for Ascertaining the Mode of Disposing of Lands in the Western Territory.

Be it ordained by the United States in Congress assembled, that the territory ceded by individual States in the United States, which has been purchased of the Indian inhabitants, shall be disposed of in the following manner:

A surveyor from each state shall be appointed by Congress, or a committee of the States, who shall take an Oath for the faithful discharge of his duty, before the Geographer of the United States, who is hereby empowered and directed to administer the same; and the like oath shall be administered to each chain carrier, by the surveyor under whom he acts.

The Geographer, under whose direction the surveyors shall act, shall occasionally form such regulations for their conduct, as he shall deem necessary; and shall have authority to suspend them for misconduct in Office, and shall make report of the same to Congress, or to the Committee of the States; and he shall make report in case of sickness, death, or resignation of any surveyor.

The Surveyors, as they are respectively qualified, shall proceed to divide the said territory into townships of six miles square, by lines running due north and south, and others crossing these at right angles, as near as may be, unless where the boundaries of the late

SOURCE: John C. Fitzpatrick (ed.), Journals of the Continental Congress, 1774–1789 (Washington, D.C.: Government Printing Office, 1933), XXVIII (1785), Jan. 11—June 30.

Indian purchases may render the same impracticable, and then they shall depart from this rule no farther than such particular circumstances may require; and each surveyor shall be allowed and paid at the rate of two dollars for every mile, in length, he shall run, including the wages of chain carriers, markers, and every other expense attending the same.

The first line, running north and south as aforesaid, shall begin on the river Ohio, at a point that shall be found to be due north from the western termination of a line, which has been run as the southern boundary of the state of Pennsylvania; and the first line, running east and west, shall begin at the same point, and shall extend throughout the whole territory. Provided, that nothing herein shall be construed, as fixing the western boundary of the state of Pennsylvania. The geographer shall designate the townships, or fractional parts of townships, by numbers progressively from south to north; always beginning each range with number one; and the ranges shall be distinguished by their progressive numbers to the westward. The first range, extending from the Ohio to the lake Erie, being marked number one. The Geographer shall personally attend to the running of the first east and west line; and shall take the latitude of the extremes of the first north and south line, and of the mouths of the principal rivers.

The lines shall be measured with a chain; shall be plainly marked by chaps on the trees, and exactly described on a plat; whereon shall be noted by the surveyor, at their proper distances, all mines, salt springs, salt licks and mill seats, that shall come to his knowledge, and all water courses, mountains and other remarkable and permanent things, over and near which such lines shall pass, and also the quality of the lands.

The plats of the townships respectively, shall be marked by subdivisions into lots of one mile square, or 640 acres, in the same direction as the external lines, and numbered from 1 to 36; always beginning the succeeding range of the lots with the number next to that with which the preceding one concluded. And where, from the causes before mentioned, only a fractional part of a township shall be surveyed, the lots, protracted thereon, shall bear the same numbers as if the township had been entire. And the surveyors, in running the external lines of the townships, shall, at the interval of every mile, mark corners for the lots which are adjacent, always designating the same in a different manner from those of the townships.

· · ·

The board of treasury shall transmit a copy of the original plats, previously noting thereon, the townships, and fractional parts of townships, which shall have fallen to the several states, by the distribution aforesaid, to the Commissioners of the loan office of the several states, who, after giving notice of not less than two nor more than six months, by causing advertisements to be posted up at the court houses, or other noted places in every county, and to be inserted in one newspaper, published in the states of their residence respectively, shall proceed to sell the townships, or fractional parts of townships, at public vendue, in the following manner, viz: The township, or fractional part of a township, N 1, in the first range, shall be sold entire; and N 2, in the same range, entire; and so in alternate order through the whole of the second range; and the third range shall be sold in the same manner as the first, and the fourth in the same manner as the second, and thus alternately throughout all the ranges; provided, that none of the lands, within the said territory, be sold under the price of one dollar the acre, to be paid in specie, or loan office certificates, reduced to specie value, by the scale of depreciation, or certificates of liquidated debts of the United States, including interest, besides the expense of the survey and other charges thereon, which are hereby rated at thirty six dollars the township, in specie, or certificates as aforesaid, and so in the same proportion for a fractional part of a township, or of a lot, to be paid at the time of sales; on failure of which payment, the said lands shall again be offered for sale.

There shall be reserved for the United States out of every township, the four lots, being numbered 8, 11, 26, 29 and out of every fractional part of a township, so many lots of the same numbers as shall be found thereon, for future sale. There shall be reserved the lot N 16, of every township, for the maintenance of public schools, within the said township; also one third part of all gold, silver, lead and copper mines, to be sold, or otherwise disposed of as Congress shall hereafter direct.

When any township, or fractional part of a township, shall have been sold as aforesaid, and the money or certificates received therefor, the loan officer shall deliver a deed in the following terms:

The United States of America, to all to whom these presents shall come, greeting:

Know ye, That for the consideration of —— dollars, we have granted, and hereby do grant and confirm unto —— the township, (or fractional part of a township, as the case may be) numbered —— in the range —— excepting therefrom, and reserving one third part of all gold, silver, lead and copper mines within the same; and the lots Ns8, 11, 26, and 29, for future sale or disposition, and the lot N 16, for the maintenance of public schools. To have to the said —— his heirs and assigns for ever; (or if more than one purchaser, to the said —— their heirs and assigns forever as tenants in Common.) In witness whereof, (A. B.) Commissioner of the loan office, in the State of —— hath, in conformity to the Ordinance passed by the United States in Congress assembled, the twentieth day of May, in the year of our Lord one thousand seven hundred and eighty-five, hereunto set his hand, and affixed his seal, this day of —— in the year of our Lord —— and of the independence of the United States of America ——

And when any township, or fractional part of a township, shall be sold by lots as aforesaid, the Commissioner of the loan office shall deliver a deed therefor in the following form:

The United States of America, to all to whom these presents shall come, Greeting:

Know ye, That for the consideration of —— dollars, we have granted, and hereby do grant and confirm unto —— the lot (or lots, as the case may be, in the township or fractional part of the township, as the case may be) numbered —— in the range —— excepting and reserving one third part of all gold, silver, lead and copper mines within the same, for future sale or disposition. To have to the said —— his heirs and assigns for ever; (or if more than one purchaser, to the said —— their heirs and assigns for ever as tenants in common.) In witness whereof, (A. B.) Commissioner of the continental loan office in the state of —— hath, in conformity to the Ordinance passed by the United States in Congress assembled, the twentieth day of May, in the year of our Lord 1785, hereunto set his hand, and affixed his seal, this —— day of —— in the year of our Lord —— and of the independence of the United States of America ——

Which deeds shall be recorded in proper books, by the commissioner of the loan office, and shall be certified to have been recorded, previous to their being delivered to the purchaser, and shall be good and valid to convey the lands in the same described.

The commissioners of the loan offices respectively, shall transmit to the board of treasury every three months, an account of the townships, fractional parts of townships, and lots committed to their charge; specifying therein the names of the persons to whom sold, and the sums of money or certificates received for the same; and shall cause all certificates by them received, to be struck through with a circular punch; and they shall be duly charged in the books of the treasury, with the amount of the moneys or certificates, distinguishing the same, by them received as aforesaid.

If any township, or fractional part of a township or lot, remains unsold for eighteen months after the plat shall have been received, by the commissioners of the loan office, the same shall be returned to the board of treasury, and shall be sold in such manner as Congress may hereafter direct.

And whereas Congress, by their resolutions of September 16 and 18 in the year 1776, and the 12th of August, 1780, stipulated grants of land to certain officers and soldiers of the late continental army, and by the resolution of the 22d September, 1780, stipulated grants of land to certain officers in the hospital department of the late continental army; for complying therefore with such engagements, Be it ordained, That the secretary at war, from the returns in his office, or such other sufficient evidence as the nature of the case may admit, determine who are the objects of the above resolutions and engagements, and the quantity of land to which such persons or their representatives are respectively entitled, and cause the townships, or fractional parts of townships, hereinbefore reserved for the use of the late continental army, to be drawn for in such manner as he shall deem expedient, to answer the purpose of an impartial distribution. He shall, from time to time, transmit certificates to the commissioners of the loan offices of the different states, to the lines of which the military claimants have respectively belonged, specifying the name and rank of the party, the terms of his engagement and time of his service, and the division, brigade, regiment or company to which he belonged, the quantity of land he is entitled to, and the township, or fractional part of a township, and range out of which his portion is to be taken.

The commissioners of the loan offices shall execute deeds for such undivided portions in manner and form herein beforementioned, varying only in such a degree as to make the same conformable to the certificate from the Secretary at War.

Where any military claimants of bounty in lands shall not have belonged to the line of any particular state, similar certificates shall be sent to the board of treasury, who shall execute deeds to the parties for the same.

The Secretary at War, from the proper returns, shall transmit to the board of treasury, a certificate, specifying the name and rank of the several claimants of the hospital department of the late continental army, together with the quantity of land each claimant is entitled to, and the township, or fractional part of a township, and range out of which his portion is to be taken; and thereupon the board of treasury shall proceed to execute deeds to such claimants.

38. Trade Relations with Europe

In the turbulent decade of the 1780's following the Revolutionary War, the new nation faced crucial problems both internally—in establishing its essential ground rules and developing its economy—and externally, in reorganizing its trade relations with other nations. This latter adjustment had to take place in the contemporary world of mercantilism in which each nation was trying to capture all the gains of trade and commerce for itself at the expense of others. Inevitably such an attitude led to the imposition by foreign nations of innumerable restrictions on American shipping, as summarized by Thomas Jefferson in the following statement.

To sum up these restrictions, so far as they are important:
FIRST.   In Europe—
Our bread stuff is at most times under prohibitory duties in England, and considerably dutied on re-exportation from Spain to her colonies.

Our tobaccoes are heavily dutied in England, Sweden and France, and prohibited in Spain and Portugal.

Our rice is heavily dutied in England and Sweden, and prohibited in Portugal.

Our fish and salted provisions are prohibited in England, and under prohibitory duties in France.

Our whale oils are prohibited in England and Portugal.

And our vessels are denied naturalization in England, and of late in France.

SECOND.   In the West Indies—

SOURCE: Andrew A. Lipscomb (ed.), *The Writings of Thomas Jefferson* (Washington, D.C.: Thomas Jefferson Memorial Association, 1903), III, 273–4.

All intercourse is prohibited with the possessions of Spain and Portugal.

Our salted provisions and fish are prohibited by England.

Our salted pork and bread stuff (except maize) are received under temporary laws only, in the dominions of France, and our salted fish pays there a weighty duty.

THIRD.   In the article of navigation—

Our own carriage of our own tobacco is heavily dutied in Sweden, and lately in France.

We can carry no article, not of our own production, to the British ports in Europe. Nor even our own produce to her American possessions.

Such being the restrictions on the commerce and navigation of the United States; the question is, in what way they may best be removed, modified or counteracted?

39. Economic Reasons for the Constitution

The following document argues for endowing the federal government with powers to remedy the economic ills the nation suffered under the Confederation. In the main, these arguments were accepted and the requisite powers incorporated into the Constitution.

The foundations of national wealth and consequence are so firmly laid in the United States, that no foreign power can undermine or destroy them. But the enjoyment of these substantial blessings is rendered precarious by domestic circumstances. Scarcely held together by a weak and half formed federal constitution, the powers of our national government, are unequal to the complete execution of any salutary purpose, foreign or domestic. The evils resulting from this unhappy state of things have again shocked our reviving credit, produced among our people alarming instances of disobedience to the laws, and if not remedied, must destroy our property, liberties and peace. Foreign powers, however disposed to favor us, can expect neither satisfaction nor benefit from treaties with Congress, while they are unable to enforce them. We can therefore hope to secure no privileges from them, if matters are thus conducted. We must

SOURCE: Tench Coxe, *A View of the United States of America* (Philadelphia: William Hall, 1794), 28–33.

immediately remedy this defect or suffer exceedingly. Desultory commercial acts of the legislatures, formed on the impression of the moment, proceeding from no uniform or permanent principles, clashing with the laws of other states and opposing those made in the preceding year by the enacting state, can no longer be supported, if we are to continue one people. *A system which will promote the general interests with the smallest injury to particular ones has become indispensibly necessary.* Commerce is more affected by the distractions and evils arising from the uncertainty, opposition and errors of our trade laws, than by the restrictions of any one power in Europe. A negative upon all commercial acts of the legislatures, if granted to Congress wold be perfectly safe, and must have an excellent effect. If thought expedient it should be given as well with regard to those that exist, as to those that may be devised in future. Congress would thus be enabled to prevent every regulation, that might oppose the general interests, and by restraining the states from impolitic laws, would gradually bring our national commerce to order and perfection.

We have ventured to hint at prohibitory powers, but shall leave that point and the general power of regulating trade to those who may undertake to consider the political objects of the Convention, suggesting only the evident propriety of enabling Congress to prevent the importation of foreign commodities, such as can be made from our own raw materials. When any article of that kind can be supplied at home, upon as low terms as those on which it can be imported, a manufacture of *our own produce,* so well established, ought not by any means to be sacrificed to the interests of foreign trade, or subjected to injury by the wild speculations of ignorant adventurers. In all cases careful provision should be made for refunding the duties on exportation, which renders the impost a virtual excise without being liable to any of the objections which have been made against an actual one, and is a great encouragement to trade.

The restoration of public credit at home and abroad should be the first wish of our hearts, and requires every economy, every exertion we can make. The wise and virtuous axioms of our political constitutions, resulting from a lively and perfect sense of what is due from man to man, should prompt us to the discharge of debts of such peculiar obligation. We stand bound to no common creditors. The friendly foreigner, the widow and the orphan, the trustees of charity and religion, the patriotic citizen, the war-worn soldier and a magnanimous ally—these are the principal claimants upon the feelings and justice of America. Let her apply all her resources to this great duty, and wipe away the darkest stain, that has ever fallen upon her. The general impost—the sale of the lands and every other unnecessary article of public property—restraining with a firm hand every needless expence of government and private life—steady and patient industry, with proper dispositions in the people, would relieve us of part of the burden, and enable Congress to commence their payments, and with the aid of taxation, would put the sinking and funding of our debts within the power of the United States.

The violence committed on the rights of property under the authority of tender laws in some of the states, the familiarity with which that pernicious measure has been recurred to, and the shameless perseverance with which it has been persisted in after the value of the paper was confessedly gone, call aloud for some remedy. This is not merely a matter of justice between man and man. It dishonors our national character abroad, and the engine has been employed to give the coup de grace to public credit. It would not be difficult perhaps to form a new article of confederation to prevent it in future, and a question may arise whether fellowship with any state, that would refuse to admit it, can be satisfactory or safe. To remove difficulties it need not be retrospective. The present state of things instead of inviting emigrants, deters all who have the means of information, and are capable of thinking. The settlement of our lands, and the introduction of manufactories and branches of trade yet unknown among us or requiring a force of capital, which are to make our country rich and powerful, are interrupted and suspended by our want of public credit and the numerous disorders of our government.

40. The Economic Powers of the Constitution

The following excerpts from the Constitution of the United States are the foundation stones which undergirded the new central government with critically important economic powers. These are essentially the powers called for in the previous document.

By these provisions, set forth in Articles I and VI, the government could levy taxes, without which no society could have been organized.

It could assume and redeem the debts incurred by the several states, thereby enabling a capital market to develop. It could coin money and control the money supply—equally important in the development of a capital market and of commercial activities. It was granted central authority over foreign affairs, tariffs, and the negotiation of treaties. And it was given powers which would ultimately lead to central control over interstate commerce. This last authority, after being tested and vindicated in many court cases, prevented the erection of state barriers to trade and was to prove vital in the regulation of national economic activity.

It should be emphasized, however, that the most important contribution of the Constitution to the nation's economic soundness lay less in specific economic provisions than in the underlying ground rules it laid for an orderly society. Because it provided for the protection of private property and the enforcement of contracts, this document ensured a growing stability in which uncertainty—and therefore the risk inherent in any economic undertaking—was held to a minimum.

ARTICLE I

Section 8

General Powers of Congress

The Congress shall have Power.—1. To lay and collect Taxes, Duties, Imposts and Excises, to pay the Debts and provide for the common Defence and general Welfare of the United States, but all Duties, Imposts and Excises shall be uniform throughout the United States;

Borrowing of money.—2. To borrow Money on the credit of the United States;

Regulation of commerce.—3. To regulate Commerce with foreign Nations, and among the several States, and with the Indian Tribes;

Naturalization and bankruptcy.—4. To establish an uniform Rule of Naturalization, and uniform Laws on the subject of Bankruptcies throughout the United States;

Money, weights and measures.—5. To coin Money, regulate the Value thereof, and of foreign Coin, and fix the Standard of Weights and Measures;

Counterfeiting.—6. To provide for the Punishment of counterfeiting the Securities and current Coin of the United States;

SOURCE: The Constitution of the United States.

Post offices.—7. To establish Post Offices and post Roads;

Patents and copyrights.—8. To promote the Progress of Science and useful Arts, by securing for limited Times to Authors and Inventors the exclusive Right to their respective Writings and Discoveries;

To enact laws necessary to enforce Constitution.—18. To make all Laws which shall be necessary and proper for carrying into Execution the foregoing Powers, and all other Powers vested by this Constitution in the Government of the United States, or in any Department or Officer thereof.

Section 9

Capitation and other direct taxes.—4. No capitation, or other direct, Tax shall be laid, unless in Proportion to the Census or Enumeration herein before directed to be taken.

Exports not to be taxed.—5. No Tax or Duty shall be laid on Articles exported from any State.

No preference to be given to ports of any State: interstate shipping.—6. No Preference shall be given by any Regulation of Commerce or Revenue to the Ports of one State over those of another: nor shall Vessels bound to, or from, one State, be obliged to enter, clear, or pay Duties in another.

Money, how drawn from treasury; financial statements to be published.—7. No money shall be drawn from the Treasury, but in Consequence of Appropriations made by Law; and a regular Statement and Account of the Receipts and Expenditures of all public Money shall be published from time to time.

Section 10

Limitations of the powers of the several States.—1. No State shall enter into any Treaty, Alliance, or Confederation; grant Letters of Marque and Reprisal; coin Money; emit Bills of Credit; make any Thing but gold and silver Coin a Tender in Payment of Debts; pass any Bill of Attainder, ex post facto Law, or Law impairing the Obligation of Contracts, or grant any Title of Nobility.

State imposts and duties.—2. No State shall, without the Consent of the Congress, lay any Imposts or Duties on Imports or Exports, except what may be absolutely necessary for executing its inspection Laws: and the net Produce of all Duties and Imposts, laid by any State on Imports or Exports, shall be for the Use of the Treasury of the United States; and all such Laws shall be subject to the Revision and Control of the Congress.

Further restrictions on powers of States.—3.   No State shall, without the Consent of Congress, lay any Duty of Tonnage, keep Troops, or Ships of War in time of Peace, enter into any Agreement or Compact with another State, or with a foreign Power, or engage in War, unless actually invaded, or in such imminent Danger as will not admit of delay.

ARTICLE VI

Debts contracted under the confederation secured.—1.   All debts contracted and Engagements entered into, before the Adoption of this Constitution, shall be as valid against the United States under this Constitution, as under the Confederation.

Constitution, laws and treaties of the United States to be supreme.—2.   This Constitution, and the Laws of the United States which shall be made in Pursuance thereof; and all Treaties made, or which shall be made, under the Authority of the United States, shall be the supreme Law of the Land; and the Judges in every State shall be bound thereby, any Thing in the Constitution or Laws of any State to the Contrary notwithstanding.

41. The Establishment of the Public Credit

It would be hard to overestimate the role of Alexander Hamilton in developing the structure of an efficient economic order in the new United States. He was instrumental in establishing the banking system, in creating the mint, in setting up a system of public credit, and indeed even in designing the Constitution itself. Characteristic of Hamilton's views on the necessity for an orderly society was his approach to the highly controversial question of the financial obligations of the new government. He took the common-sense attitude that the government must fully redeem its obligations if an efficient credit market were to emerge. In this selection he defends his view that the federal government should assume and redeem at par the debts previously incurred by the several states—a topic of furious debate in the early history of the American economy.

SOURCE: Henry Cabot Lodge (ed.), *The Works of Alexander Hamilton* (2nd edn.; New York: G. P. Putnam's Sons, 1904), III, 12–5.

NUMBER THREE

My last number contained a concise and simple statement of facts tending to show that the public debt was neither created nor increased by the funding system, and, consequently, that it is not responsible either for the existence or the magnitude of the debt.

It will be proper next to examine the allegations which have been made of a contrary tendency.

In the first place, it is asserted that the debt is greater than it ought to be, because, from the state of depreciation in which the government found it, a much less provision for it than that which was made might have sufficed. A saving of nearly one half, it is said, might have been made by providing for it in the hands of alienees, at least at 8s. or 10s. in the pound, who, having come by it at a much less rate, would have been well compensated by such a provision.

To a man who entertains correct notions of public faith, and who feels as he ought to feel for the reputation and dignity of the country, it is mortifying to reflect that there are partisans enough of such a doctrine to render it worth the while to combat it. It is still more mortifying to know that in that class are comprehended some men who are in other respects sober-minded and upright, friends to order, and strenuous advocates for the rights of property.

In reasoning upon all subjects, it is necessary to take, as a point of departure, some principle in which reasonable and sound minds will agree. Without this there can be no argument, no conclusion, in moral or political more than in physical or mathematical disquisitions.

The principle which shall be assumed here is this, that the established rules of morality and justice are applicable to nations as well as to individuals; that the former as well as the latter are bound to keep their promises; to fulfil their engagements to respect the rights of property which others have acquired under contracts with them. Without this there is an end of all distinct ideas of right or wrong, justice or injustice, in relation to society or government. There can be no such thing as rights, no such thing as property or liberty; all the boasted advantages of a constitution of government vanish into air. Every thing must float on the variable and vague opinions of the governing party, of whomsoever composed.

To this it may be answered that the doctrine, as a general one, is true, but that there are certain great cases which operate as exceptions to the rule, and in which the public good may demand and justify a departure from it.

It shall not be denied that there are such cases; but as the admission of them is one of the most common as well as the most fruitful sources of error and abuse, it is of the greatest importance that just ideas should be formed of their true nature, foundation, and extent. To minds which are either depraved or feeble, or under the influence of any particular passion or prejudice, it is enough that cases are only attended with some extraordinary circumstances to induce their being considered as among the exceptions. Convenience is with them a substitute for necessity, and some temporary, partial advantage is an equivalent for a fundamental and permanent interest of society. We have too often seen in the United States examples of this species of levity. The treaties of the United States, the sacred rights of private property, have been too frequently sported with, from a too great facility in admitting exceptions to the maxims of public faith and the general rules of property. A desire to escape from this evil was a principal cause of the union which took place among good men to establish the national government; and it behoved its friends to have been particularly cautious how they set an example of equal relaxation in the practice of that very government.

42. Hamilton on the Subject of Manufactures

Although Alexander Hamilton possessed extraordinary insight into the essentials of an efficient economic order, he also at times wore the blinders of the prevalent mercantilistic philosophy. On the subject of manufactures, he showed on the one hand full awareness of the importance of developing a manufacturing system; on the other hand he advocated government protection and subsidies, failing to observe that these would result in the very inefficiencies so criticized by Adam Smith in The Wealth of Nations. *In the following selection, Hamilton draws heavily on Adam Smith in setting forth his plea for the development of manufacturing, then he radically parts company with Smith in contending that the government should play a key role in subsidizing such development.*

SOURCE: Henry Cabot Lodge (ed.), *The Works of Alexander Hamilton* (2nd edn.; New York: G. P. Putnam's Sons, 1904), 86–95, 193–5, 197–8.

It is now proper to proceed a step further, and to enumerate the principal circumstances from which it may be inferred that manufacturing establishments not only occasion a positive augmentation of the produce and revenue of the society, but that they contribute essentially to rendering them greater than they could possibly be without such establishments. These circumstances are:

1. The division of labor.

2. An extension of the use of machinery.

3. Additional employment to classes of the community not ordinarily engaged in the business.

4. The promoting of emigration from foreign countries.

5. The furnishing greater scope for the diversity of talents and dispositions, which discriminate men from each other.

6. The affording a more ample and various field for enterprise.

7. The creating, in some instances, a new, and securing, in all, a more certain and steady demand for the surplus produce of the soil.

Each of these circumstances has a considerable influence upon the total mass of industrious effort in a community; together, they add to it a degree of energy and effect which is not easily conceived. Some comments upon each of them, in the order in which they have been stated, may serve to explain their importance.

1. As to the division of labor

It has justly been observed, that there is scarcely any thing of greater moment in the economy of a nation than the proper division of labor. The separation of occupations causes each to be carried to a much greater perfection than it could possibly acquire if they were blended. This arises principally from three circumstances:

1st. The greater skill and dexterity naturally resulting from a constant and undivided application to a single object. It is evident that these properties must increase in proportion to the separation and simplification of objects, and the steadiness of the attention devoted to each; and must be less in proportion to the complication of objects, and the number among which the attention is distracted.

2d. The economy of time, by avoiding the loss of it, incident to a frequent transition from one operation to another of a different nature. This depends on various circumstances: the transition itself, the orderly disposition of the implements, machines, and materials employed in the operation to be relinquished, the preparatory steps to the commencement of a new one, the interruption of the impulse which the mind of the workman acquires from being engaged in a particular operation, the distractions, hesitations, and reluctances which attend the passage from one kind of business to another.

3d. An extension of the use of machinery. A man occupied on a single object will have it more in his power, and will be more naturally led to exert his imagination, in devising methods to facilitate and abridge labor, than if he were perplexed by a variety of independent and dissimilar operations. Besides this the fabrication of machines, in numerous instances, becoming itself a distinct trade, the artist who follows it has all the advantages which have been enumerated, for improvement in his particular art; and, in both ways, the invention and application of machinery are extended.

And from these causes united, the mere separation of the occupation of the cultivator from that of the artificer, has the effect of augmenting the productive powers of labor, and with them, the total mass of the produce or revenue of a country. In this single view of the subject, therefore, the utility of artificers or manufacturers, towards producing an increase of productive industry, is apparent.

2. As to an extension of the use of machinery, a point which, though partly anticipated, requires to be placed in one or two additional lights

The employment of machinery forms an item of great importance in the general mass of national industry. It is an artificial force brought in aid of the natural force of man; and, to all the purposes of labor, is an increase of hands, an accession of strength, unencumbered too by the expense of maintaining the laborer. May it not, therefore, be fairly inferred, that those occupations which give greatest scope to the use of this auxiliary, contribute most to the general stock of industrious effort, and, in consequence, to the general product of industry?

.   .   .

3. As to the additional employment of classes of the community not originally engaged in the particular business

This is not among the least valuable of the means by which manufacturing institutions contribute to augment the general stock of industry and production. In places where those institutions prevail, besides the persons regularly engaged in them, they afford occasional and extra employment to industrious individuals and families, who are willing to devote the leisure resulting from the intermissions of their ordinary pursuits to collateral labors, as a resource for multiplying their acquisitions or their enjoyments. The husbandman himself experiences a new source of profit and support from the increased industry of his wife and daughters, invited and stimulated by the demands of the neighboring manufactories.

·   ·   ·

4. As to the promoting of emigration from foreign countries

Men reluctantly quit one course of occupation and livelihood for another, unless invited to it by very apparent and proximate advantages. Many who would go from one country to another, if they had a prospect of continuing with more benefit the callings to which they have been educated, will often not be tempted to change their situation by the hope of doing better in some other way. Manufacturers who, listening to the powerful invitations of a better price for their fabrics or their labor, of greater cheapness of provisions and raw materials, of an exemption from the chief part of the taxes, burthens, and restraints which they endure in the Old World, of greater personal independence and consequence, under the operation of a more equal government, and of what is far more precious than mere religious toleration, a perfect equality of religious privileges, would probably flock from Europe to the United States, to pursue their own trades or professions, if they were once made sensible of the advantages they would enjoy, and were inspired with an assurance of encouragement and employment, will, with difficulty, be induced to transplant themselves, with a view to becoming cultivators of land.

If it be true, then, that it is the interest of the United States to open every possible avenue to emigration from abroad, it affords a weighty argument for the encouragement of manufactures; which, for the reasons just assigned, will have the strongest tendency to multiply the inducements to it.

Here is perceived an important resource, not only for extending the population, and with it the useful and productive labor of the country, but likewise for the prosecution of manufactures, without deducting from the number of hands which might otherwise be drawn to tillage, and even for the indemnification of agriculture for such as might happen to be diverted from it. Many, whom manufacturing views would induce to emigrate, would, afterwards, yield to the temptations which the particular situation of this country holds out to agricultural pursuits. And while agriculture would, in other respects, derive many signal and unmingled advantages from the growth of manufactures, it is a problem whether it would gain or lose, as to the article of the number of persons employed in carrying it on.

5. As to the furnishing greater scope for the diversity of talents and dispositions, which discriminate men from each other

This is a much more powerful means of augmenting the fund of national industry, than may at first sight appear. It is a just observation, that minds of the strongest and most active powers for their proper objects, fall below mediocrity, and labor without effect, if confined to uncongenial pursuits. And it is thence to be inferred, that the results of human exertion may be immensely increased by diversifying its objects. When all the different kinds of industry obtain in a community, each individual can find his proper element, and can call into activity the whole vigor of his nature. And the community is benefited by the services of its respective members, in the manner in which each can serve it with most effect.

If there be any thing in a remark often to be met with, namely, that there is, in the genius of the people of this country, a peculiar aptitude for mechanic improvements, it would operate as a forcible reason for giving opportunities to the exercise of that species of talent, by the propagation of manufactures.

6. As to the affording a more ample and various field for enterprise

This also is of greater consequence in the general scale of national exertion than might, perhaps, on a superficial view be supposed, and has effects not altogether dissimilar from those of the circumstance last noticed. To cherish and stimulate the activity of the human mind, by multiplying the objects of enterprise, is not among the least considerable of the expedients by which the wealth of a nation may be promoted. Even things in themselves not positively advantageous sometimes become so, by their tendency to provoke exertion. Every new scene which is opened to the busy nature of man to rouse and exert itself, is the addition of a new energy to the general stock of effort.

The spirit of enterprise, useful and prolific as it is, must necessarily be contracted or expanded, in proportion to the simplicity or variety of the occupations and productions which are to be found in a society. It must be less in a nation of mere cultivators, than in a nation of cultivators and merchants; less in a nation of cultivators and merchants, than in a nation of cultivators, artificers, and merchants.

7. As to the creating, in some instances, a new, and securing, in all, a more certain and steady demand for the surplus produce of the soil

This is among the most important of the circumstances which have been indicated. It is a principal means by which the establishment of manufactures contributes to an augmentation of the produce or revenue of a country, and has an immediate and direct relation to the prosperity of agriculture.

It is evident that the exertions of the husbandman will be steady or fluctuating, vigorous or feeble, in proportion to the steadiness or fluctuation, adequateness or inadequateness, of the markets on which he must depend for the vent of the surplus which may be produced by his labor; and that such surplus, in the ordinary course of things, will be greater or less in the same proportion.

. . .

Previously to a further discussion of the objections to the encouragement of manufactures, which have been stated, it will be of use to see what can be said, in reference to the particular situation of the United States, against the conclusions appearing to result from what has been already offered.

It may be observed, and the idea is of no inconsiderable weight, that however true it might be that a state which, possessing large tracts of vacant and fertile territory, was, at the same time, secluded from foreign commerce, would find its interest and the interest of agriculture in diverting a part of its population from tillage to manufactures, yet it will not follow, that the same is true of a state which, having such vacant and fertile territory, has, at the same time, ample opportunity of procuring from abroad, on good terms, all the fabrics of which it stands in need, for the supply of its inhabitants. The power of doing this, at least secures the great advantage of a division of labor, leaving the farmer free to pursue, exclusively, the culture of his land, and enabling him to procure with its products the manufactured supplies requisite either to his wants or to his enjoyments.

•   •   •

The foregoing heads comprise the most important of the several kinds of manufactures which have occurred as requiring, and, at the same time, as most proper for public encouragement; and such measures for affording it as have appeared best calculated to answer the end, have been suggested.

The observations which have accompanied this delineation of objects, supersede the necessity of many supplementary remarks. One or two, however, may not be altogether superfluous.

Bounties are, in various instances, proposed as one species of encouragement.

It is a familiar objection to them that they are difficult to be managed, and liable to frauds. But neither that difficulty nor this danger seems sufficiently great to countervail the advantages of which they are productive when rightly applied. And it is presumed to have been shown that they are, in some cases, particularly in the infancy of new enterprises, indispensable.

It will, however, be necessary to guard, with extraordinary circumspection, the manner of dispensing them. The requisite precautions have been thought of, but to enter into the detail would swell this report, already voluminous, to a size too inconvenient.

If the principle shall not be deemed inadmissible, the means of avoiding an abuse of it will not be likely to present unsurmountable obstacles. There are useful guides from practice in other quarters.

It shall, therefore, only be remarked here, in relation to this point, that any bounty which may be applied to the manufacture of an article, cannot, with safety, extend beyond those manufactories at which the making of the article is a regular trade. It would be impossible to annex adequate precautions to a benefit of that nature, if extended to every private family in which the manufacture was incidentally carried on; and, being a merely incidental occupation which engages a portion of time that would otherwise be lost, it can be advantageously carried on without so special an aid.

The possibility of a diminution of the revenue may also present itself as an objection to the arrangements which have been submitted.

But there is no truth which may be more firmly relied upon, than

that the interests of the revenue are promoted by whatever pro-
motes an increase of national industry and wealth.

In proportion to the degree of these, is the capacity of every country to contribute to the public treasury; and where the capacity to
pay is increased, or even is not decreased, the only consequence of
measures which diminish any particular resource, is a change of the
object. If, by encouraging the manufacture of an article at home,
the revenue which has been wont to accrue from its importation
should be lessened, an indemnification can easily be found, either
out of the manufacture itself, or from some other object which may
be deemed more convenient.

The measures, however, which have been submitted, taken ag-
gregately, will, for a long time to come, rather augment than decrease the public revenue.

There is little room to hope, that the progress of manufactures
will so equally keep pace with the progress of population, as to prevent even a gradual augmentation of the product of the duties on
imported articles.

As, nevertheless, an abolition in some instances, and a reduction
in others, of duties which have been pledged for the public debt, is
proposed, it is essential that it should be accompanied with a competent substitute. In order to this, it is requisite that all the additional duties which shall be laid, be appropriated, in the first instance, to replace all defalcations which may proceed from any such
abolition or diminution. It is evident, at first glance, that they will
not only be adequate to this, but will yield a considerable surplus.
This surplus will serve:

First. To constitute a fund for paying the bounties which shall
have been decreed.

. . .

The propriety of stimulating by rewards the invention and introduction of useful improvements, is admitted without difficulty. But
the success of attempts in this way must evidently depend much
on the manner of conducting them. It is probable that the placing
of the dispensation of those rewards under some proper discretion-
ary direction, where they may be accompanied by collateral expedients, will serve to give them the surest efficacy. It seems impracticable to apportion, by general rules, specific compensations for discoveries of unknown and disproportionate utility.

The great use which may be made of a fund of this nature, to procure and import foreign improvements, is particularly obvious. Among these, the article of machines would form a most important item.

The operation and utility of premiums have been adverted to, together with the advantages which have resulted from their dispensation, under the direction of certain public and private societies. Of this, some experience has been had, in the instance of the Pennsylvania Society for the promotion of manufactures and useful arts; but the funds of that association have been too contracted to produce more than a very small portion of the good to which the principles of it would have led. It may confidently be affirmed, that there is scarcely any thing which has been devised, better calculated to excite a general spirit of improvement than the institutions of this nature. They are truly invaluable.

In countries where there is great private wealth, much may be effected by the voluntary contributions of patriotic individuals; but in a community situated like that of the United States, the public purse must supply the deficiency of private resource. In what can it be so useful, as in prompting and improving the efforts of industry?

All which is humbly submitted.

ALEXANDER HAMILTON,
Secretary of the Treasury.

43. The Condition of the Economy in the 1790's

By the end of the 1780's, and indeed even before the Constitution went into effect, it became evident that the American economy was beginning to expand. One observer, Tench Coxe, published in 1794 his enthusiastic View of the United States of America, predicting boundless progress for the new nation.

The people of the United States have exploded those principles, by the operation of which religious oppressions and restrictions of whatever description, have been imposed upon mankind, and, rejecting mere toleration, they have placed upon one common and equal footing every church, sect or society of religious men.

They have exploded, in like manner, those principles, by the op-

SOURCE: Tench Coxe, A View of the United States of America (Philadelphia, 1794), 427–31, 440–3.

eration of which, civil oppressions have been inflicted upon mankind; and they have made an unexceeded progress in their practice upon the principles of free government.

．　　・　　・

The public debt is smaller in proportion to the present wealth and population of the United States than the public debt of any other civilized nation.

The United States (including the operations of the individual states) have sunk a much greater proportion of their public debt in the last ten years, than any other nation in the world.

The expences of the government are very much less, in proportion to wealth and numbers, than those of any nation in Europe.

There is no land tax among the national revenues, nor is there any interior tax, or excise upon food, drink, fuel, lights, or any native or foreign manufacture, or native or foreign production, except a duty of about four pence sterling upon domestic distilled spirits. The greatest part of the public burdens are paid by an import duty on foreign goods, which being drawn back on exportation, it remains only on what is actually consumed. It is in that view the lowest in the world, and operates greatly in favour of American manufactures.

Trade has been encouraged by a drawback of all the import duty on foreign goods, when they are exported, excepting only a very few commodities of a particular nature, which are not desired to be much imported into, or consumed in the United States.

A national mint is established under the direction of the ablest practical man in the arts and sciences which this country contains —David Rittenhouse. It is provided by law that the purity and intrinsic value of the silver coin shall be equal to that of Spain, and of the gold coins to those of the strictest European nations. The government of the United States foregoes all profit from the coinage: a political and wholesome forbearance.

The banks established in the several cities of Philadelphia, New-York, Boston, Baltimore, Charleston, Alexandria, &c. divide a profit of seven and an half to eight and an half per cent. per annum at present, which is paid half yearly.

The interest of the public debt of the United States is paid quarter yearly with a punctuality absolute and perfect. There is no tax on property in the funds and banks.

The shipbuilding of the United States was greater in the year

1792, than in any former year since the settlement of the country, and it is much greater in the current year, than it was in the last. Generally speaking, the art of shipbuilding was never so well understood, never so well executed, nor was there ever a time when so many of the manufactures requisite for the furniture, tackle, apparel and arming of vessels were made in the United States.

The value of the manufactures of the United States is certainly greater than double the value of their exports in native commodities.

The value of the manufactures of the United States, is much greater than the gross value of all their imports, including the value of goods exported again.

The manufactures of the United States consist generally of articles of comfort, utility, and necessity. Articles of luxury, elegance, and shew are not manufactured in America, excepting a few kinds.

The manufactures of the United States have increased very rapidly since the commencement of the revolutionary war, and particularly in the last five years.

Household manufactures are carried on within the families of almost all the farmers and planters, and of a great proportion of the inhabitants of the villages and towns. This practice is increasing under the animating influences of private interest and public spirit.

• • •

The education of youth has engaged a great share of the attention of the legislatures of the states.

Night schools for young men and boys, who are employed at labour or business in the day time, have been long and beneficially supported, and the idea of Sunday schools has been zealously adopted in some places. Free schools for both sexes have been increased. Greater attention, than heretofore, is paid to female education.

The people of the United States are ingenious in the invention, and prompt, and accurate in the execution of mechanism and workmanship for purposes in science, arts, manufactures, navigation, and agriculture. Rittenhouse's planetarium, Franklin's electrical conductor, Godfrey's quadrant improved by Hadley, Rumsey's and Fitch's steam-engines, Leslie's rod pendulum and other horological inventions, the construction of ships, the New-England whale-boat, the construction of flour-mills, the wire-cutter and bender for card makers, Folsom's and Brigg's machinery for cutting nails out of rolled iron, the Philadelphia dray with an inclined plane, Mason's engine for extinguishing fire, the Connecticut steeple clock, which is wound up by the wind, the Franklin fire-place, the Rittenhouse stove, Anderson's threshing machine, Rittenhouse's instrument for taking levels, Donnaldson's hippopotamos and balance lock, and Wynkoop's underlators, are a few of the numerous examples.

· · ·

A large proportion of the most successful manufacturers in the United States are persons, who were journeymen, and in a few instances were foremen in the work-shops and manufactories of Europe, who having been skilfull, sober and frugal, and having thus saved a little money, have set up for themselves with great advantage in America. Few have failed to succeed. There appears to be least opening for those, who have been used to make very fine and costly articles of luxury and shew. There is not so much chance of success for those luxurious branches, *unless they are capable of being carried on in a considerable degree by machinery or water works;* in which case they also will thrive if the necessary capital be employed.— There is already some consumption of these fine goods in America, and as free an exportation of them (without duty, or excise) as from any country in the world.

44. The Invention of the Cotton Gin

The year 1793 marks a turning point in the history of American economic growth; in that year the cotton gin was invented by Eli Whitney. By drastically reducing the cost of separating cotton lint from the seeds, the cotton gin opened the way to the production of inexpensive textiles. In the process, it ushered in a new era for the American South, the American economy, and for the world's textile industry.

NEW HAVEN, Sept. 11th, 1793.

DEAR PARENT,—I received your letter of the 16th of August with peculiar satisfaction and delight. It gave me no small pleasure to hear of your health and was very happy to be informed that your health and that of the family has been so good since I saw you. I have fortunately just heard from you by Mr. Robbinson who says you were well when he left Westboro. When I wrote you last I

SOURCE: *Correspondence of Eli Whitney,* in *American Historical Review* (New York, 1898), III, 99–101.

expected to have been able to come to Westboro' sooner than I now fear will be in my power. I presume, sir, you are desirous to hear how I have spent my time since I left College. This I conceive you have a right to know and that it is my duty to inform you and should have done it before this time; but I thought I could do it better by verbal communication than by writing, and expecting to see you soon, I omitted it. As I now have a safe and direct opportunity to send by Mr. Robbinson, I will give you a sumary account of my southern expedition.

I went from N. York with the family of the late Major General Greene to Georgia. I went immediately with the family to their Plantation about twelve miles from Savannah with an expectation of spending four or five days and then proceed into Carolina to take the school as I have mentioned in former letters. During this time I heard much said of the extreme difficulty of ginning Cotton, that is, seperating it from its seeds. There were a number of very respectable Gentlemen at Mrs. Greene's who all agreed that if a machine could be invented which would clean the cotton with expedition, it would be a great thing both to the Country and to the inventor. I involuntarily happened to be thinking on the subject and struck out a plan of a Machine in my mind, which I communicated to Miller, (who is agent to the Executors of Genl. Greene and resides in the family, a man of respectibility and property) he was pleased with the Plan and said if I would pursue it and try an experiment to see if it would answer, he would be at the whole expense, I should loose nothing but my time, and if I succeeded we would share the profits. Previous to this I found I was like to be disappointed in my school, that is, instead of a hundred, I found I could get only fifty Guineas a year. I however held the refusal of the school untill I tried some experiments. In about ten Days I made a little model, for which I was offered, if I would give up all right and title to it, a Hundred Guineas. I concluded to relinquish my school and turn my attention to perfecting the Machine. I made one before I came away which required the labor of one man to turn it and with which one man will clean ten times as much cotton as he can in any other way before known and also cleanse it much better than in the usual mode. This machine may be turned by water or with a horse, with the greatest ease, and one man and a horse will do more than fifty men with the old machines. It makes the labor fifty times less, without throwing any class of People out of business.

I returned to the Northward for the purpose of having a machine made on a large scale and obtaining a Patent for the invintion. . . . How advantageous this business will eventually prove to me, I cannot say. It is generally said by those who know anything about it, that I shall make a Fortune by it. I have no expectation that I shall make an independent fortune by it, but think I had better pursue it than any other business into which I can enter. Something which cannot be foreseen may frustrate my expectations and defeat my Plan; but I am now so sure of success that ten thousand dollars, if I saw the money counted out to me, would not tempt me to give up my right and relinquish the object. I wish you, sir, not to show this letter nor communicate anything of its contents to any body except My Brothers and Sister, *enjoining* it on them to keep the whole a *profound secret.*

. . .

With respects to Mama I am,
kind Parent, your most obt. Son

Mr. Eli Whitney.   Eli Whitney, Junr.

45. A Beneficial Consequence of the Napoleonic Wars

Another event occurred in 1793 that led to the expansion of the American economy: the outbreak in Europe of a war of such proportions that it might justly be called the "world war" of the period. Except for a two-year interruption the conflict lasted until 1814, ultimately involving the United States in the War of 1812. However, between 1793 and 1807 the United States prospered mightily as a neutral trader and carrier. A perspicacious observer of the period, Adam Seybert, in the following document comments with mixed emotions on the source of prosperity of the period.

Independent of our newly acquired political character, circumstances arose in Europe, by which a new and extensive field was presented for our commercial enterprize. The most memorable of revo-

SOURCE: Adam Seybert, *Statistical Annals: Embracing Views . . . of the United States of America* (Philadelphia, 1818), 59–60.

lutions was commenced in France, in 1789; the wars, consequent to that event, created a demand for our exports, and invited our shipping for the carrying trade of a very considerable portion of Europe; we not only carried the colonial productions to the several parent states, but we also became the purchasers of them in the French, Spanish and Dutch colonies. A new era was established in our commercial history; the individuals, who partook of these advantages, were numerous; our catalogue of merchants was swelled much beyond what it was entitled to be from the state of our population. Many persons, who had secured moderate capitals, from mechanical pursuits, soon became the most adventurous.[1] The predominant spirit of that time has had a powerful effect in determining the character of the rising generation in the United States. The brilliant prospects held out by commerce, caused our citizens to neglect the mechanical and manufacturing branches of industry; fallacious views, founded on temporary circumstances, carried us from these pursuits, which must ultimately constitute the resources, wealth and power of this nation. Temporary benefits were mistaken for permanent advantages; so certain were the profits on the foreign voyages, that commerce was only pursued as an art; all the knowledge, which former experience had considered as essentially necessary, was now unattended to; the philosophy of commerce, if I am allowed the expression, was totally neglected; the nature of foreign productions was but little investigated by the shippers in the United States; the demand in Europe for foreign merchandise, especially for that of the West Indies and South America, secured to all these cargoes a ready sale, with a great profit. The most adventurous became the most wealthy, and that without the knowledge of any of the principles which govern commerce under ordinary circumstances. No one was limited to any one branch of trade; the same individual was concerned in voyages to Asia, South America, the West Indies and Europe. Our tonnage increased in a ratio, with the extended catalogue of the exports; we seemed to have arrived at the maximum of human prosperity; in proportion to our population we ranked as the most commercial nation; in point of value, our trade was only second to that of Great Britain.

[1] We have no trading companies under the authority of the United States. The occupations here are voluntary; it is very common for persons to change their pursuits frequently; foreigners enjoy the same commercial privileges as the citizens of the United States, except, that *aliens* cannot, in the whole or in part, be the owners of American vessels.

By our extended intercourse with other nations we not only augmented our pecuniary resources, but we thereby became acquainted with their habits, manners, science, arts, resources, wealth and power. At home we imitated them in much that was useful and adapted to our condition; fixed and permanent improvements were established throughout the United States; the accumulated capital of our merchants, enabled them to explore new sources of wealth; our cities were augmented and embellished, our agriculture was improved, our population was increased, and our debt was diminished. The merchants who had been long engaged in trade, were confounded by the changes which were so suddenly effected; the less experienced considered the newly acquired advantages as matters of right, and that they would remain to us; they did not contemplate a period of general peace, when each nation will carry its own productions, when discriminations will be made in favour of domestic tonnage, when foreign commerce will be limited to enumerated articles, and when much circumspection will be necessary in all our commercial transactions.

46. The Growth of Foreign Commerce

The tremendous expansion in shipping and in the export trade which took place in the early period of the French and Napoleonic Wars is documented by statistics, presented by Timothy Pitkin in a book published in 1816, setting down the annual tonnage of ships engaged in foreign commerce. Pitkin's figures reflect accurately the tremendous expansion up until the embargo, the fall-off in trade and shipping that took place during the embargo years, and then the more substantial decline that followed when the United States became involved in war with England in 1812.

The increase of the tonnage of the United States has been without example, in the history of the commercial world. This has been owing to the increased quantity of bulky articles of domestic produce exported, to the increase of their population, and to the extent of their carrying trade.

The actual tonnage was not ascertained, at the Treasury Department, until the year 1793. Previous to that time, the only account

SOURCE: Timothy Pitkin, A *Statistical View of the Commerce of the United States of America* (Hartford, Conn., 1816), 387, 389–91, 35–7.

of the tonnage kept at the Treasury was that, on which duties were collected, and which included the repeated voyages made by the same vessels in the course of the year.

The following is the amount of tonnage on which duties were collected from 1789 to 1792 inclusive, with its employment, in the foreign trade, coasting trade, and fisheries:—

	Foreign trade	Coasting trade	Fisheries
1789	123,893	68,607	9,062
1790	346,254	103,775	28,348
1791	363,110	106,494	32,542
1792	411,438	120,957	32,062

. . .

The amount of registered tonnage, employed in foreign trade, from 1793, to 1813, was as follows, viz.—

TABLE I

	Tons	95ths
1793	367,734	23
1794	438,862	71
1795	529,470	63
1796	576,733	25
1797	597,777	43
1798	603,376	37
1799	669,197	19
1800	669,921	35
1801	718,549	60
1802	560,380	63
1803	597,157	05
1804	672,530	18
1805	749,341	22
1806	808,284	68
1807	848,306	85
1808	769,053	54
1809	910,059	23
1810	984,269	05
1811	768,852	21
1812	760,624	40
1813	674,853	44

And the following tonnage was employed in the coasting trade, from 1793 to 1812.

TABLE II

	Enrolled		Licensed Under 20 tons	
	Tons	95ths	Tons	95ths
1793	114,853	10	7,217	53
1794	167,227	42	16,977	36
1795	164,795	91	19,601	59
1796	195,423	64	22,416	66
1797	214,077	5	23,325	66
1798	227,343	79	24,099	43
1799	220,904	46	25,736	8
1800	245,295	4	27,196	91
1801	246,255	34	28,296	91
1802	260,543	16	29,079	58
1803	268,676	12	30,384	34
1804	286,840	1	30,696	56
1805	301,366	38	31,296	73
1806	309,977	5	30,562	54
1807	318,189	93	30,838	39
1808	387,684	43	33,135	33
1809	371,500	56	33,661	75
1810	371,114	12	34,232	57
1811	Enrolled and licensed, 420,362			
1812	do. do. 477,971			

The increase of the registered tonnage, or that employed in foreign trade, from 1793 to 1801, was three hundred and fifty thousand eight hundred and fifteen tons and thirty-seven ninety-fifths, having nearly doubled, in that short period. From 1793 to 1810, a period of seventeen years, the increase of tonnage, employed in foreign trade, was six hundred sixteen thousand five hundred and thirty-five tons and eighty-two ninety-fifths. In 1793, the tonnage employed in the coasting trade, was one hundred twenty-two thousand and seventy tons and sixty-three ninety-fifths, and in 1801, amounted to two hundred seventy-four thousand five hundred and fifty-one tons, making a difference of one hundred fifty-two thousand four hundred and eighty-one tons; and from 1793 to 1810, the increase was two hundred eighty-three thousand two hundred and seventy-six tons. We have before stated the amount of tonnage employed in the fisheries; the increase from 1793 to 1807, was about forty thousand tons. Tables No. I. and II. contain the amount of tonnage, annually employed, in foreign trade, and in the coasting trade, owned in each state, from 1793 to 1810.

We shall begin with the exports—those consist of articles of the growth, produce, and manufacture of the United States, and of those which are of foreign growth and produce. Provision was made at the Treasury, at an early period of the present government, to ascertain the quantity and value of all the exports of the country; but in the general accounts no discrimination was made between the value of domestic or foreign articles, until 1802. In order to ascertain the value of the exports, directions are given, from the Treasury department, to the several collectors of the customs, to add, in their quarterly returns of duties the quantity of the various articles exported, and also their prices at the places of exportation. The quantity of the articles exported is furnished the collectors, by the exporters, and may sometimes fall short, and sometimes exceed the real quantity. At the Treasury, an average is made of the prices returned by the collectors, from the principal ports, and the value of the articles exported is calculated from the average price thus ascertained.

The whole value of exports in each year, from 1790 to 1814, and the value of those of domestic and foreign origin, since 1803, was as follows:—

to[1] Sept. 30	Total value of exports Dollars	Value of exports of domestic origin Dollars	Value of exports of foreign origin Dollars
1791	19,012,041		
1792	20,753,098		
1793	26,109,572		
1794	33,026,233		
1795	47,989,472		
1796	67,064,097		
1797	56,850,206		
1798	61,527,097		
1799	78,665,522		
1800	70,971,780		
1801	94,115,925		
1802	72,483,160		
1803	55,800,033	42,205,961	13,594,072
1804	77,699,074	41,467,477	36,231,597
1805	95,566,021	42,387,002	53,179,019
1806	101,536,963	41,253,727	60,283,236
1807	108,343,150	48,699,592	59,643,558
1808	22,430,960	9,433,546	12,997,414
1809	52,203,283	31,405,702	20,797,531
1810	66,757,970	42,366,675	24,391,295
1811	61,316,833	45,294,043	16,022,790
1812	38,527,236	30,032,109	8,495,127
1813	27,855,997	25,008,152	2,847,845
1814	6,927,441	6,782,272	145,169

[1] No annual return of exports had been made at the Treasury, prior to October, 1790.

47. The State of American Manufacturing in 1810

When the embargo put an end to America's wartime prosperity in 1807, the capital and labor once committed to commerce and shipping were driven to seek new outlets. In many cases, the shift was into manufacturing—a logical choice, since the embargo which curtailed America's shipping activities also cut off the imports to this country and resulted in a greatly increased demand for domestic production. By 1810, Albert Gallatin was moved to comment with due caution that America's future as a manufacturing nation was now becoming more assured.

From that imperfect sketch of American manufactures, it may, with certainty, be inferred that their annual product exceeds one hundred and twenty millions of dollars. And it is not improbable that the raw materials used, and the provisions and other articles consumed, by the manufacturers, create a home market for agricultural products not very inferior to that which arises from foreign demand. A result more favorable than might have been expected from a view of the natural causes which impede the introduction, and retard the progress of manufactures in the United States.

The most prominent of those causes are the abundance of land compared with the population, the high price of labor, and the want of a sufficient capital. The superior attractions of agricultural pursuits, the great extension of American commerce during the late European wars, and the continuance of habits after the causes which produced them have ceased to exist, may also be enumerated. Several of those obstacles have, however, been removed or lessened. The cheapness of provisions had always, to a certain extent, counterbalanced the high price of manual labor; and this is now, in many important branches, nearly superseded by the introduction of machinery; a great American capital has been acquired during the last twenty years; and the injurious violations of the neutral commerce of the United States, by forcing industry and capital into other channels, have broken inveterate habits, and given a general impulse, to which must be ascribed the great increase of manufactures during the two last years.

The revenue of the United States, being principally derived from duties on the importation of foreign merchandise, these have also

SOURCE: Albert Gallatin, in *Documents, Legislative and Executive, of the Congress of the United States*, American State Papers, Walter Lowrie (ed.) (Washington, D.C., 1832), 430–1.

operated as a premium in favor of American manufactures, whilst, on the other hand, the continuance of peace, and the frugality of Government, have rendered unnecessary any oppressive taxes, tending materially to enhance the price of labor, or impeding any species of industry.

No cause, indeed, has, perhaps, more promoted, in every respect, the general prosperity of the United States, than the absence of those systems of internal restrictions and monopoly which continue to disfigure the state of society in other countries. No law exists here, directly or indirectly, confining man to a particular occupation or place, or excluding any citizen from any branch, he may, at any time, think proper to pursue. Industry is, in every respect, perfectly free and unfettered; every species of trade, commerce, art, profession and manufacture, being equally opened to all, without requiring any previous regular apprenticeship, admission, or licence. Hence the progress of America has not been confined to the improvement of her agriculture, and to the rapid formation of new settlements and States in the wilderness; but her citizens have extended their commerce through every part of the globe, and carry on with complete success, even those branches for which a monopoly had heretofore been considered essentially necessary.

The same principle has also accelerated the introduction and progress of manufactures, and must ultimately give in that branch, as in all others, a decided superiority to the citizens of the United States over the inhabitants of countries oppressed by taxes, restrictions and monopolies. It is believed that, even at this time, the only powerful obstacle against which American manufactures have to struggle, arises from the vastly superior capital of the first manufacturing nation of Europe, which enables her merchants to give very long credits, to sell on small profits, and to make occasional sacrifices.

The information which has been obtained is not sufficient to submit, in conformity with the resolution of the House, the plan best calculated to protect and promote American manufactures. The most obvious means are bounties, increased duties on importation, and loans by Government.

Occasional premiums might be beneficial; but a general system of bounties is more applicable to articles exported than to those manufactured for home consumption.

The present system of duties may, in some respects, be equalized and improved, so as to protect some species of manufactures without effecting the revenue. But prohibitory duties are liable to the treble objection of destroying competition, of taxing the consumer, and of diverting capital and industry into channels generally less profitable to the nation than those which would have naturally been pursued by individual interest left to itself. A moderate increase will be less dangerous, and, if adopted, should be continued during a certain period; for the repeal of a duty once laid, materially injures those who have relied on its permanency, as has been exemplified in the salt manufacture.

Since, however, the comparative want of capital, is the principal obstacle to the introduction and advancement of manufactures in America, it seems that the most efficient, and most obvious remedy would consist in supplying that capital. For, although the extension of banks may give some assistance in that respect, their operation is limited to a few places, nor does it comport with the nature of those institutions to lend for periods as long as are requisite for the establishment of manufactures. The United States might create a circulating stock, bearing a low rate of interest, and lend it at par to manufacturers, on principles somewhat similar to that formerly adopted by the States of New York and Pennsylvania, in their *loan offices*. It is believed that a plan might be devised by which five millions of dollars a year, but not exceeding, in the whole, twenty millions, might be thus lent, without any material risk of ultimate loss, and without taxing or injuring any other part of the community.

All which is respectfully submitted.

TREASURY DEPARTMENT, *April 17th*, 1810.

ALBERT GALLATIN.

VII

General Introduction to the Period 1814-1860

Between the end of the second war with England and the firing on Fort Sumter, nearly fifty years of peace intervened, interrupted only briefly in this country by the Mexican War and abroad by the Crimean War.

At some unspecified time during this period, American economic growth accelerated both extensively and intensively, to set the pace which it has maintained ever since. Extensive growth involved the outward spread of population and enterprise westward toward the frontiers. Intensive growth lay in the expansion of productivity within the economy which reflected, in part, the westward movement and the resultant burgeoning of trade between the three regions of the South, the West, and the Northeast.

The pivot of this trade was the export market in cotton, which led to a demand for foodstuffs from the West to feed both the South and the Northeast (and later to be exported by them in turn). Meanwhile, stimulated by such interregional trade, the Northeast developed, first, shipping services and, next, some manufacturing. By the 1820's and 1830's, the pace of manufacturing was expanding rapidly, so that by this period every sector of the economy was spinning with activity, and an increase of efficiency and productivity was experienced alike in manufacturing, in services, and in agriculture.

48. The Disposal of the Public Lands

Questions surrounding the disposal of the public lands continued as a subject for debate throughout the nineteenth century. Endless arguments centered on the influence of land policy on economic growth, and pressure was continuous for reduction in the minimum price per acre and for changes in the credit terms. In perspective, it appears that the disposal policy as carried out accelerated both the westward movement and the over-all growth of the American economy, and that it encouraged the inpouring of capital as well as of labor from other lands and

182

from the eastern United States. In this selection, Henry Clay speaks for
the Committee on Manufactures in presenting to the Senate the pros
and cons of a possible reduction in price on public lands.

This uniform system of surveying and dividing the public lands,
applies to all the States and Territories within which they are situated. Its great advantages are manifest. It insures perfect security of
title and certainty of boundary, and consequently avoids those per-
plexing land disputes, the worst of all species of litigation, the dis-
tressing effects of which have been fatally experienced in some of
the western States. But these are not the only advantages, great as
they unquestionably are. The system lays the foundation of useful
civil institutions, the benefit of which is not confined to the present
generation, but will be transmitted to posterity.

Under the operation of the system, thus briefly sketched, the
progress of the settlement and population of the public domain of
the United States has been altogether unexampled. Views which the
committee will hereafter present, conclusively demonstrate that,
whilst the spirit of free emigration should not be checked or counteracted, it stands in no need of any fresh stimulus.

Before proceeding to perform the specific duty assigned to the
committee by the Senate, they had thought it desirable to exhibit
some general views of this great national resource. For that purpose,
a call, through the Senate for information, has been made upon the
Executive branch of the Government. A report has not yet been
made; but, as the committee are desirous of avoiding any delay, not
altogether indispensable, they have availed themselves of a report
from the Secretary of the Treasury to the House of Representatives,
under date the 6th April, 1832, and of such other information as was
accessible to them.

From that report, it appears that the aggregate of all sums of
money which have been expended by the United States in the acquisition of the public lands, including interest on account of the
purchases of Louisiana and Florida, up to the 30th day of September, 1831, and including also expenses in their sale and management, is $48,077,551.40; and that the amount of money received
at the Treasury, for proceeds of the sales of the public lands to the
30th September, 1831, is $37,272,713.31. The Government, there-

SOURCE: U. S. Congress, Senate, *Report by Henry Clay*, 22nd Cong., 1st
sess., 1832, 3–9.

fore, has not been reimbursed by $10,804,838%10. According to the same report, it appears that the estimated amount of unsold lands, on which the foreign and Indian titles have been extinguished, is 227,293,884 within the limits of the new States and Territories; and that the Indian title remains on 113,577,869 acres within the same limits. That there have been granted to Ohio, Indiana, Illinois and Alabama, for internal improvements, 2,187,665 acres; for colleges, academies and universities in the new States and Territories, the quantity of 508,009; for education, being the thirty-sixth part of the public lands appropriated for common schools, the amount of 7,952,538 acres; and for seats of Government in some of the new States and Territories, 21,589 acres. By a report of the Commissioner of the General Land Office, communicated to Congress with the annual message of the President of the United States in December, 1827, the total quantity of the public lands, beyond the boundaries of the new States and Territories, was estimated to be 750,000,000. The aggregate, therefore, of all the unsold and unappropriated public lands of the United States, surveyed and unsurveyed, on which the Indian title remains or has been extinguished, lying within, and without the boundaries of the new States and Territories, agreeably to the two reports now referred to, is 1,090,-871,753 acres. There had been 138,988,224 acres surveyed, and the quantity only of 19,239,412 acres sold up to the 1st January, 1826. When the information called for shall be received, the subsequent surveys and sales up to the present period will be ascertained.

The committee are instructed by the Senate to inquire into the expediency of reducing the price of the public lands, and also of ceding them to the several States in which they are situated on reasonable terms. The committee will proceed to examine these two subjects of inquiry distinctly, beginning first with that which relates to a reduction of price.

I. According to the existing mode of selling the public lands, they are first offered at public auction for what they will bring in a free and fair competition among the purchasers; when the public sales cease, the lands remaining unsold may be bought, from time to time, at the established rate of one dollar and a quarter per acre. The price was reduced to that sum in 1820, from $2 per acre, at which it had previously stood from the first establishment of the present system of selling the public lands. A leading consideration with Congress in the reduction of the price, was that of substituting cash sales for the credits which had been before allowed, and which, on many accounts, it was deemed expedient to abolish. A further reduction of the price, if called for by the public interests, must be required, either, 1st. Because the Government now demands more than a fair price for the public lands; or, 2dly. Because the existing price retards, injuriously, the settlement and population of the new States and Territories. These suggestions deserve separate and serious consideration.

1. The committee possess no means of determining the exact value of all the public lands now in market; nor is it material, at the present time, that the precise worth of each township or section should be accurately known. It is presumable that a considerable portion of the immense quantity offered to sale, or held by the United States, would not now command, and may not be intrinsically worth the minimum price fixed by law; on the other hand, it is certain that a large part is worth more. If there could be a discrimination made, and the Government had any motive to hasten the sales beyond the regular demands of the population, it might be proper to establish different rates, according to the classes of land; but the Government having no inducement to such acceleration, has hitherto proceeded on the liberal policy of establishing a moderate price, and by subdivisions of the sections so as to accommodate the poorer citizens, has placed the acquisition of a home within the reach of every industrious man. For $100 any one may now purchase eighty, or for $50, forty acres of first rate land, yielding, with proper cultivation, from fifty to eighty bushels of Indian corn, per acre, or other equivalent crops.

There is no more satisfactory criterion of the fairness of the price of an article, than that arising from the briskness of sales when it is offered in the market. On applying this rule, the conclusion would seem to be irresistible, that the established price is not too high. The amount of the sales in the year 1828, was $1,018,308.75; in 1829, $1,517,175.13; in 1830, $2,329,356.14; and, during the year 1831, $3,000,000. And the Secretary of the Treasury observes in his annual report, at the commencement of this session, that "the receipts from the public lands, during the present year, it will be perceived, have likewise exceeded the estimates, and indeed *have gone beyond all former example*. It is believed that, notwithstanding the large amount of scrip and forfeited land stock that may still be absorbed in payment for lands, yet if the surveys now projected be completed, the receipts from this source of revenue will not fall greatly below those of the present year." And he estimates the receipts during the current year, from this source, at three millions of dollars. It is incredible to suppose that the amount of sales would have risen to so large a sum, if the price had been unreasonably high. The committee are aware that the annual receipts may be expected to fluctuate, as fresh lands, in favorite districts, are brought into market, and according to the activity or sluggishness of emigration in different years.

Against any considerable reduction of the price of the public lands, unless it be necessary to a more rapid population of the new States, which will be hereafter examined, there are weighty, if not decisive considerations:

1. The Government is the proprietor of much the largest quantity of the unseated lands of the United States. What it has in market, bears a large proportion to the whole of the occupied lands within their limits. If a considerable quantity of any article, land, or any commodity whatever, is in market, the price at which it is sold, will affect, in some degree, the value of the whole of that article, whether exposed to sale or not. The influence of a reduction of the price of the public lands would probably be felt throughout the Union; certainly in all the western States, and most in those which contain, or are nearest to, the public lands. There ought to be the most cogent and conclusive reasons for adopting a measure which might seriously impair the value of the property of the yeomanry of the country. Whilst it is decidedly the most important class in the community, most patient, patriotic, and acquiescent in whatever public policy is pursued, it is unable or unwilling to resort to those means of union and concert which other interests employ to make themselves heard and respected. Government should, therefore, feel itself constantly bound to guard, with sedulous care, the rights and welfare of the great body of our yeomanry. Would it be just towards those who have heretofore purchased public lands at higher prices, to say nothing as to the residue of the agricultural interest of the United States, to make such a reduction, and thereby impair the value of their property? Ought not any such plan of reduction, if adopted, to be accompanied with compensation for the injury which they would inevitably sustain?

2. A material reduction of price would excite and stimulate the

spirit of speculation, now dormant, and probably lead to a transfer of vast quantities of the public domain from the control of Government to the hands of the speculator. At the existing price, and with such extensive districts as the public constantly offers in the market, there is no great temptation to speculation. The demand is regular, keeping pace with the progress of emigration, and is supplied on known and moderate terms. If the price were much reduced, the strongest incentives to engrossment of the better lands would be presented to large capitalists; and the emigrant, instead of being able to purchase from his own Government upon uniform and established conditions, might be compelled to give much higher and more fluctuating prices to the speculator. An illustration of this effect is afforded by the military bounty lands granted during the late war. Thrown into the market at prices below the Government rate, they notoriously became an object of speculation, and have principally fallen into the hands of speculators, retarding the settlement of the districts which include them.

3. The greatest emigration that is believed now to take place from any of the States, is from Ohio, Kentucky, and Tennessee. The effects of a material reduction in the price of the public lands, would be, 1st, To lessen the value of real estate in those three States. 2d. To diminish their interest in the public domain, as a common fund for the benefit of all the States. And, 3dly. To offer what would operate as a bounty to further emigration from those States, occasioning more and more lands, situated within them, to be thrown into the market, thereby not only lessening the value of their lands, but draining them both of their population and currency.

And, lastly, Congress has, within a few years, made large and liberal grants of the public lands to several States. To Ohio, 922,-937 acres; to Indiana, 384,728 acres; to Illinois, 480,000 acres; and to Alabama, 400,000 acres; amounting, together, to 2,187,665 acres. Considerable portions of these lands yet remain unsold. The reduction of the price of the public lands, generally, would impair the value of those grants, as well as injuriously affect that of the lands which have been sold in virtue of them.

On the other hand, it is inferred and contended, from the large amount of public land remaining unsold, after having been so long exposed to sale, that the price at which it is held is too high. But this apparent tardiness is satisfactorily explained by the immense quantity of public lands which have been put into the market by Government. It is well known that the new States have constantly and urgently pressed the extinction of the Indian title upon lands within their respective limits; and, after its extinction, that they should be brought into market as rapidly as practicable. The liberal policy of the General Government, coinciding with the wishes of the new States, has prompted it to satisfy the wants of emigrants from every part of the Union, by exhibiting vast districts of land for sale, in all the States and Territories, thus offering every variety of climate and situation to the free choice of settlers. From these causes, it has resulted that the power of emigration has been totally incompetent to absorb the immense bodies of waste lands offered in the market. For the capacity to purchase is, after all, limited by the emigration, and the progressive increase of population. If the quantity thrown into the market had been quadrupled, the probability is that there would not have been much more annually sold than actually has been. With such extensive fields for selection before them, purchasers, embarrassed as to the choice which they should make, are sometimes probably influenced by caprice or accidental causes. Whilst the better lands remain, those of secondary value will not be purchased. A judicious farmer or planter would sooner give one dollar and a quarter per acre for first rate land, than receive as a donation land of inferior quality, if he were compelled to settle upon it.

· · ·

2. Is the reduction of the price of the public lands necessary to accelerate the settlement and population of the States within which they are situated? Those States are Ohio, Indiana, Illinois, Missouri, Alabama, Mississippi, and Louisiana. If their growth has been unreasonably slow and tardy, we may conclude that some fresh impulse, such as that under consideration, is needed. Prior to the treaty of Greenville, concluded in 1795, there were but few settlements within the limits of the present State of Ohio. Principally since that period, that is, within a term of about forty years, that State, from a wilderness, the haunt of savages and wild beasts, has risen into a powerful commonwealth, containing, at this time, a population of a million of souls, and holding the third or fourth rank among the largest States in the Union. During the greater part of that term, the minimum price of the public lands was two dollars

per acre; and of the large quantity with which the settlement of that State commenced, there only remain to be sold 5,586,834 acres.

The aggregate population of the United States, exclusive of the Territories, increased from the year 1820 to 1830, from 9,579,873 to 12,716,697. The rate of the increase, during the whole term of ten years, including a fraction, may be stated at thirty-three per cent. The principle of population is presumed to have full scope generally in all parts of the United States. Any State, therefore, which has exceeded or fallen short of that rate, may be fairly assumed to have gained or lost, by emigration, nearly to the extent of the excess or deficiency. From a table accompanying this report . . . it will be seen that each of eleven States exceeded, and each of thirteen fell short of an increase at the average rate of thirty-three per cent. The greatest increase, during the term, was in the State of Illinois, where it was one hundred and eighty five per cent, or at the rate of 18½ per cent. per annum; and the least was in Delaware, where it was less than six per cent. The seven States embracing the public lands, had a population, in 1820, of 1,207,165, and, in 1830, 2,238,802, exhibiting an average increase of 85 per cent. The seventeen States containing no part of the public lands, had a population, in 1820, of 8,372,707, and, in 1830, of 10,477,895. presenting an average increase of only 25 per cent. The thirteen States, whose increase, according to the table, was below 33 per cent. contained, in 1820, a population of 5,939,759, and, in 1830, of 6,966,600, exhibiting an average increase of only seventeen per cent. The increase of the seven new States upon a capital which, at the commencement of the term, was 1,207,165, has been greater than that of the thirteen, whose capital then was 5,939,759. In three of the eleven States, (Tennessee, Georgia, and Maine,) whose population exceeded the average increase of 33 per cent, there were public lands belonging to those States; and in the fourth, (New York,) the excess is probably attributable to the rapid growth of the city of New York, to waste lands in the western part of that State, and to the great development of its vast resources by means of extensive internal improvements.

These authentic views of the progress of population in the seven new States, demonstrate that it is most rapid and gratifying; that it needs no such additional stimulus as a farther reduction in the price of the public lands; and that, by preserving and persevering in the established system for selling them, the day is near at hand when those States, now respectable, may become great and powerful members of the confederacy.

49. The Role of Cotton

Between 1814 and 1860, the growth of the American economy was stimulated to a great extent by the expansion of one major product—cotton. American exports of cotton provided a major share of the world supply and contributed more than half of the value of the nation's total exports. Her external trade relations, the prosperity and expansion of the South, and the influence of the South upon other economic regions, all hinged on that one vital crop. The dominant role of cotton in the world market as well as in America's trade was emphasized by Israel D. Andrews in a report to the House of Representatives in 1853.

The cotton crop of the United States now amounts to upwards of seven-tenths of all the cotton produced in the world. The quantity annually *exported* from the United States is about eight-tenths of the aggregate of all exported by all countries.

The following estimates, compiled from the best authorities, sustain these statements:

Cotton Crop of the World, of 1851; and exports of all countries in 1852.

	lbs.	lbs. exported
United States	1,350,000,000	1,093,230,639
Egypt, &c	40,000,000	25,000,000
East Indies	200,000,000	150,000,000
West Indies	3,100,000	3,000,000
Demerara, Berbice, &c	700,000	500,000
Bahia, Macelo, &c	14,000,000	11,000,000
Maranham, &c	12,000,000	9,000,000
Pernambuco, Aracati, Ceara, &c	30,000,000	25,000,000
Brazil, China, and all other places	250,000,000	40,000,000
Total	1,899,800,000	1,366,730,639

The first column of the above states all that is estimated to be consumed, in the countries named, in "household" manufactures and for various domestic uses, as well as that used in their home

SOURCE: U. S. Congress, House, *Communication from the Secretary of the Treasury Transmitting the Report of Israel D. Andrews . . . ,* 32nd Cong., 2nd sess., 1853, 818, 824–7.

cotton manufactories, and likewise all exported to other countries. In the second column is estimated the exports to contiguous foreign countries for manufacture, as well as the exports to Europe, &c. In the East Indies such exportations, to contiguous countries, is not *less* than the amount stated. An English writer, in 1824, (Smither's History of Liverpool, p. 116,) says, with respect to China, that cotton and cotton manufactures are "estimated to employ, directly and indirectly, nearly *nine-tenths* of the immense population of that country. A very large proportion of what is made is used for internal consumption, particularly the very finest and most costly fabrics. Nankeens and chintzes form the principal articles of their exportations."

This estimate, it is believed, overrates the number of persons so employed. One-tenth of the 350,000,000 there may be so employed, but not more. The United States exported, in 1852, upwards of $2,200,000 of domestic cotton manufactures (coarse white muslins) to China. We formerly procured some nankeens from China; but our imports of cotton goods from thence are now comparatively nothing. The above estimate as to the crop in China is doubtless too small, but the production there is decreasing.

· · ·

The following table of all the exportations from the United States since 1789, up to and including 1852, will be found useful in estimating the value of the cotton crop.

From the [following] tables, and others contained in this paper, or annexed hereto it appears that cotton and domestic manufactures now constitute more than one-half of the exports of the United States of agricultural products and domestic manufactures thereof. They constitute more than two-fifths of the total exportations of all kinds, including "products of the sea," "products of the forest," as well as the "products of agriculture" and "manufactures," "bullion and specie," &c. The statements from the treasury books show, with reference to "*exportation*," how far behind cotton every other agricultural product is, as to its increase, beyond the necessary consumption of the United States, since cotton has been cultivated for the foreign market. Generally a country does not export any but its *surplus* productions. Vast as the increase of some of our other agricultural products besides cotton has been, such increase has, in but few seasons, exceeded the increased wants of our population, constantly and rapidly augmenting by emigration.

Exportations (specie, &c., included) from the United States since 1790.

Years	Total	Domestic	Foreign
1790, '91, and '92	$59,970,295	$57,166,000	$2,804,295
1793, '94, and '95	107,125,277	90,000,000	17,125,277
1796, '97, and '98	185,441,400	99,141,400	86,300,000
1779, 1800, and '1	243,753,227	112,456,629	131,296,598
1802, '3, and '4	205,982,267	120,381,627	85,600,640
1805, '6, and '7	305,446,134	132,340,321	173,105,813
1808, (embargo)	22,430,960	9,433,546	12,997,414
1809, '10, and '11	180,278,036	119,066,420	61,211,616
1812, '13, and '14 (war)	73,310,674	61,822,538	11,488,141
1815, '16, and '17	222,149,764	179,069,799	43,079,975
1818, '19, and '20	233,115,323	176,514,915	56,600,408
1821, '22, and '23	211,833,799	140,701,487	71,132,312
1824, '25, and '26	253,117,367	170,649,955	82,467,412
1827, '28, and '29	226,948,184	165,291,553	61,656,631
1830, '31, and '32	242,337,034	183,876,556	58,460,478
1833, '34, and '35	316,170,983	252,530,942	63,640,041
1836, '37, and '38	354,569,032	298,514,915	56,054,117
1839, '40, and '41	374,966,165	323,812,247	51,153,918
1842, '43, and '44	300,238,060	270,478,958	29,759,102
1845, '46, and '47	386,783,744	352,079,133	34,704,611
1848, '49, and '50	451,685,671	402,513,683	49,172,988
1851	218,388,011	196,689,718	21,698,293
1852	209,641,625	197,604,582	12,037,043

It is important, in connexion with the tables hereinbefore given, to notice the importations and exportations of bullion and specie. The following is a statement thereof since 1821:

Bullion and coin imported and exported since 1821.

Years	Value of imports	Difference	Value of exports	Difference
1821, '22, and '23	$16,532,632		$27,661,226	$11,128,594
1824, '25, and '26	21,411,566	$895,426	20,516,140	
1827, '28, and '29	23,044,483	1,862,107	21,182,376	
1830, '31, and '32	21,369,413	4,519,369	16,850,044	
1833, '34, and '35	38,113,447	26,947,213	11,166,234	
1836, '37, and '38	41,664,411	27,855,780	13,808,631	
1839, '40, and '41	19,466,622		27,228,089	7,761,467
1842, '43, and '44	32,237,780	20,449,236	11,788,544	
1845, '46, and '47	31,969,263	17,549,761	14,419,502	
1848, '49, and '50	17,640,256		28,769,262	11,129,006
1851	5,453,981		29,465,752	24,011,771
1852	5,503,544		42,674,135	37,170,591
Aggregate	274,407,398	100,078,892	265,529,935	91,201,429

It is not within the proper range of this paper to comment upon any of the different opinions entertained with respect to the causes and effects of the fluctuations exhibited in the above statement, and in the detailed table annexed hereto of these imports and exports. Some political economists contend that what is called the "balance of trade" being in favor of or against the United States, as shown by the importation or exportation of bullion and specie, is the best evidence of the prosperous or unprosperous condition of our trade and commerce. On the other hand, others insist that such importation or exportation is no true test on either side; and that when any country has a surplus of bullion and specie, it is best to export a portion of the redundant supply; and that then those articles, besides fulfilling their proper functions of being the media and regulators and equalizers of trade and commerce, become themselves legitimate subjects of trade and commerce like other products; and that this rule especially applies to a country *producing* the precious metals.

The sole object, however, of the reference now made to the importation and exportation of bullion and specie is to notice the fact, equally forcible as respects both of these theories, that but for exportations of raw cotton, according to the treasury statistics, more than forty-eight millions of bullion and specie would have been required annually, since 1821, to have been exported (in addition to all that was exported) to meet the balances of trade against us that would have existed but for those exportations of raw cotton. It is true the treasury accounts of *exports* are not safe criteria as to values, they being in the United States, as in other countries, generally undervalued; but without the exportations of cotton from the United States, the balance-sheet would be a sorry exhibit of our condition as a commercial people, and of general prosperity. Our other exports, and especially of other agricultural products, are, when separately estimated, really insignificant in comparison with cotton. A table of the exportations of the principal domestic exports, since 1821, is appended. The following statement shows the principal domestic exports in the years 1821, '22, and '23, and in the years 1850, '51, and '52:

Articles	1821, '22, and '23	1850, '51, and '52
Total exports of domestic produce	$140,701,381	$526,005,614
Cotton	64,638,062	272,265,665
Tobacco	18,154,472	29,201,556
Rice	4,878,774	7,273,513
Flour	14,363,696	29,492,044
Pork, hogs, lard, &c	4,003,337	15,683,772
Beef, hides, tallow, &c	2,282,318	4,795,645
Butter and cheese	604,106	3,119,506
Skins and furs	1,940,424	2,628,732
Fish	2,894,229	1,391,475
Lumber, &c	4,156,078	15,054,113
Manufactures of all kinds	9,013,259	51,376,348

Among other articles not specified in this statement there was exported in 1852 over $1,200,000 of oils, $1,200,000 of naval stores, $500,000 of pot and pearl ash, $2,500,000 of wheat, $2,100,000 of Indian corn and meal, and $1,100,000 of "raw produce," kind not stated in returns.

The relative importance and value of the cotton crop of the United States to the other leading agricultural products of this country, and other principal articles of our domestic and foreign commerce, is more striking when the circumstances attendant upon the progress of each crop, and the others respectively, are considered. The augmentation of our population—the vast extension of our territory—the great increase of the area of our lands in tillage —the immense additions to our agricultural labor in our native population and in foreign emigrants—have given us consequent vastly increased resources and ability for greater production. As before shown, however, the greater portions of most of the agricultural products of the United States, and of the manufactures of them, except cotton, *are consumed in the United States.* The fact that the *exportations* from the United States of many of its most important products have not increased in proportion to our increase of population, resources, and ability, and that the article of *raw cotton* is a signal exception, surely is some evidence of its value and of the real position and actual increase of the wealth and prosperity of the cotton region. When it is recollected that very little of the additional labor given by *foreign emigration* inures to the cultivation of cotton, (and it is estimated that not more than one in 600 of the agricultural emigrants go to the cotton region;) and when the extent of internal improvements in the States where cotton is not grown, to transport their produce to market, is considered, it will be seen that this advancement of the cotton region is solely the result of steady industry, regulated by the intelligence to make it advantageous. The increased labor of that region has been almost exclusively derived from those contiguous States that do not cultivate cotton. The disparity between the increase of cotton and that of other agricultural products appears much greater when these facts are considered; and the doctrine that labor advantageously applied, and not population merely, is the true foundation of a country's wealth and prosperity, is fully verified.

The treasury accounts before referred to show that the aggregate increase of our foreign *importations* of merchandise has not equalled our increased exportations of raw cotton, and that it, as before stated, has most of all other articles enabled us to keep down the balance against us created by such importations. And it should be noticed, also, that the increase of importations is mainly for the use and consumption of those portions of the country that do not produce cotton. The consumption of imported merchandise and products in the cotton region may be greater than the proportion of its white population to that of other sections, but in the aggregate it is much less, and it is also much less than the proportion of its whole population to that of the other States.

Adding the increase of the *exportations* of our domestic manufactures of cotton to the exportations of raw cotton, the comparison between it and other agricultural products is still more favorable to it. Prior to 1826, such *exportations*, if any were made, were not specified in the treasury returns, and all our importations of cotton goods specified in those returns are exclusively those of *foreign* manufacture that had been imported hither. And the nearly total decrease of the importation of foreign raw cotton, and the manufactures thereof, and the substitution therefore of our own product, and manufactures thereof, should also be estimated.

Nor is the supply furnished from the cotton crop for the numerous "household" or "home-made" manufactures used in the United States an unimportant item constituting its value. The aggregate of the value of all these manufactures was, in 1849, upwards of

$27,540,000, and it is estimated, as before stated, that the cotton consumed in them is worth annually upwards of $7,500,000. But for our own crop, this would have to be imported.

50. Internal Trade Between the West and South

While generally shaping the economic development of the whole South, the production of cotton specifically resulted in the tremendous growth of New Orleans. The city became for a time the leading export center of the United States, exporting cotton from the "new" South and also serving as entrepôt for the flow of goods down the Mississippi from the West. The growth of this vital trade between West and South and the consequent expansion of New Orleans are described in a report on the internal commerce of the United States, published in 1888.

IMMIGRATION INTO THE MISSISSIPPI VALLEY

It was just about the time of the discovery of steam as a motive power for steam-boats that a new tide of immigration started from the Atlantic coast to the river country. There had been a rapid growth of the population of the valley from the date of the purchase of Louisiana, but between 1810 and 1820 that movement received a new impetus—probably due to the war of 1812. This movement went down the Ohio and into all the region tributary to it and to the Mississippi, both the upper and the lower portions. The immigrant guide-books of those days—of which there were many—declare the river route preferable, as being cheaper, more rapid, and more satisfactory than traveling across the country where there were few, if any, roads. The river bottoms both of the Ohio and Mississippi Rivers were then regarded as very unhealthy and dangerous sections, and the immigrant was advised not to start on his trip until in the fall, after the frosts had killed the malaria. The guide-books describe the rivers as being very unpleasant during the summer season, with offensive odors coming from the shores. The immigrants were also warned against drinking river water before filtering or boiling it. On flat-boats and on pine rafts, the latter being deemed the better plan, thousands of settlers drifted down the

SOURCE: U. S. Congress, House, *Report on the Internal Commerce of the United States*, by Wm. F. Switzler, 50th Cong., 1st sess., 1888, 190–1, 198–9, 205, 214–5.

rivers each year, and in the short space of a decade the population of the Mississippi Valley doubled.

RECEIPTS OF PRODUCE

The receipts of New Orleans during the first year of successful steam navigation, 1816, amounted in value to $8,062,540. The character of produce received will furnish an excellent comparison for subsequent years by showing the lines of goods in which a trade was developed.

Articles	Quantity	Articles	Quantity
Apples, barrels	4,253	Horses, number	375
Beef, do	2,459	Hogs, do	500
Beans, do	439	Lead, cwts	5,500
Bagging, pieces	2,579	White lead, barrels	188
Bacon and hams, cwts	1,300	Linens, coarse, pieces	2,500
Butter, pounds	509	Lard, barrels	2,458
Candles, boxes	358	Oats, bushels	4,065
Cheese, cwts	30	Paper, reams	750
Cider, barrels	646	Peltries, packages	2,450
Cordage, cwts	400	Pork, barrels	9,725
Cordage baling, coils	4,798	Potatoes, do	3,750
Corn, bushels	13,775	Powder, do	294
Corn-meal, barrels	1,075	Saltpeter, cwts	175
Cotton, bales	37,371	Soap, boxes	1,538
Flaxseed oil, barrels	85	Tallow, cwts	160
Flour, do	97,419	Tobacco, hogsheads	7,282
Ginseng, do	957	Manufactured, barrels	711
Hair, bundles	356	Tobacco, carrots	8,200
Hemp-yarn, reels	1,095	Whisky, gallons	320,000
Hides, number	5,000	Bear-skins, number	2,000

Besides horned cattle, indigo, muskets, grindstones, pecan nuts, and beans.

This is independent of the produce raised in Louisiana, such as cotton, corn, indigo, molasses, rice, sugar, tafia or rum, and lumber. These were brought to the market in the planters' crafts, and often taken from the plantation direct in foreign-bound vessels, a ship loading directly with sugar and molasses, which thus never went through New Orleans. But little account was taken of this system in the commercial reports of the time, although sea-going vessels ascended the river as far as Natchez for cargoes. They were, of course, of small size, of but little more tonnage and draught than the steam-boats themselves.

The value of receipts shows to what extent the produce of the West passed through New Orleans. Cotton, which in later days rose to be 60 and even 75 per cent. in value of all the receipts, was then barely 12 per cent. At least 80 per cent. of the articles came from the West, that is, from the Ohio and the Upper Mississippi, above the Ohio. They represented the surplus products of the Mississippi Valley, for but little found any other exit to market. Much of the produce shipped from the West to New Orleans was lost en route. A rough estimate places the loss from disasters, snags, etc., at 20 per cent. Many boats, moreover, stopped along the river on their way down to sell supplies to the planters. Thus, at Natchez, flour, grain, and pork were purchased from the Kentucky boats.

From these losses and sales the shipments down the river in 1816, including the products of Louisiana, may be estimated at $13,875,-000.

The river traffic required 6 steam-boats, 594 barges, and 1,287 flat-boats, of a total tonnage of 87,670.

The effect of the use of steam-boats in the river trade was soon seen in a large increase in the shipments of produce. The value of the receipts at New Orleans shows the following advance in the next half-dozen years:

Value of Produce Received at New Orleans from the Interior

Years	Amount
1815–'16	$9,749,253
1816–'17	8,773,379
1817–'18	13,501,036
1818–'19	16,771,711
1819–'20	12,637,079
1820–'21	11,967,067

From 1802 the down commerce of the lower river had grown in 1818, sixteen years, more than fourfold. The trade up the river during the same period had been multiplied threefold.

•   •   •

The following arrivals during the season 1825–'26 (the commercial year then began in New Orleans and throughout the South October 1; it has since been changed to September 1) gives some idea of the variety of crafts employed upon the river:

Arrivals in 1825–'26

Class	Number
Steam-boats	715
Flat-boats	981
Keel-boats	57
Schooners and sloops	108
Pirogues	101
Market boats	41
Batteaux	3
Total	2,006

While the steam-boats had greatly increased in number, three-fold in four years, it will be seen that they had not yet driven out the flat-boat. Quite the contrary. The flat-boats also had increased largely. On the other hand, there was a material falling off in the number of keel-boats in use. The flat-boats were cheap, offered a cheap means of carrying bulky freight to market, and, moreover, they carried out a great deal of produce from the smaller streams where the steam-boats could not go or where they did not care to take the risk of snags and sawyers.

The average tonnage of the river vessels in 1831 was 240 tons, and of the sea-going vessels running from New Orleans, 437. The steam-boats, however, were constantly and rapidly increasing in size, whereas the sea-going vessels increased more slowly, so that in 1845 the two were about the same tonnage, and a ship could carry away from New Orleans just the cargo that one steam-boat could bring there.

During all this period, and despite all these difficulties, the number of arrivals at New Orleans and the amount of river business on the Lower Mississippi continued to steadily increase. The growth of the river traffic is well shown in [the following] table [p. 200].

In regard to the steam-boats, it should be remembered that the steady increase in arrivals each year does not fully express the increase in tonnage, because the boats were not only growing more numerous, but were increasing in size each year, and thus while they doubled in number between 1825 and 1833 they more than trebled in their carrying capacity.

In regard to the flat-boats and other craft, there is no sufficiently definite information for most of this period. It should be said, how-

River trade of New Orleans, 1813–1841

Year ending Sept. 30—	Arrivals of Steamboats	Freight Received[1]	Value of Produce[2]
		Tons	
1813–'14	21	67,560	
1814–'15	40	77,220	
1815–'16		94,560	$9,749,253
1816–'17		80,820	8,773,379
1817–'18		100,880	13,501,036
1818–'19	191	136,300	16,771,711
1819–'20	198	106,706	12,637,079
1820–'21	202	99,320	11,967,067
1821–'22	287	136,400	15,126,420
1822–'23	392	129,500	14,473,725
1823–'24	436	136,240	15,063,820
1824–'25	502	176,420	19,044,640
1825–'26	608	193,300	20,416,320
1826–'27	715	235,200	21,730,887
1827–'28	698	257,300	22,886,420
1828–'29	756	245,700	20,757,265
1829–'30	989	260,900	22,065,518
1830–'31	778	307,300	26,044,820
1831–'32	813	244,600	21,806,763
1832–'33	1,280	291,700	28,238,432
1833–'34	1,081	327,800	29,820,817
1834–'35	1,005	399,900	37,566,842
1835–'36	1,272	437,100	39,237,762
1836–'37	1,372	401,500	43,515,402
1837–'38	1,549	449,600	45,627,720
1838–'39	1,551	399,500	42,263,880
1839–'40	1,573	537,400	49,763,825
1840–'41	1,958	542,500	49,822,115

[1] This does not include articles rafted down of which no record was kept.

[2] This includes the small amount of produce received by Lake Pontchartrain, from 1 to 6 per cent. of total. It is impossible to separate it from the receipts by river, since no separate account was kept, except for cotton and a few other articles.

ever, that while the steam-boats supplanted the flat-boats in many lines of trade, they did not entirely drive them off the river for fifteen or twenty years afterwards. During all this period when the Western cities were building steam-boats the flat-boats also were increasing in numbers. They were found serviceable in carrying hay, coal, etc., and in reaching the interior streams. The Mississippi counted some hundreds of tributaries. On some of these the settlements were sparse, and the surplus products afforded at best one or two cargoes a year, and these were sent much more conveniently and cheaply in flat-boats than in steamers. The steamers had passed the flats between 1820 and 1830 in the business transacted and the freight hauled, and from this time they increased the lead steadily. The number of flats, however, arriving at New Orleans kept but little if any behind the steamers, and as late as 1840 nearly a fifth of the freight handled in the Lower Mississippi went by flat-boat, keel, or barge. The early flat-boats had depended altogether on the current of the river to carry them down. The system of towing was tried in 1829, and a small steamer, which would be called a tug to-day, was successfully used in towing keel-boats up and down stream. The idea did not seem, however, to meet with much favor, the flat-boat men having a superstition that their conjunction with a steamer was not favorable to them, and it was reserved for a later generation to definitely try in the barge the system of towing freight up and down stream.

•   •   •

As the first two decades of the century showed the settlement of the Ohio basin, and a rapid increase in population and production, so the next two resulted in the settlement of the Lower Mississippi region from Louisiana to the mouth of the Ohio. The removal of the Indian tribes to the Indian Territory, the building of levees, and the immense increase in the demand for cotton, hastened the development of West Tennessee, Mississippi, Arkansas, and Northern Louisiana. The Western products received at New Orleans, although they did not fall off, constituted a smaller percentage of the city's total trade, while cotton and sugar became each year more important items commercially. In other words, the Western trade, while not growing less, did not increase as fast as that section advanced in population and production, nor as fast as the cotton trade.

It was during this period that the South first began to insist on the sovereignty of King Cotton, and New Orleans claimed, like Mahomet, to be its prophet. The rapid development of the cotton manufacturing industries in Europe incited the planters to devote more and more acres to it, and it became highly profitable to cultivate cotton even on credit. New Orleans was overflowing with money in those flush times, and lent it readily, and the credit system of the South was firmly established, to last even to this day. The system became universal among the planters, particularly those engaged in raising cotton and sugar, and New Orleans became not only the lender of money at a high rate of interest, but the depot of western supplies, which it advanced in large quantities to the planters throughout the vast region then tributary to it. The whole agricultural country along the Lower Mississippi and its bayous and streams became, in a manner, the commercial slaves of the New Orleans factors, and were not allowed to sell to any one else or buy from them. The Western produce shipped down the river never stopped at the plantation, but was sent direct to New Orleans, and thence transshipped up the river over the same route it had just gone. When the big collapse of 1837 came the banks of New Orleans, with a circulation of $7,000,000, purported to have a capital of $34,000,000, a great majority of them being wrecked in the storm. Within a few years, however, New Orleans recovered from the shock and strengthened its hold on the planters.

COMPETITION WITH THE RIVER

While the Mississippi Valley was listening at the Memphis convention to the story of its glories to come, and river men were calculating on the immense traffic that was assured the future, New Orleans was confident of the future. Few of its people anticipated any danger of its future, and it was predicted not only in American papers but in the British Quarterly Review that it must ultimately become, on account of the Mississippi, the most important commercial city in America, if not in the world.

That eminent statistical and economical authority, Debow's Review, declared that "no city of the world has ever advanced as a mart of commerce with such gigantic and rapid strides as New Orleans."

It was no idle boast. Between 1830 and 1840 no city of the United States kept pace with it. When the census was taken it was fourth in population, exceeded only by New York, Philadelphia, and Baltimore, and third in point of commerce of the ports of the world, exceeded only by London, Liverpool, and New York, being, indeed, but a short distance behind the latter city, and ahead of it in the export of domestic products. Unfortunately, its imports were out of all proportion with its exports. It shipped coffee, hardware, and other heavy articles like this up the river, but it left the West dependent on New York and the other Atlantic cities for nearly all the finer class of manufactured goods they needed.

Later on, when the West began to go into manufacturing itself, and Cincinnati and Pittsburgh became important manufacturing centers, New Orleans imported their goods and reshipped them to the plantations. Of these shipments up-stream over 75 per cent., strange to say, were articles which had previously been sent down-stream. Cincinnati sent its lard, candles, pork, etc., to New Orleans to be carried up by the coast packets to Bayou Sara and Baton Rouge. From these latter towns were shipped so many hogsheads of sugar and barrels of molasses to New Orleans to be thence sent by the Cincinnati boats to the Ohio metropolis. There was no trade between the Western cities and the Southern plantations, very little even with the towns; it all paid tribute to New Orleans.

The upper Mississippi had from 1850 become the center of immigration and production, and New Orleans, which had formerly depended on the Ohio River country almost wholly for its supplies, now largely got them from Saint Louis. About 1850 the traffic with Saint Louis exceeded that with Cincinnati. In 1859, 32 steamboats of 48,726 tons were required for the Saint Louis and 36 of 26,932 tons for the Cincinnati trade.

.   .   .

The extent of the commercial area covered by the river traffic of New Orleans in 1860 will show what was lost in the four years of war that followed, and never fully regained. New Orleans then absolutely controlled the entire river trade, commerce, and crops of the State of Louisiana. In Texas, through the Red River, it secured the crops of the northern half of the State; through the Arkansas and the Red it secured the products of the greater portion of the Indian Territory. It controlled the trade of the southern two-thirds of Arkansas, all the Ouachita and Arkansas valleys, all the river front, and a portion of the White River trade running up into Missouri. It controlled Mississippi with the exception of the eastern portion of the State, through which ran the Mobile and Ohio railroad and the tributaries of the Alabama. All the produce of western Tennessee and half of that of middle Tennessee went to New Orleans; and in Kentucky a large proportion of the business went to the Crescent City. The bulk of the produce of the Ohio valley had been diverted to the lakes and Atlantic seaboard, but probably one-fifth of it found its way to New Orleans direct or by way of the Cincinnati and Louisville packets.

In the Upper Mississippi probably a third of the surplus, or exported crops, similarly reached market by way of New Orleans, either direct or via Saint Louis.

The territory immediately tributary to New Orleans included all Louisiana, half of the settled portion of Texas, half of the Indian Territory, three-fourths of Arkansas, three-fourths of Mississippi, a third of Tennessee, and considerable portions of Kentucky and Alabama, probably 300,000 square miles, while indirectly tributary to it, through Saint Louis, Cincinnati, and Louisville, was a region twice as great.

Yet it was admitted at the time that New Orleans and the river route were losing some trade, and it was felt that the railroads were diverting traffic away from it. They had tapped the river at various points. The tributaries running into the Upper Tennessee, had formerly sent down their produce by flat-boats to New Orleans, the boats reaching the city in fleets of thirty and forty. Railroads had diverted much of this traffic to Charleston, Savannah, and the Atlantic cities. The trade of northern Alabama had formerly come via the Tennessee to New Orleans. It was almost gone and the receipts from North Alabama were actually less in 1860 than in 1845, although the crops had grown manifold larger. The lead trade of the Upper Mississippi had been diverted from the river by the railroads. At Cincinnati a large portion of the flour and grain that had been formerly sent down the river traveled either up it to Pittsburgh or went direct from rail to New York, or by canal to Cleveland, Buffalo, and thence by the Hudson. In the twenty years between 1840 and 1860, during which the competition of river and rail had been inaugurated, the production of the Mississippi Valley had increased far more rapidly than the receipts at New Orleans. The river traffic had increased in the aggregate, but lost relatively.

The Mississippi carried a much larger tonnage, but a far smaller percentage of the total traffic of the valley. The loss was most marked in Western products. Forty years before, these had constituted 58 per cent. of the total receipts at New Orleans. In 1859–'60 they had fallen to 23 per cent. although in that period the West had made the greatest increase in population and production. What was lost here, however, was more than made good in the cotton and sugar crops, and the river trade of New Orleans therefore showed no decline but a steady, active, and positive advance.

During all this period "the levee" of New Orleans, as the river landing of that city was called, was the wonder of every visitor. It was beyond doubt the most active commercial center of the world. Here, side by side, lay the steam-boats and flat-boats of the river, the steamers, ships, and numerous ocean vessels. Here the entire business of New Orleans and of the greater portion of the valley was transacted. The levee was the landing, warehouse, commercial exchange of half a continent, and the freight handled there exceeded that to be seen on any single dock-yard of London or Liverpool.

Value of receipts of produce from the interior at New Orleans from 1840 to 1861[3]

Year	Amount
1840–'41	$49,822,115
1841–'42	45,716,045
1842–'43	53,782,054
1843–'44	60,094,716
1844–'45	57,199,122
1845–'46	77,193,464
1846–'47	90,033,256
1847–'48	79,779,151
1848–'49	81,989,692
1849–'50	96,897,873
1850–'51	196,924,083
1851–'52	108,051,708
1852–'53	134,233,735
1853–'54	115,336,798
1854–'55	117,106,823
1855–'56	144,256,081
1856–'57	158,161,369
1857–'58	167,155,546
1858–'59	172,952,664
1859–'60	185,211,254
1860–'61	155,863,564

[3] This represents the total receipts at New Orleans, from 94 to 99 per cent. of which was by river and some 1 to 6 per cent. by way of Lake Pontchartrain.

51. Internal Trade Between the West and Northeast

While trade between the West and South moved briskly along the Mississippi during the nineteenth century, the American economy was also profiting from a healthy and expanding commerce between the

East and the West. After 1825, a great part of this northern trade became waterborne, over the Erie Canal. By reducing the cost of goods in transport, the canal led to increased westward movement and significantly stimulated the East-West trade, as described in the Andrews report to Congress in 1853.

In connexion with an unequalled increase of population in the Great West, the growth of the lake trade has been so extraordinary and so rapid, that but few persons are cognizant of its present extent and value.

In 1841 the gross amount of the lake trade was sixty-five millions of dollars. In 1846 it had increased to one hundred and twenty-five millions. In 1848, according to the estimate of Colonel Abert, of the topographical engineers, the value of the commerce of the lakes was one hundred and eighty-six millions. Owing to various causes, but particularly to the great influx of foreigners, and the opening of new and extensive lines of intercommunication, it has recently increased still more largely, until, in 1851, it amounted to more than three hundred millions. And these estimates do not include the value of the property constantly changing hands, nor has any notice been taken of the cost of vessels, or the profits of the passenger trade.

It is not within the scope of this report, nor is it practicable therein, to attempt a full exposition of the trade and commerce of the Mississippi, the Missouri, or the Ohio, flowing through that great valley, unsurpassed in all the elements of wealth by any region in this or the Old World. This trade and commerce is worthy of the particular and earnest attention of American statesmen. And it is here proper to state, that one great cause of the growth of the lake trade is the fact that a cheap and expeditious route from the Atlantic to the Great West is afforded by the internal communications, by railroads and canals, opening the way through the great lakes and through the Alleghanies, instead of being restricted to the rivers flowing southward.

The following facts in relation to the trade of the Erie canal are presented as confirming the above, and justifying farther and full official investigation as to the entire internal trade of the West:[1]

SOURCE: U. S. Congress, House, Communication from the Secretary of the Treasury Transmitting the Report of Israel D. Andrews . . . , 32nd Cong., 2nd sess., 1853, 4–5, 278–9.

[1] The facts hereinafter stated with respect to the trade and commerce of

In 1835 there left the lakes by the Erie canal for tide-water, 30,-823 tons of wheat and flour. In 1851 there left the same points, on the same canal, 401,187 tons of similar articles.

In 1851 the total amount of wheat and flour which reached tide-water by the New York canals, was 457,624 tons; showing that while between the lakes and tide-water the State of New York furnished 97,729 tons, or over 75 per cent. of the whole quantity delivered, in 1851 it only furnished 56,437 tons, or about 11 per cent. of the whole.

The great lakes are not a straight line of water, but present a zigzag course. Their surplus waters all find their way to the ocean by one great outlet, the noble St. Lawrence. Notwithstanding the opinions that may be entertained adverse to that mighty river as a channel of communication between the West and the Atlantic, it is nevertheless certain to be more used, and to increase in importance, in proportion to every material stride in the prosperity and advancement of the country bordering on the lakes.

Stretching down into New York, as if for the especial accommodation of a comparatively southern region, is Lake Erie; while extending far into the regions of the northwest, to meet the requirements of that region, Lake Superior spreads his ample waters. An examination of the map prepared by Mr. Keefer, and attached to this report, under the head of Canada, will prove that nature has provided the great lakes for all the different and distant portions of this continent, and that the St. Lawrence is their natural outlet to the sea.

. . .

Previous to the construction of the canal, the cost of transportation from Lake Erie to tide-water was such as nearly to prevent all movement of merchandise. A report of the committee of the legislature, to whom was referred the whole subject of the proposed work, consisting of the most intelligent members of that body,

---

the Mississippi and its tributaries, and of the States and cities on their shores, and on the Gulf of Mexico, and connected with them, are important not only in regard to that specific trade and commerce, but for their relation to that of the lakes and, inland, by canal and railroad to the Atlantic seaboard. It has been found in some degree necessary to refer to the former in full elucidation of the latter. The great interests of the southwestern and southern States demand, however, a fuller and more perfect notice than the resolution calling for this report, and limiting it to other sections, will allow to be now made.

dated March 17, 1817, states that at that time the cost of transportation *from* Buffalo to Montreal was $30 per ton, and the *returning* transportation from $60 to $75. The expense of transportation from Buffalo to New York was stated at $100 per ton, and the ordinary length of passage *twenty days*; so that, upon the very route through which the heaviest and cheapest products of the West are now sent to market, the cost of transportation equalled nearly *three* times the market value of wheat in New York; *six* times the value of corn; *twelve* times the value of oats; and far exceeded the value of most kinds of cured provisions. These facts afford a striking illustration of the value of internal improvements to a country like the United States. It may be here stated, as an interesting fact, that prior to the construction of the Erie canal, the wheat of western New York was sent down the Susquehanna to *Baltimore*, as the cheapest and best route to market.

Although the rates of transportation over the Erie canal, at its opening, were nearly double the present charges—which range from $3 to $7 per ton, according to the character of the freight—it immediately became the convenient and favorite route for a large portion of the produce of the northwestern States, and secured to the city of New York the position which she now holds as the emporium of the Confederacy. Previous to the opening of the canal, the trade of the West was chiefly carried on through the cities of Baltimore and Philadelphia, particularly the latter, which was at that time the first city of the United States in population and wealth, and in the amount of its internal commerce.

As soon as the lakes were reached, the line of navigable water was extended through them nearly one thousand miles farther into the interior. The western States immediately commenced the construction of similar works, for the purpose of opening a communication, from the more remote portions of their territories, with this great water-line. All these works took their direction and character from the Erie canal, which in this manner became the outlet for almost the greater part of the West.

It is difficult to estimate the influence which this canal has exerted upon the commerce, growth, and prosperity of the whole country, for it is impossible to imagine what would have been the state of things without it. But for this work, the West would have held out few inducements to the settler, who would have been without a market for his most important products, and consequently without the means of supplying many of his most essential wants. That portion of the country would have remained comparatively unsettled up to the present time; and, where now exist rich and populous communities, we should find an uncultivated wilderness. The East would have been equally without the elements of growth. The canal has supplied it with cheap food, and has opened an outlet and created a market for the products of its manufactures and commerce. The increase of commerce, and the growth of the country, have been very accurately measured by the growth of the business of the canal. It has been one great bond of strength, infusing life and vigor into the whole. Commercially and politically, it has secured and maintained to the United States the characteristics of a homogeneous people.

52. The Issue of a Protective Tariff

The tariff as an instrument of American economic policy was hotly debated throughout the nineteenth century. It entered the American scene in 1816, when a protective tariff was enacted to foster infant industries. This was increased by the act of 1824, and further tariffs became a subject for debate before the 1828 elections. The shifting opinions of the period were reflected in the attitudes of Daniel Webster, who had opposed the tariff increase in 1824 but who then reversed himself to speak in favor of government protection after considering the developing manufactures of New England. Webster's speech of 1828 which follows below is a celebrated example of contemporary thinking on the subject. While it is doubtful that the tariff played a major role in developing American manufactures, it certainly did not harm this development.

Mr. President,—This subject is surrounded with embarrassments on all sides. Of itself, however wisely or temperately treated, it is full of difficulties; and these difficulties have not been diminished by the particular frame of this bill, nor by the manner hitherto pursued of proceeding with it. A diversity of interests exists, or is supposed to exist, in different parts of the country; this is one source of difficulty. Different opinions are entertained as to the constitutional power of Congress; this is another. And then, again, different members of the Senate have instructions which they feel bound to obey, and which clash with one another. We have this morning seen an

source: "Daniel Webster's Second Speech on the Tariff," *The Works of Daniel Webster* (Boston, 1872), III, 228–33.

honorable member from New York, an important motion being under consideration, lay his instructions on the table, and point to them as his power of attorney, and as containing the directions for his vote.

Those who intend to oppose this bill, under all circumstances, and in any or all forms, care not how objectionable it now is, or how bad it may be made. Others, finding their own leading objects satisfactorily secured by it, naturally enough press forward, without staying to consider deliberately how injuriously other interests may be affected. All these causes create embarrassments, and inspire just fears that a wise and useful result is hardly to be expected. There seems a strange disposition to run the hazard of extremes; and to forget that, in cases of this kind, measure, proportion, and degree are objects of inquiry, and the true rules of judgment. I have not had the slightest wish to discuss the measure; not believing that, in the present state of things, any good could be done by me in that way. But the frequent declaration that this was altogether a New England measure, a bill for securing a monopoly to the capitalists of the North, and other expressions of a similar nature, have induced me to address the Senate on the subject.

New England, Sir, has not been a leader in this policy. On the contrary, she held back herself and tried to hold others back from it, from the adoption of the Constitution to 1824. Up to 1824, she was accused of sinister and selfish designs, *because she discountenanced the progress of this policy*. It was laid to her charge then, that, having established her manufactures herself, she wished that others should not have the power of rivalling her, and for that reason opposed all legislative encouragement. Under this angry denunciation against her, the act of 1824 passed. Now, the imputation is precisely of an opposite character. The present measure is pronounced to be exclusively for the benefit of New England; to be brought forward by her agency, and designed to gratify the cupidity of the proprietors of her wealthy establishments.

Both charges, Sir, are equally without the slightest foundation. The opinion of New England up to 1824 was founded in the conviction that, on the whole, it was wisest and best, both for herself and others, that manufactures should make haste slowly. She felt a reluctance to trust great interests on the foundation of government patronage; for who could tell how long such patronage would last, or with what steadiness, skill, or perseverance it would continue to be granted? It is now nearly fifteen years since, among the first things which I ever ventured to say here, I expressed a serious doubt whether this government was fitted, by its construction, to administer aid and protection to particular pursuits; whether, having called such pursuits into being by indications of its favor, it would not afterwards desert them, should troubles come upon them, and leave them to their fate. Whether this prediction, the result, certainly, of chance, and not of sagacity, is about to be fulfilled, remains to be seen.

At the same time it is true, that, from the very first commencement of the government, those who have administered its concerns have held a tone of encouragement and invitation towards those who should embark in manufactures. All the Presidents, I believe without exception, have concurred in this general sentiment; and the very first act of Congress laying duties on imports adopted the then unusual expedient of a preamble, apparently for little other purpose than that of declaring that the duties which it imposed were laid for the encouragement and protection of manufactures. When, at the commencement of the late war, duties were doubled, we were told that we should find a mitigation of the weight of taxation in the new aid and succor which would be thus afforded to our own manufacturing labor. Like arguments were urged, and prevailed, but not by the aid of New England votes, when the tariff was afterwards arranged, at the close of the war in 1816. Finally, after a whole winter's deliberation, the act of 1824 received the sanction of both houses of Congress, and settled the policy of the country. What, then, was New England to do? She was fitted for manufacturing operations, by the amount and character of her population, by her capital, by the vigor and energy of her free labor, by the skill, economy, enterprise, and perseverance of her people. I repeat, What was she under these circumstances to do? A great and prosperous rival in her near neighborhood, threatening to draw from her a part, perhaps a great part, of her foreign commerce; was she to use, or to neglect, those other means of seeking her own prosperity which belonged to her character and her condition? Was she to hold out for ever against the course of the government, and see herself losing on one side, and yet make no effort to sustain herself on the other? No, Sir. Nothing was left to New England, after the act of 1824, but to conform herself to the will of others. Nothing was left to her, but to consider that the government had fixed and determined its own policy; and that policy was *protection*.

New England, poor in some respects, in others is as wealthy as her neighbors. Her soil would be held in low estimation by those who are acquainted with the valley of the Mississippi and the fertile plains of the South. But in industry, in habits of labor, skill, and in accumulated capital, the fruit of two centuries of industry, she may be said to be rich. After this final declaration, this solemn promulgation of the policy of the government, I again ask, What was she to do? Was she to deny herself the use of her advantages, natural and acquired? Was she to content herself with useless regrets? Was she longer to resist what she could no longer prevent? Or was she, rather, to adapt her acts to her condition; and, seeing the policy of the government thus settled and fixed, to accommodate to it as well as she could her own pursuits and her own industry? Every man will see that she had no option. Every man will confess that there remained for her but one course. She not only saw this herself, but had all along foreseen, that, if the system of protecting manufactures should be adopted, she must go largely into them. I believe, Sir, almost every man from New England who voted against the law of 1824 declared that, if, notwithstanding his opposition to that law, it should still pass, there would be no alternative but to consider the course and policy of the government as then settled and fixed, and to act accordingly. The law did pass; and a vast increase of investment in manufacturing establishments was the consequence. Those who made such investments probably entertained not the slightest doubt that as much as was promised would be effectually granted; and that if, owing to any unforeseen occurrence or untoward event, the benefit designed by the law to any branch of manufactures should not be realized, it would furnish a fair case for the consideration of government. Certainly they could not expect, after what had passed, that interests of great magnitude would be left at the mercy of the very first change of circumstances which might occur.

As a general remark, it may be said, that the interests concerned in the act of 1824 did not complain of their condition under it, excepting only those connected with the woollen manufactures. These did complain, not so much of the act itself as of a new state of circumstances, unforeseen when the law passed, but which had now arisen to thwart its beneficial operations as to them, although in one respect, perhaps, the law itself was thought to be unwisely framed.

Three causes have been generally stated as having produced the disappointment experienced by the manufacturers of wool under the law of 1824.

First, it is alleged that the price of the raw material has been raised too high by the act itself. This point had been discussed at the time, and although opinions varied, the result, so far as it depended on this part of the case, though it may be said to have been unexpected, was certainly not entirely unforeseen.

But, secondly, the manufacturers imputed their disappointment to a reduction of the price of wool in England, which took place just about the date of the law of 1824. This reduction was produced by lowering the duty on imported wool from sixpence sterling to one penny sterling per pound. The effect of this is obvious enough; but in order to see the real extent of the reduction, it may be convenient to state the matter more particularly.

The meaning of our law was doubtless to give the American manufacturer an *advantage* over his English competitors. *Protection* must mean this, or it means nothing. The English manufacturer having certain advantages on his side, such as the lower price of labor and the lower interest of money, the object of our law was to counteract these advantages by creating others, in behalf of the American manufacturer. Therefore, to see what was necessary to be done in order that the American manufacturer might sustain the competition, a comparison of the respective advantages and disadvantages was to be made. In this view the very first element to be considered was, what is the cost of the raw material to each party. On this the whole must materially depend. Now when the law of 1824 passed, the English manufacturer paid a duty of sixpence sterling per pound on imported wool. But in a very few days afterwards, this duty was reduced by Parliament from sixpence to a penny. A reduction of five pence per pound in the price of wool was estimated in Parliament to be equal to a reduction of twenty-six per cent. *ad valorem* on all imported wool; and this reduction, it is obvious, had its effect on the price of home-produced wool also. Almost, then, at the very moment that the framers of the act of 1824 were raising the price of the raw material here, as that act did raise it, it was lowered in England by the very great reduction of twenty-six per cent. Of course, this changed the whole basis of the calculation. It wrought a complete change in the relative advantages and disadvantages of the English and American competitors, and threw the preponderance of advantage most decidedly on the side of the English. If the American manufacturer had not vastly too great a preference before this reduction took place, it is clear he had too little afterwards.

53. The Controversy over the Second National Bank

Equally as controversial as the tariff was the development of a central banking system in America. The First Bank of the United States, chartered in 1791, had been allowed to die at the end of its twenty-year charter, and not until 1816 was a second Bank of the United States chartered. Both performed many of the functions of a central bank in tying together federal fiscal policy and the activities of the banking community.

But the banks were subject to wide attack; the second bank was vigorously disliked by many who felt that it represented a dangerous concentration of economic power. Certainly its leading opponent was Andrew Jackson, and the issue of a recharter became a major part of the presidential campaign of 1832. In this selection, the President records his reasons for vetoing the extension of the bank's life.

VETO MESSAGE

Washington, July 10, 1832.

To the Senate:

The bill "to modify and continue" the act entitled "An act to incorporate the subscribers to the Bank of the United States" was presented to me on the 4th July instant. Having considered it with that solemn regard to the principles of the Constitution which the day was calculated to inspire, and come to the conclusion that it ought not to become a law, I herewith return it to the Senate, in which it originated, with my objections.

A bank of the United States is in many respects convenient for the Government and useful to the people. Entertaining this opinion, and deeply impressed with the belief that some of the powers

SOURCE: Andrew Jackson, in James D. Richardson, ed., *A Compilation of the Messages and Papers of the Presidents, 1789–1897,* (Washington, D.C., 1896), II, 576–80, 586–7, 589–91.

and privileges possessed by the existing bank are unauthorized by the Constitution, subversive of the rights of the States, and dangerous to the liberties of the people, I felt it my duty at an early period of my Administration to call the attention of Congress to the practicability of organizing an institution combining all its advantages and obviating these objections. I sincerely regret that in the act before me I can perceive none of those modifications of the bank charter which are necessary, in my opinion, to make it compatible with justice, with sound policy, or with the Constitution of our country.

The present corporate body, denominated the president, directors, and company of the Bank of the United States, will have existed at the time this act is intended to take effect twenty years. It enjoys an exclusive privilege of banking under the authority of the General Government, a monopoly of its favor and support, and, as a necessary consequence, almost a monopoly of the foreign and domestic exchange. The powers, privileges, and favors bestowed upon it in the original charter, by increasing the value of the stock far above its par value, operated as a gratuity of many millions to the stockholders.

An apology may be found for the failure to guard against this result in the consideration that the effect of the original act of incorporation could not be certainly foreseen at the time of its passage. The act before me proposes another gratuity to the holders of the same stock, and in many cases to the same men, of at least seven millions more. This donation finds no apology in any uncertainty as to the effect of the act. On all hands it is conceded that its passage will increase at least 20 or 30 per cent more the market price of the stock, subject to the payment of the annuity of $200,000 per year secured by the act, thus adding in a moment one-fourth to its par value. It is not our own citizens only who are to receive the bounty of our Government. More than eight millions of the stock of this bank are held by foreigners. By this act the American Republic proposes virtually to make them a present of some millions of dollars. For these gratuities to foreigners and to some of our own opulent citizens the act secures no equivalent whatever. They are the certain gains of the present stockholders under the operation of this act, after making full allowance for the payment of the bonus.

Every monopoly and all exclusive privileges are granted at the expense of the public, which ought to receive a fair equivalent. The many millions which this act proposes to bestow on the stockholders of the existing bank must come directly or indirectly out of the earnings of the American people. It is due to them, therefore, if their Government sell monopolies and exclusive privileges, that they should at least exact for them as much as they are worth in open market. The value of the monopoly in this case may be correctly ascertained. The twenty-eight millions of stock would probably be at an advance of 50 per cent, and command in market at least $42,000,000, subject to the payment of the present bonus. The present value of the monopoly, therefore, is $17,000,000, and this the act proposes to sell for three millions, payable in fifteen annual installments of $200,000 each.

.   .   .

It has been urged as an argument in favor of rechartering the present bank that the calling in its loans will produce great embarrassment and distress. The time allowed to close its concerns is ample, and if it has been well managed its pressure will be light, and heavy only in case its management has been bad. If, therefore, it shall produce distress, the fault will be its own, and it would furnish a reason against renewing a power which has been so obviously abused. But will there ever be a time when this reason will be less powerful? To acknowledge its force is to admit that the bank ought to be perpetual, and as a consequence the present stockholders and those inheriting their rights as successors be established a privileged order, clothed both with great political power and enjoying immense pecuniary advantages from their connection with the Government.

The modifications of the existing charter proposed by this act are not such, in my view, as make it consistent with the rights of the States or the liberties of the people. The qualification of the right of the bank to hold real estate, the limitation of its power to establish branches, and the power reserved to Congress to forbid the circulation of small notes are restrictions comparatively of little value or importance. All the objectionable principles of the existing corporation, and most of its odious features, are retained without alleviation.

The fourth section provides "that the notes or bills of the said corporation, although the same be, on the faces thereof, respectively made payable at one place only, shall nevertheless be received by the said corporation at the bank or at any of the offices of discount and deposit thereof if tendered in liquidation or payment of any balance or balances due to said corporation or to such office of discount and deposit from any other incorporated bank." This provision secures to the State banks a legal privilege in the Bank of the United States which is withheld from all private citizens. If a State bank in Philadelphia owe the Bank of the United States and have notes issued by the St. Louis branch, it can pay the debt with those notes, but if a merchant, mechanic, or other private citizen be in like circumstances he can not by law pay his debt with those notes, but must sell them at a discount or send them to St. Louis to be cashed. This boon conceded to the State banks, though not unjust in itself, is most odious because it does not measure out equal justice to the high and the low, the rich and the poor. To the extent of its practical effect it is a bond of union among the banking establishments of the nation, erecting them into an interest separate from that of the people, and its necessary tendency is to unite the Bank of the United States and the State banks in any measure which may be thought conducive to their common interest.

The ninth section of the act recognizes principles of worse tendency than any provision of the present charter.

It enacts that "the cashier of the bank shall annually report to the Secretary of the Treasury the names of all stockholders who are not resident citizens of the United States, and on the application of the treasurer of any State shall make out and transmit to such treasurer a list of stockholders residing in or citizens of such State, with the amount of stock owned by each." Although this provision, taken in connection with a decision of the Supreme Court, surrenders, by its silence, the right of the States to tax the banking institutions created by this corporation under the name of branches throughout the Union, it is evidently intended to be construed as a concession of their right to tax that portion of the stock which may be held by their own citizens and residents. In this light, if the act becomes a law, it will be understood by the States, who will probably proceed to levy a tax equal to that paid upon the stock of banks incorporated by themselves. In some States that tax is now 1 per cent, either on the capital or on the shares, and that may be assumed as the amount which all citizen or resident stockholders would be taxed under the operation of this act. As it is only the stock *held* in the States and not that *employed* within them which would be subject to taxation, and as the names of foreign stockholders are not to be reported to the treasurers of the States, it is obvious that the stock held by them will be exempt from this burden. Their annual profits will therefore be 1 per cent more than the citizen stockholders, and as the annual dividends of the bank may be safely estimated at 7 per cent, the stock will be worth 10 or 15 per cent more to foreigners than to citizens of the United States. To appreciate the effects which this state of things will produce, we must take a brief review of the operations and present condition of the Bank of the United States.

By documents submitted to Congress at the present session it appears that on the 1st of January, 1832, of the twenty-eight millions of private stock in the corporation, $8,405,500 were held by foreigners, mostly of Great Britain. The amount of stock held in the nine Western and Southwestern States is $140,200, and in the four Southern States is $5,623,100, and in the Middle and Eastern States is about $13,522,000. The profits of the bank in 1831, as shown in a statement to Congress, were about $3,455,598; of this there accrued in the nine Western States about $1,640,048; in the four Southern States about $352,507, and in the Middle and Eastern States about $1,463,041. As little stock is held in the West, it is obvious that the debt of the people in that section to the bank is principally a debt to the Eastern and foreign stockholders; that the interest they pay upon it is carried into the Eastern States and into Europe, and that it is a burden upon their industry and a drain of their currency, which no country can bear without inconvenience and occasional distress. To meet this burden and equalize the exchange operations of the bank, the amount of specie drawn from those States through its branches within the last two years, as shown by its official reports, was about $6,000,000. More than half a million of this amount does not stop in the Eastern States, but passes on to Europe to pay the dividends of the foreign stockholders. In the principle of taxation recognized by this act the Western States find no adequate compensation for this perpetual burden on their industry and drain of their currency. The branch bank at Mobile made last year $95,140, yet under the provisions of this act the State of Alabama can raise no revenue from these profitable operations, because not a share of the stock is held by any of her citizens. Mississippi and Missouri are in the same condition in relation to the branches at Natchez and St. Louis, and such, in a greater or less degree, is the condition of every Western State. The tendency of the plan of taxation which this act proposes will be to place the whole United States in the same relation to foreign countries which the Western States now bear to the Eastern. When by a tax on resident stockholders the stock of this bank is made worth 10 or 15 per cent more to foreigners than to residents, most of it will inevitably leave the country.

Thus will this provision in its practical effect deprive the Eastern as well as the Southern and Western States of the means of raising a revenue from the extension of business and great profits of this institution. It will make the American people debtors to aliens in nearly the whole amount due to this bank, and send across the Atlantic from two to five millions of specie every year to pay the bank dividends.

· · ·

By its silence, considered in connection with the decision of the Supreme Court in the case of McCulloch against the State of Maryland, this act takes from the States the power to tax a portion of the banking business carried on within their limits, in subversion of one of the strongest barriers which secured them against Federal encroachments. Banking, like farming, manufacturing, or any other occupation or profession, is a *business*, the right to follow which is not originally derived from the laws. Every citizen and every company of citizens in all of our States possessed the right until the State legislatures deemed it good policy to prohibit private banking by law. If the prohibitory State laws were now repealed, every citizen would again possess the right. The State banks are a qualified restoration of the right which has been taken away by the laws against banking, guarded by such provisions and limitations as in the opinion of the State legislatures the public interest requires. These corporations, unless there be an exemption in their charter, are, like private bankers and banking companies, subject to State taxation. The manner in which these taxes shall be laid depends wholly on legislative discretion. It may be upon the bank, upon the stock, upon the profits, or in any other mode which the sovereign power shall will.

· · ·

The bank is professedly established as an agent of the executive branch of the Government, and its constitutionality is maintained on that ground. Neither upon the propriety of present action nor upon the provisions of this act was the Executive consulted. It has

had no opportunity to say that it neither needs nor wants an agent
clothed with such powers and favored by such exemptions. There is
nothing in its legitimate functions which makes it necessary or
proper. Whatever interest or influence, whether public or private,
has given birth to this act, it can not be found either in the wishes
or necessities of the executive department, by which present action
is deemed premature, and the powers conferred upon its agent not
only unnecessary, but dangerous to the Government and country.

It is to be regretted that the rich and powerful too often bend
the acts of government to their selfish purposes. Distinctions in society will always exist under every just government. Equality of talents, of education, or of wealth can not be produced by human institutions. In the full enjoyment of the gifts of Heaven and the
fruits of superior industry, economy, and virtue, every man is equally
entitled to protection by law; but when the laws undertake to add
to these natural and just advantages artificial distinctions, to grant
titles, gratuities, and exclusive privileges, to make the rich richer
and the potent more powerful, the humble members of society—
the farmers, mechanics, and laborers—who have neither the time
nor the means of securing like favors to themselves, have a right to
complain of the injustice of their Government. There are no necessary evils in government. Its evils exist only in its abuses. If it would
confine itself to equal protection, and, as Heaven does its rains,
shower its favors alike on the high and the low, the rich and the
poor, it would be an unqualified blessing. In the act before me there
seems to be a wide and unnecessary departure from these just principles.

Nor is our Government to be maintained or our Union preserved
by invasions of the rights and powers of the several States. In thus
attempting to make our General Government strong we make it
weak. Its true strength consists in leaving individuals and States as
much as possible to themselves—in making itself felt, not in its
power, but in its beneficence; not in its control, but in its protection; not in binding the States more closely to the center, but leaving each to move unobstructed in its proper orbit.

Experience should teach us wisdom. Most of the difficulties our
Government now encounters and most of the dangers which im-
pend over our Union have sprung from an abandonment of the legitimate objects of Government by our national legislation, and the
adoption of such principles as are embodied in this act. Many of our

rich men have not been content with equal protection and equal benefits, but have besought us to make them richer by act of Congress. By attempting to gratify their desires we have in the results of our legislation arrayed section against section, interest against interest, and man against man, in a fearful commotion which threatens to shake the foundations of our Union. It is time to pause in our career to review our principles, and if possible revive that devoted patriotism and spirit of compromise which distinguished the sages of the Revolution and the fathers of our Union. If we can not at once, in justice to interests vested under improvident legislation, make our Government what it ought to be, we can at least take a stand against all new grants of monopolies and exclusive privileges, against any prostitution of our Government to the advancement of the few at the expense of the many, and in favor of compromise and gradual reform in our code of laws and system of political economy.

I have now done my duty to my country. If sustained by my fellow-citizens, I shall be grateful and happy; if not, I shall find in the motives which impel me ample grounds for contentment and peace. In the difficulties which surround us and the dangers which threaten our institutions there is cause for neither dismay nor alarm. For relief and deliverance let us firmly rely on that kind Providence which I am sure watches with peculiar care over the destinies of our Republic, and on the intelligence and wisdom of our countrymen. Through *His* abundant goodness and *their* patriotic devotion our liberty and Union will be preserved.

ANDREW JACKSON

54. The Role of the Railroad

When, in 1830, the first railroad stretched its length across American soil, the ground was laid for a debate which continues to this day. How vital was the railroad to American economic development? The mere fact that rails displaced the canal when the two came into direct competition is indication enough that railroads provided more efficient transport than did alternative means by water or wagon. But how much more efficient? Much recent research and writing points to a probability that the railroad was not so all-important as was formerly believed. However, this selection by Andrews is an early-day assessment of the role of the railroad in reducing transport costs in America in the period before the Civil War.

ECONOMICAL VIEW OF THE RAILROADS OF THE UNITED STATES

The first step toward a correct idea of our railroads, as far as their uses, objects, costs, and results are concerned, is a thorough understanding of the social and industrial character of our people, the geographical and topographical features of the country, the uniformity in the pursuits of the great mass of our people, and the great distance that separates the consuming from the producing regions.

· · ·

It is well known that upon the ordinary highways, the economical limit to transportation is confined within a comparatively few miles, depending of course upon the *kind* of freight and character of the roads. Upon the average of such ways, the cost of transportation is not far from 15 cents per ton per mile, which may be considered as a sufficiently correct estimate for the whole country. Estimating at the same time the value of wheat at $1.50 per bushel, and corn at 75 cents, and that 33 bushels of each are equal to a ton, the value of the former would be equal to its cost of transportation for 330 miles, and the latter, 165 miles. At these respective distances from market, neither of the above articles would have any commercial value, with only a common *earth* road as an avenue to market.

But we find that we can move property upon railroads at the rate of 1.5 cent per ton per mile, or for one-tenth the cost upon the ordinary road. These works therefore extend the economic limit of the cost of transportation of the above articles to 3,300 and 1,650 miles respectively. At the limit of the economical movement of these articles upon the *common* highway, by the use of railroads, wheat would be worth $44.50, and corn $22.27 per ton, which sums respectively would represent the actual increase of value created by the interposition of such a work.

The following table will show the amount saved per ton, by transportation by railroad over the ordinary highways of the country.

The value of lands is affected by railroads in the same ratio as their *products*. For instance, lands lying upon a navigable watercourse, or in the immediate vicinity of a market, may be worth, for the culture of wheat, $100. Let the average crop be estimated at 22

SOURCE: U. S. Congress, House, *Communications from the Secretary of the Treasury Transmitting the Report of Israel D. Andrews* . . . , 32nd Cong., 2nd sess., 1853, 380–3.

Statement showing the value of a ton of wheat, and one of corn, at given points from market, as affected by cost of transportation by railroad, and over the ordinary road.

	Transportation by railroad		Transportation by ordinary highway	
	Wheat	Corn	Wheat	Corn
Value at market	$49.50	$24.75	$49.50	$24.75
10 miles from market	49.35	24.60	48.00	23.25
20 do do	49.20	24.45	46.50	21.75
30 do do	49.05	24.30	45.00	20.25
40 do do	48.90	24.15	43.50	18.75
50 do do	48.75	24.00	42.00	17.25
60 do do	48.60	23.85	40.50	15.75
70 do do	48.45	23.70	39.00	14.25
80 do do	48.30	23.55	37.50	12.75
90 do do	48.15	23.40	36.00	11.25
100 do do	48.00	23.25	34.50	9.75
110 do do	47.85	23.10	33.00	8.25
120 do do	47.70	22.95	31.50	6.75
130 do do	47.55	22.80	30.00	5.25
140 do do	47.40	22.65	28.50	3.75
150 do do	47.25	22.50	27.00	2.25
160 do do	47.10	22.35	25.50	.75
170 do do	46.95	22.20	24.00	.00
180 do do	46.80	22.05	22.50	
190 do do	46.65	21.90	21.00	
200 do do	46.50	21.75	19.50	
210 do do	46.35	21.60	18.00	
220 do do	46.20	21.45	16.50	
230 do do	46.05	21.30	15.00	
240 do do	45.90	21.15	13.50	
250 do do	45.75	21.00	12.00	
260 do do	45.60	20.85	10.50	
270 do do	45.45	20.70	9.00	
280 do do	45.30	20.55	7.50	
290 do do	45.15	20.40	6.00	
300 do do	45.00	20.25	4.50	
310 do do	44.85	20.10	3.00	
320 do do	44.70	19.95	1.50	
330 do do	44.55	19.80	.00	

bushels to the acre, valued at $33, and the cost of cultivation at $15, this would leave $18 per acre as the net profit. This quantity of wheat (two-thirds of a ton) could be transported 330 miles at a cost of 10 cents per mile, or $3.30, which would leave $14.70 as the net profit of land at that distance from a market, when connected with it by a railroad. The value of the land, therefore, admitting the quality to be the same in both cases, would bear the same ratio to the assumed value of $100, as the value of its products, $14.70, does to $18, or $82 per acre; which is an actual creation of value to that amount, assuming the correctness of the premises. The same calculation may, of course, be applied with equal force to any other kind and species of property. The illustration given establishes a principle entirely correct in itself, but of course liable to be modified to meet the facts of each case. Vast bodies of the finest land in the United States, and lying within 200 miles of navigable watercourses, are unsaleable, and nearly, if not quite, valueless for the culture of wheat or corn for exportation, from the cost of transportation, which in many instances far exceeds the estimate in the above table. Under such circumstances products are often fed out to live stock, and converted into higher values which will bear transportation, when the former will not. In this manner, lands are turned into account, where their immediate products would otherwise be valueless. But in such cases, the profit per acre is often very small; as, in the districts best adapted to the culture of corn, it is considered more profitable to sell it for 25 cents per bushel than to feed it out to animals. It will be seen that at this price, thrice its value is eaten up by the cost of transportation of 165 miles.

In this manner, railroads in this country actually add to the immediate means of our people, by the saving effected in the expenses of transportation, to a much greater extent than cost. We are, therefore, in no danger from embarrassment on account of the construction of lines called for by the business wants of the community, as these add much more to our active capital than they absorb. Only a very few years are required to enable a railroad to repay its cost of construction in the manner stated.

Railroads in the United States exert a much greater influence upon the value of property, than in other countries. Take England for example. There a railroad may be built without necessarily increasing the value of property or the profits of a particular interest. Every farmer in England lives in sight of a market. Large cities are to be found in every part of the island, which consume the products of the different portions of it almost on the spot where they are raised. Railroads are not needed to transport these products hundreds and thousands of miles to market; consequently they may be of no advantage to the farmer living upon their lines. So with many branches of manufactures. These establishments may be situated immediately upon tide-water, and as the fabrics are mostly exported, they would not be thrown upon railroads in any event. Such works may exist in that country without exerting any perceptible influence in adding to the value of the property of a community. The cases of the two countries would be parallel, were the farmer in the neighborhood of Liverpool compelled to send everything he could raise to London for a market, or were their manufacturing establishments so far from the consumers of their goods, that their value would be sunk before these could be reached. We have in this country what is equivalent to manufacturing establishments in Great Britain, in good order and well stocked for business, a fertile soil, that will produce bountifully for years without rotation or dressing. All that the farmer has to do is to cast his seed on the soil and to reap an abundant crop. The only thing wanting to our highest prosperity is markets, or their equivalents, railroads, which give access to them.

55. Immigration to the United States

Immigration of European nationals to the United States began in the early days as a trickle, largely of British origin, which rapidly increased after the ending of the second war with England and then crested into a flood with the Irish famine of the 1840's. Later, thousands of Germans elected to migrate to the new country at the end of the 1840's and in the 1850's. This influx expanded the labor supply in America and enriched it with the new residents' Old World talents and skills. The expansion of immigration after 1820 is described in some detail in the eighth Census of the United States.

One of the commissioners sent by the Continental Congress to Europe, Silas Deane, expressed the expectation that if the colonies established their independence, the immigration from the Old World would be prodigiously increased; and as a consequence, the cultivated lands would rise in value, and new lands would be brought into market. This anticipation has been strikingly and abundantly realized. And in connexion with the census of nativities, the records of immigration have a special importance as indicating the pro-

SOURCE: U. S. Congress, Senate, *Preliminary Report on the Eighth Census, 1860*, 37th Cong., 2nd sess., 1862, 12–9.

gressive augmentation of the immigrants who have sought to improve their fortunes in the New World.

From a survey of the irregular data previous to 1819, by Dr. Seybert, Prof. Tucker, and other statists, it appears that from 1790 to 1800, about 50,000 Europeans, or "aliens," arrived in this country; in the next ten years the foreign arrivals were about 70,000, and in the ten years following, 114,000, ending with 1820. To determine the actual settlers, a deduction of 14.5 per cent. from these numbers should probably be made for transient passengers, as hereafter described.

Louisiana was purchased from France in 1803. The portion of this territory south of the thirty-third parallel, according to the historian Hildreth, comprised a population of about 50,000, more than half of whom were slaves. With these should be counted about 10,-000 in the settlements north of that parallel, augmented by a recent immigration, with a predominance of whites. The foreign population acquired with the whole Louisiana territory may thus be reckoned at 60,000; about one-half or 30,000 being whites of French, Spanish, and British extraction; and the other 30,000 being slaves and free colored. This number of whites should evidently be added to the current immigration by sea already mentioned, in order to obtain the foreign accession to the white population of the United States during that period.

Instead of scattered notices from shipping lists, the arrival of passengers has been officially recorded at the custom-houses, since 1819, by act of Congress. There are some deficiencies perhaps in the returns of the first ten or twelve years, but the subsequent reports are considered reliable. While the classified lists exhibit the whole number of foreign passengers, the great majority of whom are emigrants, they also furnish valuable information not otherwise obtainable respecting the statistical history of immigration.

The following numbers, registered under the act of 1819, are copied from the authentic summary of Bromwell, to which the numbers for the last five years have been added from the annual reports of the State Department, thus bringing the continuation down to the year of the present census.

To arrive at the true immigration, these numbers should be largely increased for those who have come by way of Canada. On the other hand, they should be diminished for return emigrants,

Statement of the number of Alien passengers arriving in the United States by sea from foreign countries from September 30, 1819, to December 31, 1860

Year	Males	Females	Sex not stated	Total
Year ending September 30				
1820	4,871	2,393	1,121	8,385
1821	4,651	1,636	2,840	9,127
1822	3,816	1,013	2,082	6,911
1823	3,598	848	1,908	6,354
1824	4,706	1,393	1,813	7,912
1825	6,917	2,959	323	10,199
1826	7,702	3,078	57	10,837
1827	11,803	5,939	1,133	18,875
1828	17,261	10,060	61	27,382
1829	11,303	5,112	6,105	22,520
1830	6,439	3,135	13,748	23,322
1831	14,909	7,724		22,633
1832	34,596	18,583		53,179
Quarter ending December 31				
1832	4,691	2,512	100	7,303
Year ending December 31				
1833	41,546	17,094		58,610
1834	38,796	22,540	4,029	65,365
1835	28,196	17,027	151	45,374
1836	47,865	27,553	824	76,242
1837	48,837	27,653	2,850	79,340
1838	23,474	13,685	1,755	38,914
1839	42,932	25,125	12	68,069
1840	52,883	31,132	51	84,066
1841	48,082	32,031	176	80,289
1842	62,277	41,907	381	104,565
First three quarters of				
1843	30,069	22,424	3	52,496
Year ending September 30				
1844	44,431	34,184		78,615
1845	65,015	48,115	1,241	114,371
1846	87,777	65,742	897	154,416
1847	136,086	97,917	965	234,968
1848	133,906	92,149	472	226,527
1849	177,232	119,280	512	297,024
Year ending September 30				
1850	196,331	112,635	1,038	310,004
Quarter ending December 31				
1850	32,990	26,805	181	59,976

Statement of the number of Alien passengers arriving in the United States by sea from foreign countries from September 30, 1819, to December 31, 1860

Year	Males	Females	Sex not stated	Total
Year ending December 31				
1851	217,181	162,219	66	379,466
1852	212,469	157,696	1,438	371,603
1853	207,958	160,615	72	368,645
1854	256,177	171,656		427,833
1855	115,307	85,567	3	200,877
1856	115,846	84,590		200,436
1857	146,215	105,091		251,306
1858	72,824	50,002	300	123,126
1859	69,161	51,640	481	121,282
1860	88,477	65,077	86	153,640
Total	2,977,603	2,035,536	49,275	5,062,414

[By exhibiting the number of arrivals of passengers from foreign countries during periods of nearly ten years each, the following aggregates indicate the accelerated progress of immigration.]

Periods	Passengers of Foreign birth	American and Foreign
In the 10 years ending September 30, 1829	128,502	151,636
In the 10¼ years ending December 31, 1839	538,381	572,716
In the 9¾ years ending September 30, 1849	1,427,337	1,479,478
In the 11¼ years ending December 31, 1860	2,968,194	3,255,591
In the 41¼ years ending December 31, 1860	5,062,414	5,459,421

[Very nearly the following numbers are found when returns are adjusted by the aid of the quarterly reports to the periods of the decennial census.]

Three census periods	Passengers of Foreign birth
In the 10 years previous to June 1, 1840	552,000
Do do 1850	1,558,300
Do do 1860	2,707,634

Distribution of Ages on arrival

Ages	Number of ages stated from 1820 to 1860			Proportions		
	Males	Females	Total	Males	Females	Total
Under 5	218,417	200,676	419,093	4.143	3.806	7.949
5 and under 10	199,704	180,606	380,310	3.788	3.425	7.213
10 and under 15	194,580	166,833	361,413	3.691	3.164	6.855
15 and under 20	404,338	349,755	754,093	7.669	6.633	14.302
20 and under 25	669,853	428,974	1,098,827	12.706	8.136	20.842
25 and under 30	576,822	269,554	846,376	10.940	5.112	16.052
30 and under 35	352,619	163,778	516,397	6.688	3.106	9.794
35 and under 40	239,468	114,165	353,633	4.542	2.165	6.707
40 and upwards	342,022	200,322	542,344	6.487	3.799	10.286
Total	3,197,823	2,074,663	5,272,486	60.654	39.346	100.000

and for the merchants, factors, and visitors who go and come repeatedly, and are thus enumerated twice or more in the returns.

For an example of the former class, according to British registry, 17,798 emigrants returned from the United States to Great Britain in the year 1860. How numerous has been the latter class who have been counted twice or more, is not definitely known; to make note of these would constitute a desirable improvement in the future official reports.

The preceding summaries embrace passengers of foreign birth, together with 397,007 native born Americans, who were also registered as arriving from foreign ports. In the record of ages following, both classes are united; but since the foreigners are far more numerous, the result will exhibit very nearly the relative number at each age of the foreign passengers. A careful reduction of the whole number whose ages were specified, has just been completed in connexion with the census [as shown in table on p. 229].

From the foregoing table it will be seen that the distribution is materially different from that of a settled population; the females are less than the males in the ratio of two to three; almost precisely one-half of the total passengers are between fifteen and thirty years of age. It will further be noted that the sexes approach nearest to equality in children and the youthful ages, as would naturally be expected in the migration of families; while from twenty-five years of age to forty the male passengers are double the number of females. The total distribution of ages has never varied very materially from the average, as appears from the following table:

Total Proportions for different periods

Ages	1820 to 1830	1830 to 1840	1840 to 1850	1850 to 1860	1820 to 1860
Under 5	6.904	8.511	8.284	7.674	7.949
5 and under 10	5.763	7.552	7.434	7.077	7.213
10 and under 15	4.568	7.817	7.564	6.328	6.855
15 and under 20	11.052	11.830	13.059	15.762	14.302
20 and under 25	22.070	19.705	21.518	20.617	20.842
25 and under 30	19.574	16.661	15.722	15.944	16.052
30 and under 35	10.194	10.215	9.914	9.609	9.794
35 and under 40	8.171	7.875	6.563	6.466	6.707
40 and upwards	11.704	9.834	9.942	10.523	10.286
Total	100.000	100.000	100.000	100.000	100.000

The passengers from foreign ports arrive at all seasons of the year; the greatest number, however, make the passage in the second and third quarters, or in the summer months, and a smaller number in the winter months.

The deaths on the voyage during the last five years have been only about one-sixth of one per cent.; the time of passage being generally some thirty days. With regard to the question, how many of the passengers are emigrants, the reports of the State Department during the past five years—1855 to 1860—have specified the places of residence as follows:

Country where the passengers from foreign ports mean to reside; also the country where born

Country	Mean to reside in—			Born in—
	Males	Females	Total	Males & Females
United States	551,095	357,395	908,490	126,794
British America	7,682	4,044	11,726	25,443
Great Britain and Ireland	2,207	1,037	3,244	407,429
Azores	544	133	677	1,954
Spain	389	65	454	4,997
West Indies	271	72	343	5,170
France	130	47	177	19,338
Germany	140	36	176	279,957
Other countries specified	329	67	396	82,185
Not stated			50,901	23,317
Total of 5 years, 1855 to 1860			976,584	976,584

Deducting the number at the head of the last column who were born in the United States, it will be seen that in these five years 781,696 out of a total of 849,790 alien passengers, designed to make their permanent home in the United States. Further statistics of 24,848 second passages, and about 30,000 emigrants, to Canada, via New York, indicate that *the alien passengers should be diminished 14.5 per cent. to determine the number of actual settlers.*

From the first of the two following tables it will be seen that the most numerous class among the passengers is that of *laborers;* the next in order are *farmers*, mechanics, and merchants. The "seam-stresses and milliners," and nearly all of the "servants," are females; the other female passengers, with few exceptions, have been entered under the category of "not stated," and comprise about five-sevenths of that division.

It will be proper to mention that the ten trades and professions marked with a star in the table were always enumerated during the whole period. The other occupations were not reported during the four years 1856–'59, except that their aggregate only was embraced under the single title of "other occupations." But the omission could be roughly supplied by assuming the number in each trade during the four years to be the same fraction of the yearly passengers as it was in the other six years.

In 1856–'59, the deaths on the passage also were omitted in the official total of passengers, though retained in all previous years and in 1860; for the sake of uniformity this temporary omission of deaths is restored in the present collection of tables, which have been verified throughout with the greatest care.

The next following table, stating the birthplace or "country where born," will form a valuable supplement to the decennial census of nativities. Excepting the first numeric column, which commenced with small numbers October 1, 1819, the remaining columns correspond as nearly with the census periods as the official yearly reports allow without interpolation.

The total number arriving from the United Kingdom of Great Britain and Ireland on our shores is thus stated to be 2,750,874. But a recent statement from British official sources[1] gives the number emigrating to the United States in the forty-six years, 1815–'60, as 3,048,206. The difference of the two returns will be explained partly by those who emigrated in the interval, 1815–19, before our registry commenced, being about 55,000; and chiefly by the more numerous class who entered the United States by way of Canada, and so were not included in our custom-house returns.

In the same period of forty-six years it is also stated that 1,196,521 persons emigrated from the United Kingdom to the British colonies in North America. A large portion of these are known to have eventually settled in the United States. Thus it appears safe to assume that since the close of the last war with that country, in 1814, about three and a quarter millions of the natives of Great Britain

[1] *British Almanac*, 1862.

Occupation of passengers arriving in the United States from foreign countries during the forty-one years ending with 1860

Occupation	1820 to 1830	1831 to 1840	1841 to 1850	1851 to 1860	1820 to 1860
*Merchants	19,434	41,881	46,388	124,149	231,852
*Farmers	15,005	88,240	256,880	404,712	764,837
*Mechanics	6,805	56,582	164,411	179,726	407,524
*Mariners	4,995	8,004	6,398	10,087	29,484
*Miners	341	368	1,735	37,523	39,967
*Laborers	10,280	53,169	281,229	527,639	872,317
Shoemakers	1,109	1,966	63	336	3,474
Tailors	983	2,252	65	334	3,634
Seamstresses and milliners	413	1,672	2,096	1,065	5,246
Actors	183	87	233	85	588
Weavers and spinners	2,937	6,600	1,303	717	11,557
*Clergymen	415	932	1,559	1,420	4,326
Clerks	882	1,143	1,065	792	3,882
*Lawyers	244	461	831	1,140	2,676
*Physicians	805	1,959	2,116	2,229	7,109
Engineers	226	311	654	825	2,016
Artists	139	513	1,223	615	2,490
Teachers	275	267	832	154	1,528
Musicians	140	165	236	188	729
Printers	179	472	14	40	705
Painters	232	369	8	38	647
Masons	793	1,435	24	58	2,310
Hatters	137	114	1	4	256
Manufacturers	175	107	1,833	1,005	3,120
Millers	199	189	33	210	631
Butchers	329	432	76	108	945
Bakers	583	569	28	92	1,272
*Servants	1,327	2,571	24,538	21,058	49,494
Other occupations	5,466	4,004	2,892	13,844	26,206
Not stated	101,442	363,252	969,411	1,544,494	2,978,599
Total	176,473	640,086	1,768,175	2,874,687	5,459,421

* See preceding paragraphs [Ed.]

233

Country where born

Countries	1820 to 1830	1831 to 1840	1841 to 1850	1851 to 1860	1820 to 1860
England	15,837	7,611	32,092	247,125	302,665
Ireland	27,106	29,188	162,332	748,740	967,366
Scotland	3,180	2,667	3,712	38,331	47,890
Wales	170	185	1,261	6,319	7,935
Great Britain and Ireland	35,534	243,540	848,366	297,578	1,425,018
Total United Kingdom	81,827	283,191	1,047,763	1,338,093	2,750,874
France	8,868	45,575	77,262	76,358	208,063
Spain	2,616	2,125	2,209	9,298	16,248
Portugal	180	829	550	1,055	2,614
Belgium	28	22	5,074	4,738	9,862
Prussia	146	4,250	12,149	43,887	60,432
Germany	7,583	148,204	422,477	907,780	1,486,044
Holland	1,127	1,412	8,251	10,789	21,579
Denmark	189	1,063	539	3,749	5,540
Norway and Sweden	94	1,201	13,903	20,931	36,129
Poland	21	369	105	1,164	1,659
Russia	89	277	551	457	1,374
Turkey	21	7	59	83	170
Switzerland	3,257	4,821	4,644	25,011	37,733
Italy	389	2,211	1,590	7,012	11,202
Greece	20	49	16	31	116
Sicily	17	35	79	429	560
Sardinia	32	7	201	1,790	2,030
Corsica	2	5	2		9
Malta	1	35	78	5	119
Iceland				10	10
Europe	2		51	473	526
British America	2,486	13,624	41,723	59,309	117,142

234

South America	542	856	3,579	1,224	6,201
Central America	107	44	368	449	968
Mexico	4,818	6,599	3,271	3,078	17,766
West Indies	3,998	12,301	13,528	10,660	40,487
China	3	8	35	41,397	41,443
East Indies	9	39	36	43	127
Persia			7	15	22
Asia	3	1	4	19	27
Liberia	1	8	5	5	19
Egypt		4			4
Morocco		4	1		5
Algiers			2		2
Barbary States	4				4
Cape of Good Hope	2				2
Africa	10	36	47	186	279
Azores	13	29	327	2,873	3,242
Canary Islands	271	6	1	8	286
Madeira Islands	70	52	3	189	314
Cape Verd Islands	4	15	3	7	29
Sandwich Islands	1	6	28	44	79
Society Islands			1	6	7
Australia	2	3		104	109
St. Helena		1	3	13	17
Isle of France		2	1		3
South Sea Islands	79				79
New Zealand				4	4
Not stated	32,892	69,799	52,725	25,438	180,854
Total Aliens	151,824	599,125	1,713,251	2,598,214	5,062,414
United States	24,649	40,961	54,924	276,473	397,007
Total	176,473	640,086	1,768,175	2,874,687	5,459,421

and Ireland, "a population for a kingdom," have emigrated to this country.

Next in magnitude is the migration from Germany, amounting to 1,486,044 by our custom-house returns; the next is that from France, 208,063; and from the other countries, as shown in the table. A large share of the German emigrants have embarked from the port of Havre; others from Bremen, Hamburg, Antwerp; many have also crossed over and taken passage from British ports.

As our own people, following "the star of empire," have migrated to the west in vast numbers, their places have been supplied by Europeans, which has modified the character of the population, yet the great mass of the immigrants are found to cherish true patriotism for the land of their adoption.

56. A Statistical Picture of the American Economy in 1840

Unique to America was a very early effort to measure in precise statistical terms its own economic progress. Notable tracts on this subject date from the beginning of national independence. Among the works in the forefront of this attempt were Blodget's Economica, Seybert's Statistical Annals, and Pitkin's writings. George Tucker and Ezra Seaman were two other distinguished authors who attempted to determine the sources of America's economic growth by carefully delineating the characteristics of the economy. An extraordinary accomplishment is the selection by Seaman which follows, in which he presents statistics on the national economy and offers a criticism of Tucker's results. In laying out these statistical estimates, Seaman was preceding by almost a century the national-income accounting which ultimately developed throughout the world. As a trailblazer he gave a remarkably accurate and precise view of the characteristics of the American economy of the 1840's.

Let the reader compare with each other the values produced according to the estimates of Professor Tucker, of New Hampshire and Vermont—Ohio and Kentucky—Virginia and North Carolina —South Carolina and Arkansas—Michigan and Tennessee, and he will be at a loss to account for the great differences in the productive industry of those states, and they will strike the mind as gross in-

SOURCE: Ezra C. Seaman, *Essays on the Progress of Nations* (New York, 1846), 145–50.

consistencies apparent upon the face of the estimates. My mode of making the estimates show no inconsistencies which are not easily accounted for. Mining being more than twice as productive as farming, and the number of miners in Wisconsin being large in proportion to the population, the mining industry of that territory raised the average income of its inhabitants greatly above that of the inhabitants of Indiana, Michigan and the neighboring states. The income from commerce, and also from the culture of sugar and cotton, is nearly three times as great as from the culture of tobacco and of grain in the interior and western states. This accounts for the large average incomes in Louisiana and Mississippi, compared with those of all the agricultural states. The commerce of Missouri raises their incomes above those of Tennessee.

[The tables on pp. 238–239 and pp. 240–241] exhibit the profits of slavery in a very clear light. They show that slave labor employed in the culture of cotton in the southern slave States, is more profitable and productive, than free labor employed in agriculture in the free States; and that the culture of sugar in Louisiana must be still more profitable than the culture of cotton. They show also, that the culture of tobacco and Indian corn in the northern slave States is greatly depressed, and much less productive than the culture of cotton at the south, and of wheat, corn, &c., in the manufacturing and commercial States of the north and east. . . .

Though the annual net products of labor and capital in the northern slave States amounts to only about forty-four dollars to each person, and only fifty-one dollars for each free person, after allowing twenty-five dollars for the support of each slave, as is shown in the foregoing table; yet this does not include the profits of slave breeding, which amounts to over $10,000,000 per annum, and about three dollars to each free person. Adding this sum, and it makes about fifty-four dollars for the average income of each free person in the northern slave States. . . .

It needs but a glance at the tables in Sec. 15, in relation to commerce, and to table A, in Sec. 22, to see that both labor and capital employed either in mining, manufactures or commerce, are more than twice, and nearly twice and a half as productive as when they are employed in agriculture, except in the culture of sugar and cotton. When the reader takes this into consideration, he need be at no loss for the cause of the incomes of the people of the commercial and manufacturing States of Massachusetts and Rhode Island being

Statement of the values produced in each of the departments of industry, in each of the United States

SEC. 20. VALUES PRODUCED by LABOR AND CAPITAL in 1840, according to the census of the United States; estimated upon the principles heretofore stated in sections 13 to 18 inclusive

	Agriculture	Manufactures	Mining	Commerce	Forest	Fisheries
Maine	$11,933,578	$5,742,261	$302,766	$5,407,221	$1,513,245	$1,080,475
New Hampshire	8,587,073	5,654,951	72,704	1,492,685	362,033	98,203
Vermont	10,727,168	3,071,050	363,000	1,277,669	353,602	
Massachusetts	13,909,170	40,449,501	1,488,794	15,801,105	308,205	5,974,146
Rhode Island	1,962,457	8,383,753	146,580	1,702,782	35,723	633,396
Connecticut	9,637,253	12,037,892	705,339	3,117,344	152,005	841,430
New York:						
Southern District	18,968,100	21,228,952	1,063,410	27,283,758	300,833	977,566
Northern District	52,209,110	25,999,305	4,167,407	16,762,483	3,733,234	119,621
New Jersey	14,350,888	10,094,327	730,000	3,876,701	306,948	104,164
Pennsylvania	51,786,365	31,597,102	9,661,095	20,777,206	973,534	24,545
Ohio	35,723,200	13,368,358	1,803,135	12,238,382	954,000	21,000
Indiana	16,265,951	3,565,643	73,503	3,248,386	567,422	1,111
Illinois	11,926,555	2,948,990	323,243	2,563,516	209,138	
Michigan	5,089,898	1,321,808	20,730	972,485	379,077	99,210
Wisconsin	690,506	292,705	374,300	475,476	290,132	49,258
Iowa	808,861	170,178	13,350	320,488	73,868	
FREE STATES	$264,576,133	$185,926,776	$21,314,556	$117,317,687	$10,512,999	$10,024,125

Delaware	2,880,012	1,487,355	34,702	589,004	12,563	237,143
Maryland	14,124,775	5,900,345	745,170	5,559,831	195,799	395,928
District of Columbia	157,282	868,549		691,244		145,170
Virginia	39,983,938	7,966,393	1,838,508	7,966,828	514,966	167,666
North Carolina	23,960,555	2,455,294	327,803	2,058,056	1,641,481	424,594
Tennessee	22,608,115	2,651,491	903,072	2,706,378	184,994	
Kentucky	22,538,069	4,828,044	1,117,199	3,953,916	158,034	
Missouri	10,406,008	2,235,570	201,311	3,508,451	441,068	
NORTHERN SLAVE STATES	$136,658,754	$28,393,041	$5,167,765	$27,033,708	$3,148,905	$1,370,501
South Carolina	22,543,344	2,231,745	124,968	2,923,986	442,090	2,300
Georgia	28,120,912	2,155,214	213,891	3,169,666	94,629	84
Alabama	21,744,850	1,645,938	79,943	2,992,051	143,467	
Mississippi	23,709,109	1,507,712		1,633,602	168,987	
Louisiana	21,350,043	2,683,591	96,640	13,737,483	58,530	
Arkansas	3,906,193	¹601,622	17,515	378,149	182,214	
Florida	1,704,336	410,828	5,050	773,561	23,281	192,086
SOUTHERN SLAVE STATES	$123,078,787	$11,236,650	$538,007	$25,608,498	$1,113,198	$194,470
SLAVE STATES	$259,737,541	$39,629,691	$5,705,772	$52,642,206	$4,262,103	$1,564,971
UNITED STATES	$524,313,674	$225,556,467	$27,020,328	$169,959,893	$14,775,102	$11,589,096

¹ Deducted for error in the value of dwelling houses, $780,000.

239

Population and values produced in each of the States, according to my estimate, and also that of Professor Tucker

SEC. 21. POPULATION and AGGREGATE OF VALUES PRODUCED BY LABOR AND CAPITAL in the several States, according to the census of 1840; the amount to each person, and the amount to each free person after deducting twenty-five dollars for the cost of supporting each slave; also, the aggregate amount, and the amount to each person, according to the estimates of Professor Tucker.

	Population	Values produced	Amount to each	Per Professor Tucker: Value produced	Per Professor Tucker: To each person
Maine	501,793	$25,979,546	$51¾	$26,462,705	$52
New Hampshire	284,574	16,267,649	57⅛	19,556,141	68
Vermont	291,948	15,792,489	54	25,143,191	85
Massachusetts	737,699	77,930,921	105⅝	75,470,297	103
Rhode Island	108,830	12,864,691	118	13,001,223	119
Connecticut	309,978	26,491,463	85½	28,023,737	90
N. Y.: Southern District	745,853	69,822,619	93⅝ }	193,806,433	79
N. Y.: Northern District	1,683,068	102,991,160	61 1-5 }		
New Jersey	373,306	29,463,028	79⅞	29,672,426	79
Pennsylvania	1,724,033	114,819,847	66⅝	131,033,655	76
Ohio	1,519,467	64,108,075	42	63,906,678	42
Indiana	685,866	23,722,016	34½	23,532,631	34
Illinois	476,183	17,971,442	37⅔	18,981,985	39
Michigan	212,267	7,883,208	37	7,026,390	33
Wisconsin	30,945	2,177,377	70	1,905,600	61½
Iowa	43,112	1,386,745	32	1,132,106	27
FREE STATES	9,728,922	$609,672,276	$62¾	$658,655,198	$67⅛

	Population	Values produced	Amount to each	Amount to each free person	Per Professor Tucker Value produced	Per Professor Tucker To each person
Delaware	78,085	$5,240,779	$67 1-5	$68	$5,252,535	$67
Maryland	470,019	26,921,848	57¼	65	28,821,661	61
District of Columbia	43,712	1,862,245	42½	45	1,971,593	45
Virginia	1,239,797	58,438,299	47⅛	59	76,769,053	62
North Carolina	753,419	30,867,783	41	49	32,422,198	44
Tennessee	829,210	29,054,050	35	38	37,973,360	45
Kentucky	779,828	32,595,262	41¾	47	38,624,191	49
Missouri	383,702	16,792,408	43⅔	47	15,830,444	41
NORTHERN SLAVE STATES	4,577,772	$201,772,674	$44	$51	$237,665,035	$51⅞
South Carolina	594,398	28,268,433	47½	75	27,173,536	45
Georgia	691,392	33,754,396	48¾	65	35,980,363	52
Alabama	590,756	26,606,249	45	60	28,961,325	49
Mississippi	375,651	27,019,410	72	122	29,739,338	79
Louisiana	352,411	37,926,287	107	183	35,044,959	99
Arkansas	97,574	5,085,693	50	60	6,888,395	70
Florida	54,477	3,109,142	57	85	2,976,687	54
SOUTHERN SLAVE STATES	2,756,659	$161,769,610	$58¾	$88	$166,764,603	$62
SLAVE STATES	7,334,431	$363,542,284	49⅝		$404,429,638	55
UNITED STATES	17,063,353	$973,214,560	57		$1,063,084,836	62¼
IN NAVY	6,100					

about twice as great to each inhabitant as they are in the agricultural State of Vermont. He will see at once the reason why the incomes of the people of the rich soil of Ohio and the north-western States are so low, when compared with those of the manufacturing and commercial States. He will see that agriculture in the southern district of New York, in the vicinity of a great commercial city with $1,618 capital to each person employed, is only about half as productive as manufacturing in Massachusetts, Rhode Island, Connecticut and New Jersey, with one-third part as much capital in proportion to the number of laborers employed. He will also see, that though the great Erie Canal, the most magnificent work of the age, has poured much wealth into the city of New York, and perhaps nearly doubled the population, business and wealth of that great commercial emporium; it has at present very little perceptible influence in raising the incomes and increasing the wealth of the inhabitants of the northern district of New York. This great and splendid work, together with the canals and railroads of Ohio and the western States, have had an influence in dispersing the population, spreading it over a wide surface, and deluding the people with the idea, that nothing but internal improvements, agricultural industry and commercial enterprise, are necessary to make a country wealthy.

On comparing the foregoing table with the tables in Sections 8, 9, and 10, and more particularly with table D, in Sec. 10, the reader will see that the productive industry of the United States as a whole, compares very favorably with that of France, Holland, and Belgium; and also with that of Great Britain prior to the nineteenth century. He will see that the productive industry of Massachusetts and Rhode Island exceeds all Europe in proportion to the population, and is equalled only by Louisiana, and perhaps Cuba, and some other sugar and coffee growing countries of the torrid zone.

When the reader looks back to Sections 8, 9, and 10, and contemplates the progressive steps in the productive industry of England, France, and the Netherlands; and reflects that a century since, and before the invention of the Steam Engine, of the Spinning Jenny, and of the machinery for rolling iron, all the manufactures of the metals, as well as of cloths, were by hand labor; he need be at no loss for the reason why the productive industry and wealth of those countries was small a century since, compared with what it is now; and why it is now small in France, Ireland, and our agricultural

States of the west, in comparison with Great Britain and our manufacturing States.

57. The Progress of American Agriculture

Agriculture was another aspect of the national economy which made
striking progress before the Civil War. The westward movement opened
up vast areas of rich land. More land, more labor, more capital, all were
put into production, and the result was amplified by better machinery
and equipment. An excerpt from the eighth census briefly reviews this
development.

AGRICULTURE

View of the Condition and Progress of Agriculture
in the United States

It appears from the returns of the last census, that the ratio of
increase of the principal agricultural products of the United States
has more than kept pace with the increase of population. Indeed,
there appears no reason to doubt the continuance of an abundant
supply of all the great staple articles, equal to the necessities of any
possible increase of population or national contingency for ages to
come. It is also gratifying to note the evidences of improvement in
some of the most important agricultural operations, proving that
our farmers are fully in sympathy with the progressive spirit of the
age, and not behind their fellow-citizens engaged in other industrial
occupations. The products of the great west are giving a tone to the
markets of Great Britain and the continent. Chicago has become
one of the first grain markets in the world, and as the boundless
region still further west is being developed, every channel of communication with the Atlantic coast will teem with the products of
the soil. Illinois alone sends now to the great market at New York
an average of two thousand head of cattle weekly, and other States,
comprising regions almost unknown at the former census, and still
more distant from the seaboard, are adding and increasing their contributions.

New plants and animals have been introduced in the past decade.
From the products of the sugar cane—*sorghum saccharatum*—

SOURCE: U. S. Congress, Senate, *Preliminary Report on the Eighth Census,*
1860, 37th Cong., 2nd sess., 1862, pp. 80–2.

transplanted from the Chinese empire, the west is furnished with a new article of domestic luxury and utility, and rendered comparatively independent of the sugar cane of more southern States.

The great dairy interest in our country during this period has increased the production of cheese and butter, and already American cheese is as well known in English markets at the best English dairy cheese.

Indian corn is now an indispensable article for Great Britain, and each succeeding year is increasing the demand for this important product of our country, which is raised in every State and Territory of our Union.

While it is admitted that very much remains to be accomplished by the agricultural interest of our country, it cannot be doubted that the past ten years has shown to the world that the United States has within its own territory the resources which will enable us to compete with the older nations of the world in every department of domestic industry.

The London exhibition in 1851 made known that the United States had the means of supplying the implements and machinery needed in every country in Europe. Since that time our reapers and mowers, ploughs, steam-engines, and railroad cars have found their way to the Old World, and an American in taking the tour of the continent will, in the great empire of Russia, find himself on board of an American railroad car drawn by an American locomotive on a railroad built by an American engineer. We point to these advances as evidence that the enterprise of our countrymen, with so wide a scope for its development at home, manifests itself wherever a profitable field opens for its exercise abroad.

At a period like the present, when, for the preservation of the national life and character, the resources of the country are subjected to a greater strain than they have ever yet borne, when a large portion of its effective labor is diverted to the same sacred duty, and all the productive forces of the Union are controlled to an unprecedented extent by causes more pervading and subversive in their effects than any which could possibly arise from extraneous sources, it is a subject of the highest gratification that we are blessed with the amplest returns from the labors of the husbandman. The crops of hay and grain, as the result of a favorable season and a broader cultivation of land, are believed especially to have afforded abundant and timely harvests. Regarded either as a source of cheap and ample supply for a vast commissariat with the least possible drain upon the public chest, of cheap and plenary subsistence to the numerous unemployed and dependent classes, or as a source of exports and employment for the commercial and shipping interests, the bounty of our land is at the present time a subject of national congratulation and thankfulness.

The increasing annual products of agriculture in our highly-favored country, and the hay and grain crops in particular, furnish striking illustrations of the close interdependence and connexion of all branches of the national industry. The dependence of agriculture upon the results of mechanical skill, as well as the astonishing progress of the latter within the last half century, is strongly exemplified in the application of labor-saving appliances, which become still more valuable, in emergencies like the present, in all the operations of the farm. The saving effected by new and improved implements in Great Britain within a dozen years preceding 1851 was stated by a competent authority to be not less than one-half on all the main branches of farm labor. Our own progress in this respect is believed to have been more rapid than that of any other agricultural people, and to be in advance of our application of the fruits of purely scientific research in the improvement of agriculture. In nearly every department of rural industry mechanical power has wrought a revolution. The inventive genius of the country has not only contrived to make it prepare the crop for market and to sew or knit the family apparel of the farmer, but to rock and "tend" the infant as well as to rend from the embrace of earth the century-rooted oak which our fathers were forced to leave to the slow eradication of time. Whether the superior agricultural advantages and the demand for improved implements and machinery in the United States have stimulated the facile ingenuity of our mechanics, or have only been seconded by its ready contributions to industry, we shall not stop to inquire. The greatest triumphs of mechanical skill in its application to agriculture are witnessed in the instruments adapted to the tillage, harvesting, and subsequent handling of the immense grain crops of the country, and particularly upon the western prairies. Without the improvements in ploughs and other implements of tillage which have been multiplied to an incredible extent, and now are apparently about to culminate in the steam plough, the vast wheat and corn crops of those fertile plains could not probably be raised. But were it possible to produce wheat upon the scale that it is now raised, much of the profit and not a little of the product would be lost were the farmer compelled to wait upon the slow process of the sickle, the cradle, and the hand-rake for securing it when ripe. The reaping-machine, the harvester, and machines for threshing, winnowing, and cleaning his wheat for the market have become quite indispensable to every large grain grower. The commercial importance of the wheat crop and its various relations to the subject of domestic and foreign supply, to markets, the means of transportation, storage, &c., make it highly important that the producer shall have the means of putting his crop in the market at the earliest or most favorable time and with the greatest precision.

58. The Progress of American Manufactures

Even more than the growth in agriculture or in trade and commerce, the spectacular acceleration of American manufacturing dominated the country's economic scene by the time of the Civil War. Tools and machinery displayed by Americans in the Crystal Palace exhibition in England in 1851 were greeted there with amazement and admiration, and British investigators were subsequently sent to the United States to study American methods and to explore the sources of such extraordinary success. One such commission, headed by Messrs. Whitworth and Wallace, produced a lengthy report from which the following excerpts are taken. After describing some of the characteristics of American manufacturing, the authors undertake to assess why these methods succeed. High on their list of reasons they give credit to the size of the American market and to the existence of an educated populace.

The industry of the United States has to be estimated by the peculiar circumstances of the country to which it has been devoted. In the States the labour-market is higher than with ourselves, especially as respects skilled labour. It has, therefore, been a principal aim as much as possible to apply machinery for the purpose of supplying this want, and, as the consequence, it will be seen that some of the principal achievements of American inventors have been acquired in this department. To this very want of human skill, and the absolute necessity for supplying it, may be attributed the ex-

SOURCE: *The Industry of the United States in Machinery, Manufactures, and Useful and Ornamental Arts, Compiled from the Official Reports of Messrs. Whitworth and Wallace to the British Government* (London, 1854), pp. iv–ix, 160–2.

traordinary ingenuity displayed in many of their labour-saving machines, where automatic action so completely supplies the place of the more abundant hand-labour of older manufacturing countries.

Of this we have an illustration in the machine for the manufacture of the seamless grain-bags, the loom for which is described as a perfect self-actor, or automaton, commencing the bag, and continuing the process until the work is turned out complete.

For another curious illustration of this automatic action we have the manufacture of ladies' hair-pins at Waterbury. A quantity of wire is coiled upon a drum or cylinder, and turns round upon its axis, as suspended from the ceiling of the workshop. The point of the wire being inserted into the machine, and the power applied, the wire is cut off to the requisite length, carried forward and bent to the proper angle, and then pointed with the necessary blunt points, and finally dropped into a receiver, quite finished, all but the lacquering or japanning. These pins are made at the rate of 180 per minute.

The reader is referred also to the automaton machine for shanking buttons. The blanks being cut in thin brass, are put into a curved feeding-pipe, in which they descend to the level of the machine, by which a hole is stamped in the centre of each. Then the shank is formed by another portion of the machine, from a continuous wire carried along horizontally, the wire being shaped into the shank, and pushed up into its proper place. These operations are completed at the rate of 200 a minute, the only attendance required being that of one person to feed this automaton with the blanks and the wires, which he is so well able to work up to the satisfaction of his masters.

There is, of course, nothing to boast of on the ground of superiority on account of these inventions; but it is much to the credit of the American inventor, that he is able so to meet the necessities of his case, and supply the want of fingers, which are at present so scarce.

Another peculiarity observable in American industry, is the want of that division of labour which is one of the great causes of excellence in the productions of our own and other of the older countries in which art is carried to a high point of perfection. With us, trades and manufactures branch out into a variety of subdivisions, from which, besides the perfection noticed, we have a great economy of time, and, consequently, of expense. The citizen of the United

States knows that matters are different with him, and seems really to pride himself in not remaining over long at any particular occupation, and being able to turn his hand to some dozen different pursuits in the course of his life.

This knowledge of two or three departments of one trade, or even the pursuit of several trades, by one individual, does not interfere so much with the systematic division of labour as may be supposed. In most instances the change of employment is made at convenient periods, or as a relief to the workman from the monotony of always doing the same thing. This change and variety of occupation is, in many respects, favourable to the man, as distinguished from the operative or the artist. In many cases our economic laws enhance the work or the value of time, when they degrade the workmen, between whom and the perfection of their works a singular contrast exists. While our American operative is a man and a citizen, he is often found wanting in that perfect skill of hand and marvellous accuracy which distinguish the workmen of this country. So much is there to check the national tendencies of self-gratulation and boasting on either side of the Atlantic, and to promote respect and good feeling among us all.

The machinery of a country will naturally correspond with its wants, and with the history and state of its people. Testing the machinery of the United States by this rule of adaptation, the mechanical appliances in use must call forth much admiration. A large proportion of the mechanical power of the States has, from its earliest application, been, from the circumstances of the country, directed to wood, this being the material on which it has been requisite to operate for so many purposes, and which is presented in the greatest abundance. Stone, for a similar reason, has been subdued to man's use by the application of machinery, of which we have an instance in the fact that one man is able to perform as much work by machinery in stone-dressing, as twenty persons by hand. In common with our own and other great manufacturing countries, the Union presents remarkable illustrations of the amazingly productive power of machinery, as compared with mere manual operations. Into the details of these triumphs of machinery it is unnecessary here to enter. It may suffice to refer to the improvements effected in spinning-machinery, by which one man can attend to a mule containing 1,088 spindles, each spinning three hanks, or 3,264 hanks a day; so that, as compared with the operations of the most expert spinner in Hindoostan, the American operative can perform the work of 3,000 men.

The Law of Limited Liability, which is now engaging public attention, is an important source of the prosperity which attends the industry of the United States. This law affords the most ample facilities for the investment of capital, and has led to a much greater development of the industrial resources and skill of that country than could have resulted under other circumstances for many years to come. In the United States, the agent or secretary, manager, treasurer, and directors being also shareholders, are held by the law responsible to the extent of their means for the results of the management intrusted to them. The limited responsibility is confined to the non-managing shareholders only. It will be seen from the several illustrations given in the following pages, that this law works well in America; and these facts will strengthen the case of those who advocate its application to our country.

The comparative density of the old and the new countries, differing as they do, will account for the very different feelings with which the increase of machinery has been regarded in many parts of this country and the United States, where the workmen hail with satisfaction all mechanical improvements, the importance and value of which, as releasing them from the drudgery of unskilled labour, they are enabled by education to understand and appreciate. This statement is not intended to disparage the operatives of our own country, who in many respects are placed in a position different from that of their class in the United States, where the principles that ought to regulate the relations between the employer and the employed are thoroughly understood, and where the law of limited liability, to which we have just referred, affords the most ample facilities for the investment of capital in business, and where the skilled labourer is in many respects furnished with many opportunities of advancement which he has not among us. Particularly it should be noticed that no taxation of any kind is suffered to interfere with the free development of the press, and that the humblest labourer can indulge in the luxury of his daily paper, so that everybody reads, and intelligence penetrates through the lowest grades of society. . . .

The compulsory educational clauses adopted in the laws of most of the States, and especially those of New England, by which some three months of every year must be spent at school by the young factory operative under 14 or 15 years of age, secure every child from the cupidity of the parent, or the neglect of the manufacturer; since to profit by the child's labour during *three-fourths* of the year, he or she must be regularly in attendance in some public or private school conducted by some authorized teacher during the other fourth.

This lays the foundation for that wide-spread intelligence which prevails amongst the factory operatives of the United States; and though at first sight the manufacturer may appear to be restricted in the free use of the labour offered to him, the system re-acts to the permanent advantage of both employer and employed.

The skill of hand which comes of experience is, notwithstanding present defects, rapidly following the perceptive power so keenly awakened by early intellectual training. Quickly learning from the skilful European artisans thrown amongst them by emigration, or imported as instructors, with minds, as already stated, prepared by sound practical education, the Americans have laid the foundation of a wide-spread system of manufacturing operations, the influence of which cannot be calculated upon, and are daily improving upon the lessons obtained from their older and more experienced com-peers of Europe.

Commercially, advantages of no ordinary kind are presented to the manufacturing States of the American Union. The immense development of its resources in the west, the demands of a popu-lation increasing daily by emigration from Europe, as also by the results of a healthy natural process of inter-emigration, which tends to spread over an enlarged surface the population of the Atlantic States; the facilities of communication by lakes, rivers, and railways; and the cultivation of European tastes, and consequently of Euro-pean wants; all tend to the encouragement of those arts and manu-factures which it is the interest of the citizens of the older States to cultivate, and in which they have so far succeeded that their markets may be said to be secured to them as much as manufacturers, as they have hitherto been, and will doubtless continue to be, as mer-chants. For whether the supply is derived from the home or foreign manufacturer, the demand cannot fail to be greater than the indus-try of both can supply. This once fairly recognised, those jealousies which have ever tended to retard the progress of nations in the peaceful arts, will be no longer suffered to interfere, by taking the form of restrictions on commerce and the free intercourse of peoples.

The extent to which the people of the United States have as yet succeeded in manufactures may be attributed to indomitable energy and an educated intelligence, as also to the ready welcome accorded to the skilled workmen of Europe, rather than to any peculiar native advantages; since these latter have only developed themselves as manufacturing skill and industry have progressed. Only one obstacle of any importance stands in the way of constant advance towards greater perfection, and that is the conviction that perfection is already attained. This opinion, which prevails to a large extent, is unworthy of that intelligence which has overcome so many difficulties, and which can only be prevented from achieving all it aspires to, by a vain-glorious conviction that it has nothing more to do.